ADDICTED TO LUST

ADDICTED TO LUST

PORNOGRAPHY IN THE LIVES OF
CONSERVATIVE PROTESTANTS

SAMUEL L. PERRY

OXFORD
UNIVERSITY PRESS

OXFORD

UNIVERSITY PRESS

Oxford University Press is a department of the University of Oxford. It furthers
the University's objective of excellence in research, scholarship, and education
by publishing worldwide. Oxford is a registered trade mark of Oxford University
Press in the UK and certain other countries.

Published in the United States of America by Oxford University Press
198 Madison Avenue, New York, NY 10016, United States of America.

Library of Congress Cataloging-in-Publication Data
Names: Perry, Samuel L., author.
Title: Addicted to Lust : Pornography in the Lives of Conservative
Protestants / Samuel L. Perry.
Description: New York : Oxford University Press, 2019. |
Includes bibliographical references and index.
Identifiers: LCCN 2018054212 | ISBN 9780190844219 (hardcover) |
ISBN 9780190844240 (online content)
Subjects: LCSH: Pornography—Religious aspects—Christianity. |
Protestants—Sexual behavior—United States. |
Christian conservatism—United States.
Classification: LCC BV4597.6 .P47 2019 | DDC 241/.667—dc23
LC record available at https://lccn.loc.gov/2018054212

1 3 5 7 9 8 6 4 2

Printed by Sheridan Books, Inc., United States of America

To Jill,
the strongest, bravest woman I know.
You're a total badass.

CONTENTS

PREFACE

—⟫•◇•⟪—

This book is about the curious relationship between pornography and conservative Protestants in the United States. By "pornography" I mean the standard definition of sexually explicit material made with the intent of arousing the viewer, and these days, accessed primarily through the internet.[1] And by "conservative Protestants" I mean American Christians who believe that faith in Jesus Christ *alone* grants them eternal salvation (Protestant), and who view the Bible as inerrant, supremely authoritative, and best interpreted literally (conservative). While I will occasionally settle for an alternative definition of "conservative Protestant" depending on the dataset I have available (e.g., by the denomination believers affiliate with, self-identifying as "evangelical" or "fundamentalist") throughout the book, my preference will be to focus on *theological beliefs* as the key identifying marker of conservative Protestants.

Empirically, this book represents my attempt to understand the social etiology and consequences of an ongoing paradox. On the one hand, conservative Protestants almost unanimously consider pornography not only morally wrong or sinful but dangerously so, and in some ways *unique* in its sinfulness. Sexual sin within the conservative Protestant subculture holds a special place among threats to personal godliness and society in general—more so than, say, greed, bigotry, or gossip (a perspective I call "sexual exceptionalism"). And yet, despite their essentially unanimous moral rejection of pornography use, conservative Protestants, depending on how you define them, view pornography only slightly less often than other Americans. There *is* a consistent difference, to be sure, but certainly not as great as one might expect. This paradox—that conservative Protestants both morally reject *and* regularly view pornography—is in some ways an inevitable consequence for a subculture that repudiates the sexual mores of the dominant culture while simultaneously (and quite intentionally) refusing to disengage from that culture, particularly in terms of technology and media consumption. This book takes stock of how that paradox plays itself out in the community life, mental health, and intimate relationships of conservative Protestants.

But the theoretical punch of this book is bigger than just elucidating how conservative Protestants deal with porn or sexual sin more broadly. While I will develop a number of concepts and make several more minor arguments throughout, a central aim of this book is to advance our understanding of what I call "moral incongruence." In simple terms, moral incongruence is the experience of violating socially learned and sacralized moral values.[2] Applied to pornography use, the concept of moral incongruence helps us understand how the "effects" of pornography use in our society are often less about what the practice of viewing explicit sexual media *does* to peoples' brains or standards and more about what that practice *means* within our own moral context. Applied to the experience of conservative Protestants, I show how moral incongruence creates a situation in which pornography affects conservative Protestants' lives in ways that are not only unique but also, as we will see, uniquely damaging compared to other Americans who may use pornography more often, but who lack the deeply inculcated and socially reinforced moral condemnations against it. This damage can also be exacerbated by other subcultural distinctives among conservative Protestants, including their pietistic idealism, biblicism, sexual exceptionalism, complementarian gender ideology, and contentious understandings of mental health and change. (I'll explain all those terms and ideas in good time.)

There is no way around it. The topic of pornography is loaded with moral and political implications. Some scholars view it as irredeemably oppressive and misogynistic—a cancer for society.[3] Others, applying a more social constructivist interpretation, challenge the very idea that "pornography" is itself "a thing," rather than an arbitrary label dominant groups give to sexual ideas and images that fall outside their parochial standards of acceptability.[4] The former group sees porn as *im*moral and to be rejected, while the latter group sees it as *a*moral and valuable for pushing the boundaries of sexual freedom. And of course, many (myself included) fall somewhere between these two extremes.

Readers should know that social science is inextricably linked with issues of morality and politics. This is so because social science involves statements about what human beings are like, and inevitably involves assumptions about the sorts of goals and priorities around which societies should be organized. Scientists are human. (That's a nice way of saying they are prone to bias.) As such, they do not approach the issues of human flourishing, fairness, and moral imperatives without preformed and deeply held beliefs. Moreover, as the moral psychologist Jonathan Haidt has argued so powerfully, scientists, like all humans, tend to be "groupish." Rather than choose our intellectual tribes on the basis of pure reason, we like to emotionally identify with groups first, and then use reasoning to defend our group's beliefs against others whom we conclude to be either stupid, or evil, or both.[5] I am not saying that is how social science *ought* to be; but that's how it *is*, nevertheless.

Why do I say this at the onset? In my experience, pornography research is a unique field because there is little established dogma that groups in power use to exclude scholars from the conversation. That is a good thing. Different scholarly camps approach the subject of porn with different ideological presuppositions and different conclusions that they like to draw. This is not the case for all sexuality research certainly, but it has been true in research on pornography.[6] In some disciplines or fields, one ideological position on an issue eventually comes to dominate the narrative and ultimately takes on a moral quality. Even attempting to question the established doctrine on such subjects would show that you are not only ignorant on an issue most consider settled; there may also be something *morally* wrong with you. But the subject of pornography's positive or negative influence on society is not like such issues. On the contrary, differing arguments on the subject of porn's "effects" are published in nearly every issue of the top sexuality journals like the *Archives of Sexual Behavior* or the *Journal of Sex Research*, both of which I currently serve as an editorial board member. The debates about porn are wide open. That is good for science, and for me.

Still, readers will almost certainly have their own moral and political views on the subject of porn. And they may be curious whether I have an agenda in writing about it. (I consider it a point of professional pride that in 2017 I was accused of having a pro-porn agenda by anti-porn activists and having an anti-porn agenda by pro-porn activists *in the same week*!) It is best to address the issue of my own potential biases from the outset. I am not a robot or a sociopath, and so of course I have my own moral views regarding issues like pornography, sexuality, religion, family functioning, and so on. But this book is not written to moralize about the dangers of pornography. In fact, people who read this book hoping to find ammunition for a political crusade against pornography will ultimately be guilty of cherry-picking findings. My arguments in this book regarding pornography's place in the lives of conservative Protestants are nuanced, contextualized, and in some ways surprising and contradictory. They certainly do not fit neatly into a "porn is always harmful" narrative. And nothing in my findings suggests pornography should be banned or outlawed—a proposition that I find imprudent and implausible.[7]

But with that said, neither will I avoid discussing the vast and growing body of literature suggesting that pornography use, under certain circumstances, can be detrimental to romantic and family relationships, sexual functioning, mental health, and even our relationships with strangers. And even the staunchest pro-porn advocates have to recognize how so much of the content of mainstream pornography is filled with misogynistic and racist messages.[8] Having published over twenty peer-reviewed articles and now a book on the subject, my scholarly opinion on pornography is not neutral. On balance, I don't think there is much evidence that porn (especially in its most mainstream form and as it is most often produced and used) makes the world a more humane and equitable place. But my goal in writing this book is neither to moralize against nor advocate for pornography. Rather, I wish to understand how it is experienced by a large, but specific portion of American men and women.

A few more caveats. Readers will likely notice that my interview sample and focus are selective in at least two ways I wish to acknowledge here.

First, the majority of men and women I interviewed are college educated and live in urban or suburban regions of the country. As a result, conservative Protestants from rural, working-class areas of the United States are not well represented, which means I'm also likely missing representation from more charismatic, Pentecostal expressions of conservative Protestantism often found in such regions. This is largely a result of the networks I had available to recruit interview participants. Though unfortunate, this is not as problematic as it might seem for a study of conservative Protestants and pornography use, since education, income, urban residence, and knowledge of computers are shown to predict regular pornography use.[9] Thus, my interview sample comprises the conservative Protestants most likely to be affected by pornography's availability.

Second, because I am writing about what I consider to be "mainstream" conservative Protestantism, my examples and arguments will be more about conservative Protestants on the whole (in a statistical sense) rather than small pockets of conservative Protestants who may deviate in important ways from those in the mainstream. One important example where readers might see this is in my almost exclusive focus on *heterosexual* conservative Protestants, who constitute around 99% of that group, according to the General Social Surveys.[10] To be sure, there are conservative Protestant men and women who privately are attracted to the same sex (likely a much larger percentage than we know) or who may openly identify as gay or lesbian. I don't intend my lack of focus on these men and women to indicate that I am somehow unconsciously being heteronormative; and I certainly do not intend it as a form of erasure (acting like they don't exist). I do write about these men and women at points in the book, but I fail to do their unique experiences justice. I hope other scholars will fill in this and other canyon-sized gaps that this book has left.

ACKNOWLEDGMENTS

—⟫◆⟪—

Curious friends often ask me, "Do you enjoy writing books?" Whenever I hear this, I'm reminded of the missionary Jim Elliot's statement about wrestling. Elliot was a champion college wrestler and someone once asked him if he really liked wrestling. He responded, "Before the match, I'm terrified; during the match, I'm in agony; and after the match, I'm exhausted. But yes, I love wrestling."[11] That echoes my experience in book writing. Though few feelings match that sense of accomplishment you get when you finish a book, the actual day-to-day writing of a book is difficult, slogging work, and it would be impossible without tremendous help. Owing to that help, I accrued a large number of debts in writing this book. Some can be repaid with thanks; other debts would take a lifetime to repay. But the least I can do for now is acknowledge my gratitude in these pages and let that be a start.

First and foremost, I wish to thank the men and women, pastors and laypersons, believers, unbelievers, and everyone in between who were willing to share their experiences with and evaluations of pornography use. Because of the moral stigma surrounding pornography use and masturbation in our culture, talking about these activities openly can be difficult, but I was often pleasantly surprised at how candid people could be. Two research assistants, Kara Snawder (currently a sociology doctoral student at Indiana University) and Hunter Harwood (currently a psychology doctoral student at Biola University), also deserve special thanks in this regard for conducting many of the interviews themselves. This research benefited greatly from their commitment to excellence in research, as well as their enthusiasm for people and the topics covered in the interviews.

A number of colleagues and friends around the country provided feedback on book proposals, drafts of chapters, or even undeveloped thoughts that I had bouncing around in my head. The most significant help in this regard came from Andrew Whitehead, my longtime coauthor and good friend, and Joshua Grubbs, also a coauthor and friend, as well as the leading expert on moral incongruence and pornography use. Other helpful feedback came from Kelsy Burke, Cynthia Graham, George Hayward, Annette Mahoney, Gerardo Marti, Mark Regnerus, Landon Schnabel, Jeremy Thomas, Nicholas Wolfinger, Paul Wright, and Kenneth Zucker. George Hayward also provided invaluable statistical help with the fixed effects regression models in chapter 3 (as well as on our *Social Forces* article using those same data), and Jeremy Thomas generously provided his cache of *Christianity Today* articles on pornography from 1956 to 2010, which I reference several times throughout the book.

My colleagues and students at the University of Oklahoma also deserve thanks. Cyrus Schleifer has been a coauthor on a number of the studies I cite in these pages and has been a sounding board for countless ideas in the book. Conversations with Joshua Davis also helped me process thoughts for different chapters. Kenneth Frantz, during our bimonthly chats over coffee, would periodically ask how the book was coming along; and some days that was the motivation I needed to sit back in my chair and write a few more lines. Lastly, the qualitative data collection and initial writing for this book benefited tremendously from a Junior Faculty Summer Stipend provided by the College of Arts and Sciences at OU.

Theo Calderara at Oxford University Press had vision for this project from our first conversation. He and his team, including Hannah Campeanu, were excellent at each stage of the process. I am also grateful to the two anonymous readers who provided helpful feedback that pushed me to add more complexity to the story that I was trying to tell.

Lastly, my family deserves special thanks. I love the academic life, but it can be rather difficult for one's immediate family at times. It seems there is always some looming deadline or another writing project to start. While I have continually tried to draw boundaries and defend my family life from encroachments from work, I have not always succeeded at this, and my wife, Jill, has been tremendously understanding during these times. I dedicate this book to her. Jill, I am so grateful for your friendship and for the miracles you work in keeping our family going. Thanks for having a sense of humor about being married to "the porn guy" for the last few years. Now let's get back to Cancun!

My family also experienced some health issues over the past two years and we could not have made life work without the support of my in-laws, Melinda Jobe-Palvado and D. E. Palvado, Dave and Debbie Jobe, and Ann Wynia, as well as my parents, David and Kay Perry. Your help with the kids, housework, meals, and just about everything else made it possible for me to keep my job. Words can't do justice to the debt we owe, but thank you. A million times, thank you.

Lastly, to my daughter, Ryan, and my sons, Beau and Whitman, you inspire me to do my job with excellence. (And someday, when you're all older, I won't have to change the subject when you ask what the book is about!) I am thrilled to see what the future holds for each of you. Your mom and I are so very proud of you all.

Introduction: "The Greatest Threat"

I would personally say from all my knowledge now that pornography's probably the greatest threat to the cause of Christ in the history of the world. It's that serious.

—Josh McDowell, interview with Christian
Broadcasting Network News, 2015

Pornography is the greatest cancer in the church today.

—Chuck Swindoll, print advertisement for
the Set Free Summit, 2015

Pornography is perhaps the most destructive moral crisis facing the church today. . . . It is difficult to overstate the extent of the issue. . . .[Pornography] is like a cancer that slowly destroys a person.

—Russell Moore and Phillip Bethancourt, *"Christianity's Pornography
Crisis," LifeWay MEN blog,* August 22, 2017

I think that pornography represents the greatest moral crisis in the history of the church. . . . [P]orn is something evangelicals can do in a dark room behind a shut door after they have railed against homosexual marriage and talked about conservative theology. . . . I think the greatest threat to the church today is the Christian pastor, the Christian school teacher, the Christian college and seminary student who exalts sound theology, who points to the Bible, and then retreats to the basement computer to indulge in an hour or three of Internet pornography.

—Heath Lambert, Ethics & Religious Liberty
Commission Summit, 2014

"THE MAGNITUDE OF PORNOGRAPHY IN THE WORLD," began Christian apologist Josh McDowell, his voice nearly lowering to a whisper, "is beyond comprehension." Addressing the 2016 Set Free Global Summit, the white-haired McDowell folded his arms, looked thoughtfully at his notes, and began rattling off astronomical figures on the scale of pornography consumption worldwide. "One of the top pornographic websites," he shared, "receives 100 million page views per day!" A world-class orator, McDowell rarely uses the colloquial term "porn," almost always saying the full word "pornography" with a slower intonation, conveying both gravitas and disgust. He pauses after each statement, letting the statistics sink in. "The total number of pornographic videos on *all* websites watched in a day," McDowell explained, "is over 17.2 billion . . . over 6.3 trillion a year . . . and over 190 billion pornographic photos are viewed every month."[1]

To put things into perspective for his audience, McDowell fired off a fusillade of statistics. "One pornography site monthly distributes porn equal to 58,000 years of music played continuously." "Another pornographic website transfers nearly 4,000 pages of porn per second," the equivalent, he said, of twenty DVDs. Hitting his stride, he added, "If all the data [from an unspecified pornographic website] was printed on 8.5 by 11-inch paper, it would fill 540 million four-drawer filing cabinets." One day's worth of those pieces of paper "would fill an Empire State Building!" And "one month of photos would be 1,392,000 miles long, if placed side by side, it would wrap around the equator 58 times."

By the time McDowell took the stage for his closing address, entitled "A Call to Arms," the audience had sat through nearly two dozen talks on how porn alters the brain, destroys families, and promotes sex trafficking. Now, McDowell attempted to rouse them to fight. McDowell quoted British abolitionist William Wilberforce ("You may choose to look the other way, but you can never say again that you did not know") and the German theologian Dietrich Bonhoeffer, who was martyred in a plot to kill Hitler ("Silence in the face of evil is itself evil—God will not hold us guiltless. Not to speak is to speak. Not to act is to act."). He then challenged his audience: "We need a Wilberforce, a Mother Theresa, and a Bonhoeffer in the church today who have the courage to battle the devastation of porn as they did slavery and Nazism." McDowell concluded his talk with a solemn charge: "Each one of us has a responsibility. To have the knowledge that everybody has gained this week, and go back and be silent is complicity in pornography and child sex trafficking. . . . We have a job to do."

The four-day conference was hosted by Josh McDowell Ministries (a subsidiary of Cru, formerly Campus Crusade for Christ) and Covenant Eyes, a Christian firm that sells internet accountability software and filters. Nearly a thousand pastors and lay leaders (the vast majority of them men) representing over three hundred organizations from nineteen countries traveled to the Summit to learn about the growing threat of pornography and the resources available to help those in their churches break free from their "addictions" to porn. The list of twenty-five speakers, addressing topics such as "Brain Science and Porn," "The Power of Accountability," "Counseling Towards Recovery," and "Healing a Wife's Wounded Heart," included pastors, activists, Ivy League professors, therapists, neuroscientists, medical professionals, and pollsters, many of whom write books or run organizations dedicated to liberating Christians from pornography. Regardless of their profession, however, nearly all presenters were, like Josh McDowell, squarely within the evangelical Protestant tradition.[2] Their messages were, likewise, unified: pornography is destroying Christian families and the witness of the church; it is horrifyingly addicting; viewing porn directly supports sexual violence, including rape and child sex trafficking; and the only hope is found in the gospel of Jesus Christ.

From "A Scourge on Society" to a Scourge on the Church

Conservative Protestants have been warring against sexually explicit media since the mid-1800s. In the latter half of the twentieth century, influential fundamentalist leaders such as Jerry Falwell, Tim LaHaye, David Jeremiah, Pat Robertson, and D. James Kennedy, as well as flagship evangelical publications like *Christianity Today*, inveighed against the growing presence of pornography in American life, and increasingly, in the lives of believers themselves.[3] And conservative Protestant leaders were optimistic that they would turn back the rising tide of pornography. In his 1982 book *The Battle for the Family*, LaHaye assured readers, "It is just a matter of time before one of our Moral Majority organizations or our pro-moral senators put together a well-organized campaign to outlaw [pornography]. Together with outraged and fearful women throughout the country, we will succeed in putting pornographers out of business."[4]

To say that LaHaye was wrong is an understatement that borders on the comical. Pornography has never been a more accepted and visible part of the American cultural landscape. And it has never been more widely consumed.[5] While accurate statistics on porn viewership have always been difficult to obtain, economist Joseph Price and his colleagues used data from the General Social Survey to show that the percentage of American men below age 45 who reported viewing an X-rated movie in the previous year increased by roughly 20% between the mid-1970s and late 2000s. Porn use among American women also increased about 10% during this period. How frequently are Americans viewing porn these days? Data from a large probability sample of American adults surveyed in 2014 show that well over half of men and over a quarter of women under age 40 seek out pornographic material monthly, and over 45% of men and 16% of women under 40 intentionally view porn *in a given week*.[6]

What accounts for this increase? While Americans have become less likely to see pornography as immoral, much of the rise in porn viewership can be attributed to accessibility and anonymity.[7] The rise of smartphones means more Americans are being introduced to pornographic material at younger ages.[8] It should not be a surprise, then, that most of the increase in porn viewership has happened among younger cohorts of Americans.[9] Yet porn use is increasing among older Americans as well. Historically, watching pornography had been an activity for young people, and particularly single men. Age and family obligations would either make porn less desirable, less accessible, or both. However, Joseph Price and his colleagues have shown that that recent cohorts of Americans—the first to grow up with the internet as adolescents—are more likely to view pornography at older ages compared to previous cohorts.[10] Here, then, is the situation: more Americans today (men and women) watch porn than ever before, and many watch it regularly; they are more likely to start viewing it earlier; and they are continuing to view it later into their adult years. As famous as he was for writing fiction about apocalyptic prophesy, LaHaye's greatest work of prophetic fiction turned out to be his claim that pornography would be stamped out. Porn has never been more mainstream than it is today.

But conservative Protestants didn't just lose the political and cultural battles over porn. Committed Christians are losing the *personal* battle with porn. In their 2016 book *The Porn Phenomenon*, produced in partnership with Josh McDowell and Cru, the Christian-based polling firm Barna Group makes sobering claims about the prevalence of pornography use among committed Christians, such as:

• About half of Americans ages 18–30 who are "practicing Christians" actively seek out porn at some point in a given year.[11]
• One-fifth of practicing Christian young adults (ages 18–24) actively seek out porn at least weekly, and 44% come across porn at least weekly even if they are not actively seeking it out.
• Over one in three practicing Christian millennials (ages 25–30) actively seek out porn at least monthly.
• Nearly one in five practicing Christian married men actively seek out porn at least monthly.
• Over one in five youth pastors currently "struggle" with porn use and well over half of these pastors consider themselves "addicted."
• Over 94% of youth pastors and 92% of senior pastors believe porn is a bigger problem for the church now than it was twenty years ago.[12]

And as we will see later on, these numbers are quite modest compared to the figures spouted by McDowell and other Christian anti-porn activists, which often veer into the outrageous. But regardless of their statistical accuracy, conservative Protestants no longer talk about pornography as something *outside* the church. On the contrary, they are now scrambling to navigate a world in which committed Christian men (and increasingly women) can now so easily evade the traditional barriers to viewing sexually explicit media and have unlimited hardcore porn at their fingertips.

In one important sense, the "struggle" is self-induced. Conservative Protestants live in the world. Influenced by the spirit of evangelicalism, most refuse to fully detach from secular media and technology; in fact, they often enthusiastically embrace it for the sake of "engaging the culture."[13] Consequently, conservative Protestants are often indistinguishable from other Americans when it comes to media consumption. Table I.1 shows that Protestants who believe the Bible is "the actual word of God and is to be taken literally, word for word" or who affiliate with a denomination scholars categorize as "fundamentalist" are statistically identical to other Americans in most social media use. The only difference is that biblical literalists are about 10% less likely to use Facebook than other Americans, and both literalists and fundamentalists use LinkedIn less. Regarding internet access and use, biblical literalists are only slightly less likely than other Americans to say they use the internet or apps "more than occasionally," and fundamentalist Protestants are roughly 2.5% less likely than others to access the internet through a phone or tablet. Despite these small differences, however, the reported frequency of internet use and TV watching are statistically indistinguishable across all groups. Conservative Protestants, in other words, are just as engaged in the modern digital culture as other Americans.

But the price of their engagement with secular media and technology means conservative Protestants are routinely exposed to seductive messages about sexuality from a culture that is daily growing more brazen, and more at odds with their traditional, Christian sexual ethic. Deluged with sexual imagery and temptation at every turn, devout Christians, male and female, young and old, have nearly limitless opportunities to violate their own values by committing virtual fornication with images on a screen. Conservative Protestants, more than anyone else, recognize they are losing this battle on multiple fronts. This is why Josh McDowell explained to one Christian news source, "I would personally say from all my knowledge now that pornography's probably the greatest threat to the cause of Christ in the history of the world. It's that serious."[14]

This book is about pornography in the lives of conservative Protestants. Specifically, it provides the first comprehensive, sociological examination of how conservative Protestants experience porn use, its consequences in their lives, and how they are trying to respond individually and collectively. But beneath all this, it is a book about culture. It represents an attempt to understand how subcultures bound by a particular set of moral values and standards (in this case, a traditionalist sexual ethic) negotiate a world in which technological advances and broader cultural transitions make that ethic difficult to uphold.

TABLE I.1 Comparison of Social Media, Internet Use, and TV Watching Using Two Indicators of Conservative Protestantism

	Protestant Biblical Literalist[a]	Other Americans	Protestant Fundamentalist[b]	Other Americans
Social Media Use (listed alphabetically)				
Classmates	0.0	2.0	0.0	1.9
Facebook	71.8*	82.5	75.2	81.8
Flickr	1.9	2.8	2.6	2.5
Google+	35.3	36.3	35.6	36.2
Instagram	55.9	48.8	51.3	49.5
LinkedIn	18.6*	28.4	19.7*	28.8
Pinterest	31.4	36.5	41.5	35.0
Snapchat	41.2	41.3	45.3	40.3
Tumblr	4.9	7.9	3.4	8.5
Twitter	21.6	27.1	25.6	26.7
WhatsApp	14.7	16.2	11.1	17.4
Internet and App Use				
Use Internet/Apps from Phone or Tablet	97.1	99.1	96.6*	99.2
Used Internet/Apps Yesterday	92.2	94.5	90.8	94.8
Use Internet/Apps More Than Occasionally	82.3*	89.2	83.7	88.8
Use Home Internet Via Mobile Device	82.4	70.1	73.9	72.6
Hours of Internet Use on Weekdays	3.51	3.43	3.59	3.35
Hours of Internet Use on Weekends	3.97	3.51	4.01	3.45
Minutes of Internet Use on Weekdays	5.21	3.31	4.32	3.52
Minutes of Internet Use on Weekends	3.68	3.55	3.50	3.57
Hours of TV Watching per Day	2.68	2.28	2.57	2.31

Source: General Social Survey, 2016 (adults 18–39).
* Statistically significant difference from other Americans at the .05 level (two-tailed test).
[a] This is a Protestant who affirms "The Bible is the actual word of God and is to be taken literally, word for word."
[b] This is a Protestant who affiliates with a denomination that the GSS framers categorize as "fundamentalist" as opposed to "moderate" or "liberal."

Building on this idea, the book also explores what we might call the experience of *moral incongruence* and its consequences. All of us behave in ways that contradict what we say we value or how we would like to think of ourselves. For instance, most of us would say patience, kindness, and generosity are good *moral* qualities. We esteem those traits in others and try to teach them to our children. But we are often not as patient, kind, or generous as we wish we were. We are inconsistent. That may be unpleasant to think about, but it probably does not keep us awake at night. But what if we found ourselves consistently, and *willfully*, violating a moral value that sat at the core of our social identities? What if, say, generosity represented one of the core indicators of personal worth and goodness for our social group—to the point where your status as a group member was determined largely by how generous you were? Conversely, what if ungenerous people were notoriously stigmatized and whispered about? What if we each had internalized this value, measuring our own worth by our generosity, and desperately wanted to exemplify that quality, but each day we struggled with an overwhelming desire to be miserly and selfish, often succumbing to that temptation? Now imagine if situations like this were happening all the time, where we were constantly failing to live up to the standards of our group or ourselves (or our God). How might these experiences of moral incongruence influence our sense of self? Our social identity? Our most important relationships? To the extent that moral incongruence is happening collectively, how might this affect the group itself? Habitual pornography use, for conservative Protestants, is just such a case.

While this book tells us something important about American religion and culture, it also tells about pornography itself. Within academic research on pornography, debates continue to swirl regarding pornography's supposed effects on psychological health, relationship outcomes, sexual violence, and gender equality. Scholars on one side of the debate see porn as having wholly negative consequences. Some argue, for example, that habitual porn use can influence cognition and even neurochemical activity in pathological ways, contributing to hypersexual disorder (sex addiction) or sexually violent behavior. Others in this camp argue that heavy porn consumption can make men chronically impotent. Taking a more interpersonal approach, some scholars in this group argue that habitual porn viewing can make men dissatisfied with their sexual partners, or conversely, that pornography use by one's (typically male) partner lowers women's self-esteem and attachment to the relationship. And still others argue that habitual exposure to violent pornography actually incites rape and child abuse.[15]

On the other side of the debate, however, numerous scholars and clinicians challenge research linking porn use to negative outcomes. They argue, rather, that most opposition to porn use is rooted in old-fashioned, puritanical views about sexuality; that porn use is harmless (perhaps even beneficial); and that "self-selection" explains any observed associations between porn use and negative psychological, sexual, or social outcomes. That is to say, rather than pornography use actually *causing* sexual violence or relational dysfunction, individuals who are more prone to these problems are simply more likely to seek out porn in the first place.[16]

Lacking a broader sociological perspective, both sides of the debate often ignore the role of culture in connecting sexual practices to human identity, belonging, and relationships. This book supports an emerging body of research showing that the connection between porn use and intrapersonal or relational dysfunction is often less about viewing sexual images on a computer screen, and more about how one's community, and the values it holds dear, indelibly shapes the *meaning* of that activity for men and women, with very real consequences in their lives and relationships. Conservative Protestants, I will show, experience pornography in ways that are not only unique among Americans, even compared to other religious groups, but also uniquely damaging to their mental health, spiritual lives, and families.

But first, I need to lay some groundwork. The following section provides a brief introduction to the social scientific research on pornography and its influence in people's lives. It also sets the stage for understanding what a book about conservative Protestants contributes to that discussion.

What We Know About Pornography's Effects—And What We Don't

As an empirical social scientist, I am interested in how pornography use influences people's lives, but I argue that this question cannot be accurately answered without taking into consideration issues of cultural context, power, and interpretation.

How do we define "pornography," given that it can be a somewhat amorphous term? The standard dictionary definition of "pornography" is media depicting explicit sexual content intended for the primary purpose of arousal. But "explicit sexual content" is extremely general and subjective, and not all pornographic content is the same. While I will repeatedly acknowledge that there is a variety of pornographic content available, and will draw some of that out in the interviews, the book proceeds under the basic idea that "pornography" is whatever has become the market standard, the most common, readily available content—basically, whatever comes up when you Google "porn." To examine the effects of porn on people's lives, you can't look at edge cases—you need to focus on what people are most likely to see.

So, is there empirical evidence that pornography consumption changes humans' thought processes and relationships? Yes, but with qualifications. For instance, one major line of research has explored whether viewing pornography can contribute to someone's becoming sexually violent or at least more accepting of sexual violence later on.[17] Experimental studies consistently find that exposure to violent pornography in particular increases viewers' proneness to aggressive behavior or their acceptance of "rape myths" (basically that victims bare responsibility for their own rape).[18] Other studies have suggested that pornography use is associated with both verbal and physical forms of sexual violence.[19] But it's also important to emphasize that violent pornography is most likely to lead to forms of aggression when it is viewed by individuals who are *already* at risk to engage in these activities, such as misogynists or men with impersonal orientations toward sex.[20] So, both self-selection *and* porn use itself likely play a role.

A large number of studies have also explored pornography's connection to other important issues like mental health, romantic and family relationships, and even religion, each of which I will take up in later chapters. One thing that the majority of these studies have in common is their focus on the ways viewing pornography potentially influences the *psychological* (for the neuroscientists, also neurological or physiological) functioning of individuals.

What has my own discipline of sociology had to say about the subject? Far too little, I am afraid.[21] Despite nearly half of American men and over one-sixth of women under age 40 viewing porn at least weekly, you will search in vain for any studies focusing on pornography use in the flagship journals of American sociology.[22] This is not only a missed opportunity for the discipline but also has resulted in a glaring gap in the research itself. Because the vast majority of research on pornography use has been conducted by scholars operating within a (social) psychology or neuroscience theoretical framework, with few exceptions, the empirical focus has been almost entirely on the *individual* porn viewer or perhaps a couple. Moreover, because of this focus, the data have been almost exclusively quantitative and too often based on "convenience samples" of online respondents or undergraduates. The result is that studies by and large have been unable to step back and locate the observed associations between pornography use and, say, mental health or marriage outcomes, within a broader cultural context. Most of the pornography research, as a result, is unable to speak to the ways individuals interpret their pornography use and the implications of *these interpretations themselves* for those individuals or broader groups.

When I say that this book provides a *sociological* examination of pornography in the lives of conservative Protestants, I mean that it conceives of things like sexuality, pornography, and morality as *fundamentally* about social groups. Most people view pornography alone. But we are never alone. Certainly, conservative Protestants believe God is watching, but that is not what I am talking about. Wherever we are, we bring with us the influences of our parents, friends, class background, mass media, and so on, and these shape the lenses through which we interpret our own behavior and relate toward others. Conservative Protestants, as individuals and as a group, bring to the experience of pornography a deeply inculcated rejection of just about everything that is portrayed on the screen (and what they are likely doing with their hands and genitals while watching). And yet, conservative Protestants *are* watching porn. They hate it; yet they watch it. What is more, conservative Protestants as a group are self-reflectively aware that they watch it. What are the practical consequences of this incongruence, not only for their lives as individuals but also for their intimate relationships, their parenting, their faith communities, and the conservative Protestant subculture it-self? How are they trying to respond?

Studying Conservative Protestants and Pornography

While I offered something of a parenthetical definition of conserva-tive Protestants in the preface, I need to further qualify exactly what I mean by "conservative Protestants" and why I use that particular label. First, my focus in this book and all my contemporary examples of conservative Protestants are entirely American. The people about whom I am writing are inextricably connected to their American-ness in terms of culture and identity, a fact that should influence any arguments about how this subculture is negotiating the broader cul-tural and sexual milieu. Most generally, I use "conservative Protestant" to refer to American Protestants who are *theologically conservative*. By theologically conservative, I mean they hold to orthodox creeds (the Trinity, virgin birth, substitutionary atonement, bodily resurrection) and view the Bible as their primary authority for how they should live. Because my quantitative data include different measures of religion, I often operationalize "conservative Protestant" by self-identification as an "evangelical" or a "fundamentalist" Protestant or affiliation with theologically conservative denominations, and, when possible, in com-bination with other measures of Bible belief. In qualitative interviews, all those whom I label "conservative Protestant" in this book would identify as theologically conservative in the way I describe. I should also stress, however, that when I refer to "conservative Protestants" as a group, I do not wish to give the impression that I view the 60 million or so American conservative Protestants as a monolith or that I be-lieve that conservative Protestants think exactly the same way about sexuality, pornography, or other issues. Quite the contrary, much of this book will highlight some of the important theological distinctions within large subgroups of conservative Protestants (e.g., reformed camps vs. broadly evangelical camps) and how that influences their experience of pornography use.[23]

Conservative Protestants—and especially those of the more "re-formed" or Calvinistic variety—largely subscribe to a view I call *pi-etistic idealism*, by which I mean that they believe that ideas and intentions are of paramount importance. God is chiefly concerned not with a person's actions but with her motivations. The flip side of this is that conservative Protestants—more so than Catholics, Mormons, Orthodox Christians, Jews, or really most other religions—have a weak "theology of the body."[24] Simply put, for conservative Protestants, the obedience that God demands is not about bodily actions so much as it is about a person's heart.

Such is also the case for sin. As I will show, pietistic idealism is vitally important for understanding how conservative Protestants think about sexual impurity. The Bible's teachings on sexuality are understood to mean that sexual activity outside of heterosexual marriage is a sin *primarily* because of the inordinate desires in someone's heart—also called "lust" or sexual idolatry. This is why, as we will see, conservative Protestants are unequivocally opposed to viewing pornography (the very purpose of which is to lust with one's heart), but hold a far more ambiguous relationship with masturbation, especially if it does not involve pornography. Indeed, it often seems that the primary reason for condemning masturbation *at all* is that it involves lusting in one's heart. The concept of pietistic idealism will also help us understand why (reformed) conservative Protestant strategies for defeating "porn addiction" almost always prioritize heart transformation over bodily discipline, which they view as potentially useful but insufficient for *true* purity in God's eyes.

Elsewhere in the book, I use the term *sexual exceptionalism* to describe the tendency among conservative Protestants to view sexual sin as *supremely* corrupting—the worst of all possible sins. This is not necessarily unique to conservative Protestantism, since we can see this in Christianity throughout history. But among contemporary conservative Protestants, this emphasis contributes to greater feelings of social stigma for acts of "sexual immorality," including homosexuality, adultery, premarital sex, and pornography/masturbation, but also individual feelings of guilt and shame for repeatedly committing such acts. Many conservative Protestant men, as we will see, evaluate their entire spiritual condition in terms of whether they have looked at porn and/or masturbated recently. This emphasis also contributes to greater feelings of betrayal, insecurity, and second-hand shame for spouses and other family members.

Also, one could not discuss conservative Protestantism's relationship to pornography without considering how their particular views regarding gender and sexual orientation come into play. Whether conservative Protestants actually live out different gender roles in their day-to-day relationships is up for debate, but they often formally affirm *complementarianism*, subscribing to the belief that God designed men to be initiators, leaders, and protectors, while women are designed to be responders, helpers, and nurturers. How does this relate to pornography use? Within the conservative Protestant subculture, *male* pornography use and masturbation are extremely sinful, but they are also normalized by complementarianism. Men are seen as natural sexual initiators and are understood to "struggle" with issues of lust more than women. In fact, Christian men might be thought abnormal (or lying) if they did *not* confess to struggling with lust. Porn use, then, may actually in a way affirm one's God-given masculinity. Women, on the other hand, are perceived as sexual responders, not prone to visual lusting and masturbation—certainly not as a man is thought to be. Conservative Protestant women who view porn, as a result, describe experiencing heightened sexual shame for not only corrupting their own sexuality but also for violating God's design for gender—sinning "like a man."

Male same-sex attraction also provides an interesting lens through which to view the importance of gender for conservative Protestants in interpreting pornography use. On the one hand, conservative Protestants are often thought of as viewing homosexuality as the ultimate perversion. Christian pastors and authors, for example, often discourage porn use and masturbation among men either by equating it with homosexuality ("a man touches your penis and brings you to orgasm") or by warning that homosexuality is where their path leads ("porn will lead you to more deviant sexual tastes"). However, unlike conservative Protestant women who view porn, men who struggle with watching gay-male porn often feel more free to confess that to pastors or other groups of men, because even homosexual lust is still consistent with God's design for masculinity. Feminine lust, I show, is even more shameful and isolating.

Last, in this book I highlight how theology influences conservative Protestants' experiences with pornography. More than any other moral struggle for conservative Protestants, recurrent pornography use exposes several *practical tensions* in Christian theology that conservative Protestants find difficult to resolve. On the one hand, for instance, conservative Protestants believe a certain level of guilt or shame about one's sin is entirely appropriate. In fact, guilt about sin is indicative of a changed heart or true conversion. On the other hand, conservative Protestants believe those who have placed their faith in Jesus have been forgiven of all sins—past, present, and future. They no longer need to feel shame for their sin because it has been washed away. Too much guilt and shame, then, ultimately indicates an inadequate understanding of the gospel. It can overwhelm believers, leading them to hide the sin by withdrawing from other Christians and from God himself (my respondents often liken this pattern to Adam and Eve covering themselves with fig leaves). Therein lies a tremendous tension: continuing in sin without guilt or shame shows that you do not fully understand the gospel, but so does beating yourself up over the sin in your life.

A similar tension is related to habitual, willful sin in the believer's life. With the exception of some Holiness traditions that subscribe to "Christian perfectionism," most conservative Protestant traditions hold that believers will never be morally perfect in this life. So, on some level, sin is expected. However, virtually all conservative Protestant traditions are in agreement that a *true* believer's behavior will be noticeably different from that of an unbeliever. After you accept Jesus, you will not go on sinning as before. Pornography use and porn-fueled masturbation are extremely problematic in this regard because they are not only recurrent but also almost always conscious and premeditated, unlike other "reflex" sins such as pride, selfishness, or impatience. Recurrent pornography use, then, often causes extreme psychological dissonance and unrest in the lives of many conservative Protestant men and women. On the one hand, they know they will struggle with sin because they are imperfect. But as believers, they are no longer slaves to sin and indeed *must* be on an upward trajectory in terms of obedience. Otherwise, there is reason to doubt their own salvation.

Before I discuss these contemporary issues further, some historical context in order. As I mentioned at the beginning of this chapter, conservative Protestants' relationship to pornography has actually changed quite a bit since the middle of the twentieth Century. The following chapter tells that story.

I

From Obscenity *Outside* to Addiction *Within*

Words like "Christian," "porn," and "addiction" would not have been used in the same sentence just a few decades ago. . . . "Those videos" were in that other section of the store. "Those movies" were only available at the XXX store downtown or late at night on HBO, Showtime, or Cinemax. "Those people" only hung out in that part of town. . . . The Internet changed everything. The Internet took the far away, the forbidden, the hard-to-access, and the expensive, and made it accessible, affordable, and relatively anonymous. No barrier to entry. No passwords. No limits.

—Chris McKenna, "Your Church Is Looking at Porn,"
Covenanteyes blog, May 18, 2017

A FEW MONTHS BEFORE our interview, Brian, a 35-year-old Southern Baptist, and his wife, Lauren, had volunteered to help an elderly woman in their church, Mary, into an assisted-living facility. Mary's late husband, Ted, a World War II veteran, had been an accounting professor and dean at the local college and a staple in their community. He had also been a deacon and an enormously popular Sunday school teacher at their large Southern Baptist church since the 1950s. Brian and Lauren were tasked with helping Mary clean out the house in which she had lived for nearly seventy years. After Ted died, Mary hadn't wanted to throw away any of his things. Apparently, she had not even sorted through them.

As Brian and Lauren rummaged through one of the musty closets in a spare bedroom, they found an old, tattered three-ring binder hidden in the back, caked with dust. The label on the spine read "Fundamental Concepts and of Principles of Accounting." Brian and Lauren opened the binder, and much to their surprise, they did not see mathematical formulas or notes on depreciation. Instead, they were greeted with reams of plastic pages displaying photos of naked women in racy poses: Ted's collection of pornographic postcards likely accumulated during the war. Always gracious, and more than a little embarrassed, Lauren immediately tried to give Ted the benefit of the doubt as a "collector of all kinds of things," but Brian recognized a porn stash when he saw one. "Why else would it have been mislabeled and tucked into the back of the closet?" he asked. Brian had seen similar collections of pornography in the closets of his friends' dads growing up.

The dates on the postcards suggested the longtime Baptist deacon and beloved Sunday school teacher was hiding that cache of pornography since before *Playboy* even existed. It all seemed so primitive compared to how people access porn today, or even compared to how people viewed porn when Brian and I were growing up in the days before high-speed internet and smartphones. Ted might as well have been painting erotic stick figures on a cave wall! I asked Brian whether he thought anyone else in Ted's life might have known about the postcards. Certainly not anyone at church, Brian felt. "It would've been a complete scandal!" he exclaimed. Not because no one else was doing that sort of thing, Brian thought, but because "I just can't imagine those old-school Southern Baptists talking about [their porn use] with each other."

Clearly, pornography has been an issue confronting conservative Protestants for a long time. Ted is hardly the first conservative Protestant man to occasionally view sexually explicit material and hide it from his family. Data going back to the 1960s show that over half of men who attended church at least monthly reported at least "some" exposure to pornographic materials.[1] And more than one-fifth of Protestant "fundamentalist" men in the early-1970s (and roughly a third of those Ted's age at the time) reported viewing an X-rated movie the year they were surveyed. Another constant is that, unlike Americans more broadly, conservative Protestants are just as opposed to pornography today as they were four decades ago.

But Ted's story also highlights several new developments. Most obvious is the cultural and technological tidal wave that has simultaneously placed limitless, free, anonymous porn into the hands of every Christian with a smartphone. The world of pornography has changed considerably since "brother Ted" was tucking away his bawdy binder in the back of his closet. While conservative Protestants are just as opposed to pornography as ever, they find themselves increasingly in a context where pornography seems nearly unavoidable. And try as they might, they are losing the battle with pornography. The focus is no longer on shutting down pornographers or ensuring the faithful protect themselves and society from "filth" and "smut." It is instead on helping believers, their families, and their faith communities recover from their "enslavement" to pornography "addictions." How did conservative Protestants get to this place?

Conservative Protestants Confront the Threat of Pornography

Until the middle of the twentieth century, conservative Protestants showed relatively little interest in mobilizing political action against pornography. This was primarily because they viewed pornography as something *external* to their communities, being made and viewed by "those people," as Chris McKenna put it.[2] The 1960s and '70s witnessed two major, interrelated cultural shifts that would ignite the war between conservative Protestantism and pornography. The first was the sexual revolution, which represented a dethroning of traditional sexual mores in favor of an ethos that separated sex from the nuclear family and allowed women greater agency in sexual relationships. This sexual revolution in combination with other cultural and demographic transitions precipitated the second cultural shift—namely, the massive re-engagement of conservative Protestants into the public sphere.[3] Provoked by a variety of perceived encroachments from the federal government along with a culture clearly becoming unmoored from its traditional Christian heritage, fundamentalist leaders sought to provoke cultural and political engagement from the people in the pews. Pervasive pornography was one of the key issues conservative Protestant leaders sought to address, but almost always from the perspective of warning against a deadly threat to personal godliness and traditional family values. The war with porn had not been lost; it was only just beginning.

Books written by pastors like Jerry Falwell, Tim LaHaye, and David Jeremiah in the early 1980s show how conservative Protestant leaders were confronting the social menace of pornography both *outside* and *within* the church. One consistent theme is that pornography must be denounced as a threat to the morality of the entire nation. Jerry Falwell called pornography "a cancer that is changing the character of our republic."[4] And Tim LaHaye deemed pornography, "the single most inflammatory force for evil in our society."[5] How did pornography corrupt society? Falwell, LaHaye, and Jeremiah each argued that rampant pornography inflamed lust and promoted perversion, which caused a rapid increase in sexually transmitted diseases and all manner of depravity, including rape, homosexuality, group sex, and child molesting, as well as lesser evils like divorce. LaHaye's descriptions of pornography were bursting with these sorts of claims:

- "If proper investigation were made, I am confident that pornographic literature and movies would be declared the prime causes of today's sex crimes."[6]
- "Many of the most shocking crimes today are inspired when morally sick words and living-color pictures are transmitted through the printing press, into an equally sick mind, arousing the individual to horrifying action."[7]
- "I would judge that fully two-thirds of the sexual problems in marriage today can be traced to the use of pornography."[8]
- "I am convinced that the elimination of pornography from America would reduce forcible rape by 30 to 40%, and stiffer and faster penalties for rapists would cut it another 30 to 40%."[9]
- "Evidence is also mounting up that child abusers and pornographers are actually opening day-care centers to gain access to innocent children."[10]
- "What kind of a man or boy would sexually molest a helpless girl? Here are some of their characteristics. . . . A sexually obsessed male who reads pornographic literature or views sexually explicit movies."[11]
- "Pornography is one of the most serious social scourges of our nation and is currently an $8-billion-a-year industry. We have seen rising levels of venereal disease, child sexual abuse, homosexuality, divorce,

rape, and social deterioration in American because of the spread of pornography."[12]

- "I consider this form of mental depravity [pornography] the number one cause of the alarming increase in child molestation and assault. I know of cases where teenage brothers read their father's pornographic magazines and became so emotionally overheated that they raped their own sisters. Only God knows how often this occurs, for shame and fear keep many girls from reporting the crime."[13]

Other authors made similar claims, often illustrated with horrifying stories intended to warn Christian parents about where pornography would ultimately lead their children. David Jeremiah wrote about "Marty," an affluent teenager who was seeing a psychiatrist for his headaches. Jeremiah explained that headaches were not Marty's *real* problem, however. His problems began when he saw an adult movie at a friend's house.

> The movie turned out to be a hard-core pornographic film, depicting sexual perversion of the worst kind. After the initial embarrassment, the kids were completely seduced. They began to try to outdo the adults from that moment on. By the time Marty had reached high school, he no longer got a kick out of it. He turned now to drugs and sexual fantasies. Marty's experiences with pornography sated him with sex before the process of idealization was established in his relationships with girls. Apart from a miracle, Marty will never lead a normal life. What happened to Marty could happen to your children or to mine.[14]

This story conveys another theme that runs through both early and contemporary discussions of pornography use among conservative Protestants—that of *escalation*. Pornography use only becomes more and more habitual and perverse; it is itself a gateway to other evils. Worst of all, pornography could do the same thing to *our* kids too.[15]

And conservative Protestant adults were just as susceptible. Jeremiah advised the most important thing believers could do to fight porn, aside from keeping it out of the community, was to "make sure that we keep *ourselves* unspotted by the world. With the constant bombardment facing Christians every day, more than a few have succumbed to the temptation. Recently, I learned of a gospel minister who attended late-night pornographic films until he was discovered by one of his parishioners who had also fallen into the sin of an unclean mind."[16]

But pornography was not only a threat to Christian morality and families. Falwell claimed that pornography was a threat to the very freedoms Americans enjoy by potentially facilitating a communist or fascist takeover.

> Pornography is the antipathy of the basic premise of America with regard to freedom. Pornography is enslavement. . . . Liberty cannot be represented by sexual license. Communist theoreticians readily admit that one of the ways Western societies can be weakened is through sexual laxity. When the Nazis took Poland in 1939 they flooded the bookshelves with pornography. Their theory was that they would make individuals conscious of only their personal and sensual needs and thus render them more submissive to the oppression that was to come. The Nazis knew what moral decay would do to a people. We Americans are ripe for oppression.[17]

Regardless of whether the Nazis' intentions in making pornography available to Poles were as Falwell says (and they quite likely were not), Falwell's argument is that sexual idolatry is anti-American and will lead the nation into ruin.[18]

Related to this last idea, authors ultimately argued that Christian citizens had a responsibility before God to defend America's morality through legal action. This is perhaps the greatest shift from previous conservative Protestant approaches to pornography. While commentators in the 1950s felt that censorship was un-American and that Christians ought to focus more on their own spiritual lives as individuals, conservative Protestant leaders of the 1980s saw legal action as not only righteous, but of the utmost importance.[19] Falwell, the most overtly political of the group, concluded, "Moral Americans must hold up a standard. Proliferation of pornography into our society is striking evidence of our decadence. The moral fiber of our nation is so deteriorated that we cannot possibly survive unless there is a complete and drastic turnabout soon: A permissive society that tolerates pornography has the same hedonistic attitude that destroyed ancient societies."[20] He challenged his readers, "It is time we went into the courtrooms and prosecuted and stood before the Congress and the Senate of the United States and said, 'Gentlemen, the line must be drawn. We the people of this country will no longer stand for pornography. . . . It is the responsibility of descent people to halt [pornography's] advancement."[21]

LaHaye outlined a legal strategy to fight pornography. He repeatedly called Christian citizens to action, "We will not halt this sordid, sex-crazed crime rate until we rid our nation of pornography in magazines, X-rated and 'adult' movies, and particularly 'kiddie porn.' "[22] In a chapter on pornography in *The Battle for the Family*, LaHaye actually proposed a Constitutional Amendment reminiscent of Prohibition, called the "Decency in Literature Amendment," that would "permit law-enforcement officials to close down smut peddlers and stop this very profitable and corrupting business."[23] He even assuredly outlined the contours of this legislation and how it would be implemented:

> Simply stated, the laws of our country prohibit indecent exposure, public nudity, child molesting, intercourse between an adult and minor, and many other activities. Any literature or film that portrays such illegal sex acts should likewise be declared pornographic and outlawed. The fines for such offenses should be multiple. For example, each time a publisher is fined for the same offense, the penalty should be doubled. . . . Personally I look for a ground swell of reaction to pornography that will soon demand that our elected leaders protect us from this plague.[24]

Confident in their cause and numbers—and likely emboldened by their success in electing conservative candidates like Ronald Reagan to office—conservative Protestant leaders believed the Christian community should, could, and indeed *would*, rise up to halt the "purulent infection" of pornography.[25] Their optimism didn't last.

"Your Church Is Looking at Porn": Conservative Protestants Go from Offensive to Defensive

> As pornography is increasingly targeted to the private spaces we share with our personal computers, the battle must shift from retailer to consumer and employ a new Christian strategy: an emphasis on ministry to those who are enticed and entrapped by this newest version of "the lust of the eye."
>
> —Editorial, "We've Got Porn: Online Smut Is Taking
> Its Toll on Christians. What is the Church Doing About It?"
> *Christianity Today*, June 12, 2000

Conservative Protestants' efforts to curtail the distribution of pornographic materials were washed away by the cultural and technological tsunami of the internet. As Chris McKenna wrote in a 2017 blog post, "The Internet changed everything. The Internet took the far away, the forbidden, the hard-to-access, and the expensive, and made it accessible, affordable, and relatively anonymous. No barrier to entry. No passwords. No limits."[26] To be sure, the ubiquity and growing cultural acceptance of pornography have not made conservative Protestants any more accepting of it. They have, on the contrary, been unwavering in their opposition to the distribution of pornography over time. Figure 1.1 shows that the percentage of Americans who believe "There should be laws against the distribution of pornography whatever the age." Because some of the religion questions of the General Social Surveys (GSS) were not asked until later waves, I have here focused on Protestants who affiliate with a "fundamentalist" denomination (as opposed to those denominations the GSS classifies as "moderate" or "liberal") so that I can look back at trends starting in the early 1970s.[27] Over the forty-three-year span, around 50% of fundamentalist Protestants have expressed a desire to outlaw pornography completely. That number has remained consistent. By contrast, other Americans have become more accepting of porn over time. While 42% wished to outlaw porn distribution in 1973, by 2016 this number had steadily declined to 28%.

Yet the content of conservative Protestants' resistance to pornography *has* changed over time. Sociologist Jeremy Thomas sees three dominant narratives in conservative Protestant opposition to pornography.

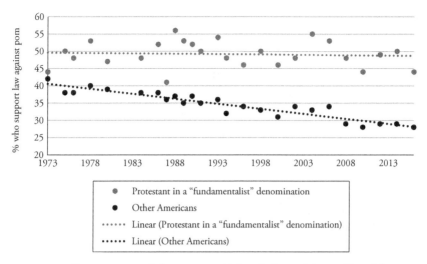

FIGURE 1.1 Percentage of Americans Who Believe There Should Be a Law Against the Distribution of Pornography at Whatever Age
Source: General Social Surveys, 1973–2016.

The first, dominant from the 1950s to around the early 1980s, was the *narrative of traditional values*. Leaders framed their opposition to pornography by using arguments about religious depravity and porn's consequences for personal purity, family stability, and societal morality. The writings I've quoted from Falwell, LaHaye, Jeremiah, and others most clearly reflect this narrative.

But two more narratives emerged starting around the mid-1970s and remain common today. One is the *narrative of public-performer harm*. This narrative originated largely with anti-porn feminists who argue against pornography because it harms both female *performers* by subjecting them to abuse, exploitation, pregnancy, disease, and later psychological harm and the *public*, by encouraging the objectification, subjugation, and abuse of women.[28]

The last narrative Thomas identifies is the *narrative of personal-viewer harm*, which is concerned with the consequences of pornography for the viewers themselves.[29] This is where much of the psychological and neuroscience research on pornography's "effects" over the past few decades comes into play. Following the growing research literature surrounding pornography's potential connection to sexual compulsion, addiction, depression, and other mental health issues, conservative Protestants have within the last few decades began to emphasize this narrative more frequently.

Thomas clearly demonstrates these transitions. Looking at articles in *Christianity Today* from its founding in 1956 all the way up to 2010, Thomas shows that from the 1950s to the mid-1970s, over 80% of all discussions of pornography fit the traditional values narrative. By 2010, this percentage declined to roughly 20%. By contrast, discussions falling under the narrative of personal-viewer harm made up roughly three-fourths of pornography references by 2010. Taking this up to the present day, I found that this remains true as of 2017 (see Figure 1.2).

But why the transition in conservative Protestants' anti-porn narratives? I believe it is the result of a growing *perception* that they are losing the war with pornography. Their stance has gone from "offensive," concerned primarily with preventing the moral filth of pornographers and porn users from corrupting their children through diligent legal campaigning, to "defensive," and concerned with addressing the

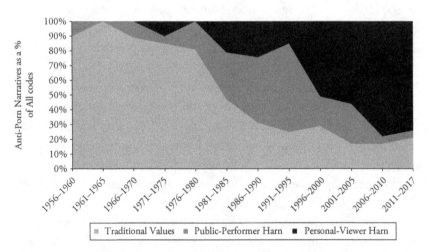

FIGURE 1.2 Coded Paragraphs Reflecting Conservative Protestants' Anti-Pornography Narratives as a Percentage of All Codes from *Christianity Today*, 1956–2017
Source: *Christianity Today*, 1956–2017 (data from Jeremy Thomas (2013, 2016) and author's complication).

problem of habitual (perhaps even compulsive) pornography use within their own ranks.

Why do I emphasize the word "perception"? Haven't more conservative Protestants, and particularly the younger cohorts, been watching pornography than in previous years? From the limited available data we have, the answer is yes and no, depending on how we define "conservative Protestant." The only data we have for viewing how the consumption of pornography has changed over the years is the GSS, which has asked a simple yes/no question about whether or not someone has viewed an "X-rated movie" since the 1970s. Since the primary focus of conservative Protestants regarding porn use has been on young men, I focus on men under age 40 in the sample. If any group of conservative Protestants would be susceptible to pornography's lure, it would be these men. (I will further explore the data on conservative Protestant women and pornography in chapter 4.)

Figure 1.3 shows the percentage of American men ages 18 to 39 who report viewing an X-rated movie in the previous year since 1973. I separate Protestants who affiliate with "fundamentalist" denominations from other Americans. Keep in mind that being classified as "fundamentalist"

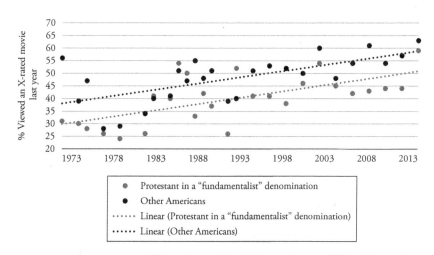

FIGURE 1.3 Percentage of American Men Below Age 40 Who Viewed an X-Rated Movie in the Previous Year By Affiliation with a Fundamentalist Denomination
Source: General Social Surveys, 1973–2016.

tells us little about the beliefs or level of commitment among these Protestants; it shows only that they affiliate with denominations historically recognized as theologically conservative as opposed to those widely thought to be more moderate or liberal. The trend lines reveal that men who are conservative Protestants by this definition are consistently less likely than others to view pornography, but their usage of pornography is increasing, and at a rate similar to others. The conservative Protestant group who viewed porn increased by about 20% from 1973 to 2016, while other Americans increased by about 21%. (The results are virtually identical if I compare those in "evangelical" denominations to other Americans.) Figure 1.3 would suggest that conservative Protestant men below age 40 are indeed succumbing to the temptation of pornography over time.

But what happens when we look at conservative Protestant men by a somewhat more reliable measure—say, their commitment to the authority of the Bible? Figure 1.4 shows trends in porn use for Protestant men who affirm that the Bible is the "actual word of God and is to be taken literally, word for word" (this question was not asked until 1984). The trend lines indicate that pornography use among these conservative

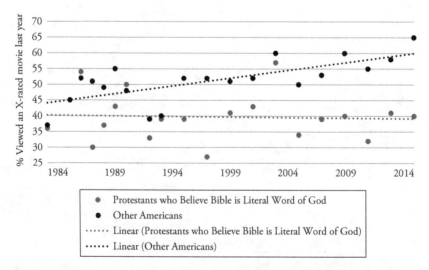

FIGURE 1.4 Percentage of American Men Below Age 40 Who Viewed an X-Rated Movie in the Previous Year By Adherence to Biblical Literalism
Source: General Social Surveys, 1984–2016.

Protestant men, on average, has not changed over time (staying at about 40%), even while it has grown over 15% for other American men under 40 (from 44 to 60%). In fact, this trend also holds true for Protestant men under age 40 who have had a "born-again experience" or have tried to convert someone to Christianity.[30] This suggests that, unlike those who simply affiliate with a fundamentalist or an evangelical denomination, conservative Protestant men for whom their faith is more meaningful and authoritative seem to be resisting the growing trend among American men to view porn, even in the midst of the internet revolution.

Now, there are a number of important limitations of the GSS porn-use measure. Some are not as consequential as they seem, while others require greater caution. I will not go into all of them here.[31] However, one key limitation I will acknowledge is that the question only asks about whether a respondent viewed pornography *at all*, not how often the respondent viewed it. It could be that conservative Protestants who do watch pornography are watching it more often today than in previous years because of its greater accessibility, anonymity, and affordability. There are no available data to track that trend, unfortunately.

Even so, the finding that young Bible-believing Protestant men are not increasingly turning to pornography is highly inconsistent with the common assumption among conservative Protestants themselves. According to Barna Group's survey of Americans and pastors, roughly three-fourths of "practicing Christians" (self-identified Protestants or Catholics who attended church within the past month and who strongly agree their faith is very important to them) and over 90% of senior pastors and youth pastors believe that pornography use is now a bigger problem for the church than it was twenty years ago.[32] Trends from Figure 1.4 would also be inconsistent with the dominant narrative coming from conservative Protestant thought-leaders and organizations. In fact, the very impetus for conferences like the 2016 Set Free Global Summit, or Barna Group's *The Porn Phenomenon*, or the popularity of accountability software and filter programs like Covenant Eyes and X3watch is the perception that pornography *is* overtaking the faithful.

Consider the following statements taken from various books, articles, blog posts, or sermons, many of which are based on statistical memes that bounce around within conservative Protestant circles.

- "A survey taken at a Promise Keepers rally revealed that over 50% of the men in attendance were involved with pornography within one week of attending the event. And that was 20 years ago."[33]
- "Forty-seven percent of Christian homes now have a major problem with pornography."[34]
- "Of those who identify themselves as Christian fundamentalist conservatives, they're 91% more likely they're watching pornography than the average non-believer."[35]
- "A recent survey conducted by the Barna Group found that approximately two-thirds (64%) of U.S. men view pornography at least monthly. Moreover, the study revealed the number of Christian men viewing pornography virtually mirrors the national average."[36]
- "One evangelical leader was skeptical of survey findings that said 50% of Christian men have looked at porn recently. So he surveyed his own congregation. He found that 60% had done so within the past year, and 25% within the past 30 days."[37]
- "Barna found porn use is up among Christians too. Some 41% of Christian men ages 13–24 and 23% of Christian men ages 25 and up said they 'frequently' used porn."[38]
- "According to a 2000 survey of clergy members conducted by *Christianity Today* and *Leadership* magazines, about 40% of clergy acknowledge visiting sexually explicit websites."[39]
- "Fifty percent of pastors regularly look at porn."[40]
- "There's roughly a fifty-fifty chance your pastor is looking at porn."[41]
- "Of evangelical, fundamental, born again youth pastors, 80 to 90% watch pornography. The ones leading our kids."[42]
- "[A] recent anonymous study done by Promise Keepers discovered that 54% of pastors had viewed porn in the previous seven days. If that is the number of *pastors*, how many people in the pews are using too? It's safe to say that some 20 million Christians [50% of those in the United States, according to the author] are using some form of illicit material *every week*. The church has become pornified (emphasis his)."[43]

The belief that a large percentage of faithful Christian men are now regularly viewing pornography is so taken for granted that writers are skeptical of any statistics saying otherwise—even their own. For one example of this, Barna Group indicates in *The Porn Phenomenon* that only 13% of "practicing Christians" reported viewing pornography at least monthly—a rather inconvenient statistic if one wants to affirm the narrative that most devout churchgoers are regularly viewing porn. Thirteen percent does not seem so bad compared to 42% of everyone else in the survey, and it is extremely low compared to the high rates of Christian porn viewership commonly claimed among conservative Protestants. Anticipating the incredulity among readers, Barna includes an asterisk by the practicing Christians statistic explaining, "It is likely practicing Christians use porn less frequently, as reported, but there may also be under-reporting since porn use within the Christian community is much less socially acceptable than in the wider culture."[44] First, it is likely that Barna Group is quite wrong about committed Christians underreporting their porn use. Research by psychologist Kyler Rasmussen and his coauthors has shown that religiously devout people are actually *more* likely to report their pornography consumption.[45] But what is important here is that Barna Group actually calls into question the accuracy of their own data in the face of findings that porn viewership is actually not as high among committed Christians as commonly thought.

None of this is to say that conservative Protestants are not viewing pornography more often than they want. *Any* pornography use for conservative Protestants is sinful, and few would be comforted by the findings in Figure 1.4 indicating that only around 40% of conservative Protestant men under age 40 view porn in a given year. My only point is that *perceptions* about pervasive porn use play a major role in determining how conservative Protestants are collectively responding to the issue. For starters, many leaders are already operating under the assumption that pornography companies have the upper hand in hooking young Christians. In his 2017 article "Your Church Is Looking at Porn" for the *Covenanteyes* blog, Chris McKenna explains that the porn companies "are winning the cultural battle" on multiple fronts by perfecting their ability to attract attention, employing cutting-edge technologies like smartphones and virtual reality, and ultimately, making porn use seem normal and healthy (even perhaps, necessary).[46] Consequently, the belief that young Christians can somehow be protected from ever seeing pornography has been abandoned as hopelessly naïve. In his 2015 chapel address at Moody Bible Institute, apologist Josh McDowell railed against this antiquated idea. Instead, he takes eventual exposure to pornography as inevitable:

> We no longer ask, "How should I prepare my child if they see porn?" That's so dumb. The intelligent basis is asking this question, "How should I prepare my child for *when* they see porn?" Because your precious little granddaughter *will see porn*. All these mothers that come to me and many of them are homeschoolers and things which I admire. They say, "I can protect my child." I will look at that mother and say, "You are the problem." . . . It would be like trying to protect your kids in our culture from ever listening to music. . . . I don't care how much you pray for them, how much you teach them the Word of God or anything else, they *will* see pornography (emphasis his).[47]

This is a far cry from the defiant optimism of Falwell and LaHaye in the early 1980s.

The Rise of the Addiction Paradigm

Beyond simply wrestling with the ubiquity of porn, and the perception that more conservative Protestants are capitulating to sinful desires in a sex-crazed culture, the dominant narrative among conservative Protestant authors and leaders has shifted toward addressing the issue of porn "addiction" in the church. Citing a widely referenced statistic, one author explains, "Not only is our culture becoming 'pornified,' so too is the church. A recent survey found that 50% of Christian men and 20% of Christian women are 'addicted to porn.' That means that in a church with one hundred adults, twenty-five men and ten women are struggling with porn: one in three."[48] Describing habitual pornography use as an "addiction" (and embracing related terminology of "sobriety," "detox," "recovery," "triggers," and "relapse") has become ubiquitous in conservative Protestant literature on sexual sin and pornography use in particular. Sometimes the addiction language is explicitly used in the titles of popular Christian porn recovery books:

- *Addicted to "Love": Understanding Dependencies of the Heart: Romance, Relationships, and Sex*
- *Porn Nation: Conquering America's # 1 Addiction*
- *Cutting It Off: Breaking Porn Addiction and How to Quit for Good*
- *False Intimacy: Understanding the Struggle of Sex Addiction*
- *Wired for Intimacy: How Pornography Hijacks the Male Brain*
- *Breaking Free: Understanding Sexual Addiction & The Healing Power of Jesus*
- *Sexual Detox: A Guide for Guys Who Are Sick of Porn*

Other times, the authors simply assume the language of addiction throughout. But in almost all popular books written by conservative Protestants on pornography use, addiction is now the dominant paradigm.[49]

Importantly, the "addiction" paradigm has increased disproportionately to actual porn use. As I will discuss further in Chapter 3, a number of studies since the mid-2000s have shown that even though committed Christians are *not* more likely to watch pornography than other Americans, they are consistently more likely to label themselves "addicted" to pornography.[50] These trends are affirmed by Barna Group's national data as well. In their 2014 survey on pornography use, they found that while self-identified Christian men were somewhat *less* likely to view pornography regularly than non-Christian men, Christian men were roughly *twice as likely* as non-Christian men to label their pornography use "excessive" or consider themselves "addicted" to pornography.[51] And in *The Porn Phenomenon*, Barna Group finds that while only 21% of youth pastors and 14% of senior pastors currently use porn, a whopping 56% of youth pastors and 33% of senior pastors who use porn believe they are addicted.[52]

Why has this porn-addiction paradigm become so pervasive among conservative Protestants? One possible reason—and the one that anti-porn activists and conservative Protestants themselves would most affirm—is that regular pornography use *is in fact* an addiction just like cigarettes, drugs, alcohol, or gambling. Conservative Protestants, in this view, are the ones being honest about their addictions, while other Americans are simply in denial about porn's stranglehold on their lives. Without wading into the issue of whether porn use is addictive in the clinical sense, at least at this moment, scholars often view this explanation with skepticism, since the term "addiction" is often thrown around by conservative Protestant men who view porn quite rarely and fail to show signs consistent with other dependencies.[53]

A slight variation on this explanation might be that conservative Protestants are disproportionately more likely than other Americans to say they are addicted to porn because they are disproportionately more likely to use it compulsively. That is, there may be something about conservative Protestants (either culturally or perhaps their underlying personality types) that makes them more susceptible to addictive behavior. When conservative Protestants use pornography, it is argued, they feel a great deal of internal condemnation, which can then spiral into a vicious cycle of porn use and shame.[54] This shame–relapse cycle is also a dominant theory among conservative Protestant authors themselves, and is one reason much of the advice in their porn recovery books centers on reducing the shame that "addicted" men and women feel by applying the principles of forgiveness and redemption.[55] Scholars have also argued for something called the "preoccupation hypothesis," which suggests that conservative individuals (either religious or political) often get caught up in the very thing they are obsessed with opposing. For conservative Protestants, their constant opposition to sexual sin means they think about it more often and thus, ironically, may be more susceptible to it.[56]

In his 2016 study tracing the increase in "porn addiction" language in *Christianity Today*, sociologist Jeremy Thomas provides another explanation. Collectively employing the concept of "addiction," Thomas argues, serves the purpose of providing a sense of psychological relief. More specifically, Thomas reasons that the "addiction" idea relieves conservative Protestants from moral responsibility for their actions. In decades past, pornography use would simply have been called "sin" (along with other colorful terms like "perversion," "depravity," "degeneracy," and "debasement"). But calling habitual pornography use an "addiction" puts some rhetorical distance between the actor and his behavior. It is no longer a sinful behavior that one is *choosing* to engage in.

An addiction is physiological—almost involuntary. You don't want to do it, but your body fights against you, and thus you are less culpable.[57] A further step in this direction of rhetorical distancing is the increasingly common use of "slavery" language in discussions of habitual porn use. One can observe this trend in popular titles like *Finally Free* and *Redemption: Freed by Jesus from the Idols We Worship and the Wounds We Carry*. If "addiction" is something physiological and largely out of the control of the porn viewer, being "in bondage," "enslaved," "trapped," or "caught in the web" of pornography is something even more involuntary. The "slavery" motif also provides a more explicitly biblical metaphor for habitual porn use than the modern term "addiction." If one is "enslaved" by one's porn addiction, the only solution is to be "set free" by God's sovereign grace.

Beyond providing psychological relief for the viewer, Thomas argues that calling widespread pornography use an "addiction" allows conservative Protestant *leaders* to placate their own consciences in failing to protect their church members from pornography's influence. The thinking goes: Pastors are supposed to be able to shepherd their flock away from sin. But how can a pastor be expected to fight physiological addictions? That is the role of therapists, counselors, and other parachurch organizations. Interestingly, Barna Group's public-opinion research on pastors lends support to this idea that pastors tend to protect their own egos in evaluating porn use in their congregation. In *The Porn Phenomenon*, Barna Group points out that while over 90% of pastors view pornography as a bigger problem for the church today than it was twenty years ago, they are far more optimistic about *their own* congregations. Less than 40% of pastors say porn use is a major or significant problem in their own congregation, and half say it is only a minor problem. Barna Group concludes, "There could be a tendency among pastors to be pessimistic about the broader Church and optimistic about their own community of faith."[58] In other words, pastors, being human beings, might be disinclined toward characterizing their flock (under *their* responsibility) as struggling with a serious porn problem. The idea and terminology of porn "addiction" might provide similar ego protection.

Thomas's arguments are persuasive. I would add that the idea of pornography "addiction" has been embraced as a rhetorical device to mobilize Christians against pornography within churches. The concept of addiction (and its association with gambling, drugs, and alcohol) carries with it implications about one's porn habit involuntarily escalating into more deviant, out-of-control behavior, ultimately resulting in the wreckage of an entire life. This can mobilize collective action by making the threat seem more imminent. Christian parents, for example, may be genuinely concerned that their kids would be exposed to graphic sexual content, but few parents would think their children capable of willfully embracing a lifestyle of sexual perversion. Parents just don't tend to think their kids are capable of such things. But "addictions" might take ahold of young people, virtually apart from their will. All it takes is exposure to porn, and they will be hooked. That idea is scary, and thus, potentially motivating.

Conclusion

Conservative Protestants' relationship to pornography, particularly within the past few decades, has been marked by both continuity and discontinuity. The faithful still oppose pornography as strongly as they ever have, perhaps even more so now that the issue of porn use is becoming so prominent within their own congregations. And while by some measures (e.g., conservative religious identity or affiliation), conservative Protestant adults do seem to be increasing in their likelihood of viewing porn, the *most* committed (those who affirm the authority of the Bible, live out their faith publicly, etc.) are not much more likely to view porn than they were before the internet came along.

Conservative Protestants have changed most noticeably in their collective orientation toward pornography. Pornography is no longer seen as a threat *outside* the church. It is, as so many conservative Protestant authors have called it, "a cancer" that is killing Christian lives and testimonies, particularly men.[59] As pastor and author Tedd Tripp asserts, "Online pornography is not just a problem for Christian men; it is THE problem."[60] With this growing perception, conservative Protestants' orientation to the problem of porn has gone from offensive to defensive, from fighting the obscenity *outside* to fighting the addiction *within*. Summarizing the trends in conservative Protestants' perspective on pornography use over the past six decades, Jeremy Thomas concludes: "Pornography use has changed from being a deviant activity that one could avoid by staying away from the seedy and disreputable part of town, to being a sinful choice that one could resist through prayer and grace, to being a 'biological disease' that one could treat and recover from."[61] This is where conservative Protestants find themselves in the fight against porn today.

2

Fifty Shades of Gray Area—On Masturbation

Is it wrong for a Christian to masturbate? There is probably no more controversial a question in the field of sex than this.

—Tim and Beverly LaHaye, *The Act of Marriage*, p. 365

Welcome to the Gray Zone.

—Stephen Arterburn, Fred Stoeker, and Mike Yorkey,
Every Young Man's Battle, p. 117

[Christian] judgments about masturbation run all the way from viewing it as a sin more serious than fornication, adultery, or rape to placing it in the same category as head scratching.

—Richard Foster, *The Challenge of the Disciplined Life*, p. 123

This is a very difficult and complex question.

—Mark and Grace Driscoll, *Real Marriage*, p. 183

It all depends.

—Lewis B. Smedes, *Sex for Christians*, p. 221

THERE IS A CURIOUS irony at the heart of conservative Protestants' unique relationship to morality, sexuality, and the body. Conservative Protestants tend to be *unambiguously* and almost *unanimously* opposed to pornography. That may seem rather obvious by now, but thus far I've spent little time empirically validating that fact. In all my interviews and focus groups with men and women, participant observation at group events, or my survey of what conservative Protestants have written about sexuality, I have not found one person make an allowance for the possi-bility that watching pornography might be morally acceptable.[1] (Several opined that watching pornography would be preferable to actually having sex with another person, but even this was viewed as a lesser of two evils, not as something morally acceptable.) Obviously, this does not mean conservative Protestants don't view porn or don't privately ra-tionalize its use *for them*; just that they don't publicly approve of it.

National data have borne this out for some time. In the 2000 Politics of Character Survey, for example, nearly three-fourths of those who considered themselves "evangelical Christians" believed viewing por-nography was "wrong for all," and this number increased to over 84% among evangelicals who believe the Bible is the literal word of God. Other more recent studies tracking public opinion have found nearly identical results.[2]

Conservative Protestant *congregations* are also unmistakably opposed to porn use. In the 2007 Baylor Religion Survey, over three-fourths of Americans in conservative Protestant denominations, and roughly 85% of those who believe the Bible is the literal word of God, said their church forbade the use of pornography. By comparison, only around 55% of conservative Protestants who take the Bible literally said their church forbade premarital sex or cohabitation, and less than three-fourths said the same for homosexuality or abortion. In other words—and this is striking—conservative Protestants who affirm the authority of the Bible are more likely to say their church condemns *watching* sexual media than they are to say it condemns *actual* unmarried sex, homosexual sex, or abortion. Clearly, for the overwhelming majority of conservative Protestant individuals and congregations, porn use is unequivocally a sin—among the worst sins, in fact.

Masturbation, however, is a different issue. Even though pornog-raphy use is typically assumed to lead to or to be done in concert with solo masturbation, conservative Protestants' opinions of masturbation on its own are often quite different from their views on porn. To be sure, most conservative Protestants I interviewed or read on the sub-ject view masturbation as something dangerous, and a majority also seem to think it should be avoided. And yet, as other sociologists have also observed, conservative Protestants seem far less willing to come down dogmatically on whether it is *always* wrong for *any* Christian to masturbate, whatever the circumstances, than they are to condemn pornography.[3]

Do we see this comparative ambivalence toward masturbation at the national level? While there are no available data on Americans' attitudes toward masturbation, we can observe conservative Protestants' more ambiguous relationship with masturbation compared to viewing pornography by comparing their porn viewing and masturbation practices. Figure 2.1 shows the percentages of American men and women who report viewing pornography at least monthly and who also reported masturbating within the past month, according to two studies.[4] Because of the limited religion measures in the data, to focus on conservative Protestants I selected Protestants who identify as "evangelical" or "fundamentalist." The obvious trend in both surveys is that conservative Protestant men and women are considerably more likely to masturbate at least monthly than they are to view porn that frequently. In the 2012 New Family Structures Study (NFSS), conservative Protestant men are over two and a half times more likely to masturbate monthly as view porn monthly, and conservative Protestant women are over eight times more likely. And while the differences in the 2014 Relationships in America (RIA) survey between porn viewing and masturbation are not quite as stark (perhaps porn use and masturbation are becoming more closely related as porn becomes ever more accessible and portable), the

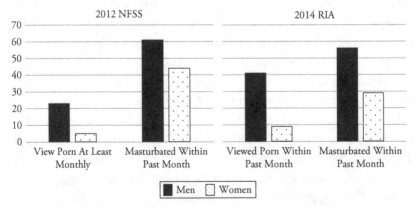

FIGURE 2.1 Monthly Pornography Use and Masturbation Among Conservative Protestant Men and Women in 2012 and 2014

trend is still the same. Clearly, we can infer from this that conservative Protestants don't seem to be quite as opposed to masturbation as they are to viewing pornography, at least not in practice.

But what is most surprising is the fact that while conservative Protestants are rather obsessed with pornography as a moral threat, they virtually ignore masturbation. There are no large-scale collective efforts among conservative Protestants to stamp out "masturbation" per se. Some might argue that masturbation is often *implied* when Christians discuss pornography use, and that is certainly true to an extent. But digging a little deeper into the Christian literature on sexual purity and lust reveals that conservative Protestants tend to consider pornography use and solo masturbation, though functionally related, as conceptually and morally distinct, with the former being far more feared. This is a fascinating paradox, since conservative Protestants at first blush would seemingly have solid theological reasons to condemn masturbation just as dogmatically as, say, pornography use or even homosexuality. If the only form of conscious orgasmic activity of which God approves takes place between two heterosexually married adults, solo masturbation falls outside those boundaries. And because masturbation is so much more habitual than porn use for both men and women (as Figure 2.1 shows), masturbation might reasonably give conservative Protestants greater cause for concern. Indeed, while "pornography addiction," as we have already seen, seems to dominate the fears of conservative Protestants within the past few decades, it would seem more sensible for them to worry about "masturbation addiction."

Ultimately, conservative Protestants' curiously ambivalent response to the practice of solo masturbation reveals deeper, persistent moral tensions within the conservative Protestant subculture when it comes to sexual morality and the body. This chapter unpacks the cultural sources and broader consequences of those moral tensions.

Why Masturbation Doesn't Arouse Conservative Protestants (to Action) Like Porn Does

Why is it that conservative Protestants have within the past few decades become so vocal and active in opposing porn use, but they have not shown the same sort of unified moral concern about solo masturbation?

Culture mediates how we interpret potential threats. Sociologist William Sewell developed the idea of "cultural schemas" to describe how cultural values, norms, and beliefs become deeply ingrained through years of socialization and experiences in our everyday social environment.[5] These cultural schemas inform our views about what is moral or immoral, sacred or profane, just or unjust, and how we respond in any given situation. Building on these observations, sociologists David Snow and Robert Benford argue that if we wish to successfully arouse and motivate an audience to confront a problem, we must ensure that we frame those issues in such a way that they align with our target audience's pre-existing cultural schemas.[6] In other words, people will generally only perceive social situations as "problems" or "threats" worth addressing if those problems correspond to their deeply held cultural and cognitive categories for immorality, impurity, and personal identity.[7]

Conservative Protestants share particular cultural schemas that shape their perceptions about what is moral and immoral, and how to respond in the face of either. While pornography use and masturbation are functionally related and are both violations of the traditional Christian standard for sexual morality, three "interpretive prisms" cause conservative Protestants to perceive, and ultimately respond to, the two issues quite differently: (1) the schema of biblicism; (2) the schema of pietistic idealism; and (3) the growing influence of psychology within conservative Protestantism.

"How It Should Be Whenever Scripture Is Silent"

In much of the conservative Protestant literature on sexuality, the immorality of pornography is virtually assumed, while such books often include special sections or entire chapters that address the "controversy" over whether masturbation is *itself* sinful.[8] There are even entire books, such as Steve Gerali's *The Struggle* (2003), dedicated to the question of whether Christians should embrace masturbation. Conservative Protestants themselves, in fact, are self-reflective about their collective moral ambiguity on the issue. Certainly not one to shy away from condemning certain sexual practices, Tim LaHaye admits, "Masturbation is one of the most controversial sexual subjects in the Christian community."[9]

But why should masturbation be controversial? The interpretive prism of biblicism provides one answer. Scholars generally regard a commitment to the authority of the Bible as a hallmark of conservative Protestantism, but "biblicism" describes how deep this commitment goes.[10] For conservative Protestants, the Bible is not only inspired by God but also is his literal word, inerrant and complete. It reveals God's will about *all* issues relevant to Christian living and thus is the Christian's only truly authoritative moral standard. Traditions, extra-biblical texts, creeds, leaders, or other sources are all subservient to it. Moreover, most conservative Protestants believe that the Bible's teachings transcend culture and are therefore just as authoritative and valid for Christians today as they were two thousand years ago. The schema of biblicism leads many conservative Protestants to adopt what sociologist Christian Smith calls the "handbook model" of interpretation. Here, the Bible is viewed as a sort of exhaustive manual or textbook containing God's instructions for Christians on every subject, including sexuality, family, science, personal finance, the environment, politics, social media, physical fitness, and so on.[11]

Thus, the morality of any practice rests largely on the issue of whether the Bible provides a clear teaching on the subject. Historically, masturbation could be condemned as an "unnatural" moral abomination that God would judge in large part because it was associated with the biblical story of Onan in Genesis 38. (Onan was struck dead by God for refusing to impregnate his dead brother's widow according to custom. In order to avoid producing children, Onan withdrew during intercourse and ejaculated on the ground.) But this idea rarely comes up anymore as an argument against masturbating. In fact, only one man in my interviews, Chet, a 28-year-old Texan with a strong Pentecostal background, made an oblique reference to Onan: "I just deem [masturbation] as morally wrong, you know? I forget where in the Bible, but basically spilling your seed on the ground is, you know, in the Bible; it's talked about as being wrong, and that's my thought process on masturbation and viewing pornography." Conservative Protestant authors, however, quite frequently cite this as a misinterpretation of the passage.[12] In fact, the consensus of virtually all pastors I interviewed and writers I surveyed is that the Bible does not contain any *explicit* teaching on masturbation. For instance, in his book *Breaking Free* (1999), author

Russell Willingham considers the common biblical texts used to argue against masturbation and concludes, "When it comes to the subject of masturbation, we can find no clear biblical prohibition."[13] And James Dobson said of masturbation, "Unfortunately, I can't speak directly for God since His Holy Word, the Bible is silent at this point."[14]

The lack of a clear biblical proscription against masturbation led most to conclude the subject was somewhat morally ambiguous. Stephen Arterburn, Fred Stoeker, and Mike Yorkey, the authors of the popular *Every Man's Battle* series of books about sexual purity, began their chapter on masturbation: "Let's get right to it, first things first. Masturbation isn't addressed in the Bible, so there's no direct, definitive scripture that says the practice is right or wrong. In other words, the issue of masturbation won't be as cut and dried as say, adultery."[15] Some take this lack of explicit biblical condemnation against masturbation as a tacit indication that it simply doesn't matter much to God. *Christianity Today* columnist Tim Stafford explains, "Masturbation is difficult to put in a good-or-evil category. . . . The Bible isn't shy about mentioning sex, but masturbation is never referred to. I think the very least you can conclude is that masturbation isn't the most important issue in the world from God's perspective."[16] Indeed, even Christian authors who argue adamantly against masturbation are forced to acknowledge its moral ambiguity. Canadian author and blogger Tim Challies, for example, affirms strongly, "Masturbation simply cannot fulfill God's design for sexuality, and thus has no place in the life of one who calls himself a Christian." And yet, he also admits, "Technically, it is accurate to say that masturbation is amoral: You can't say it is always bad or always good. This is because on very rare occasions masturbation may not be sinful."[17]

The pastors I interviewed were similarly at a loss. One evangelical Presbyterian pastor in Texas was almost evasive, insisting that the lack of clear biblical teaching precluded him from condemning the practice outright: "I think it's a gray area and I don't really have a public opinion on the issue of masturbation." When I asked specifically about the morality of single Christians masturbating, he replied, "It'd be a person-by-person kind of thing as to how I'd pastor them." Similarly, when I asked him about married persons: "I'm not going to make that judgment call for all couples." Likewise, when I asked one reformed

Baptist pastor in Tennessee whether masturbation could be permissible, he said simply: "I don't know. I just don't know. . . . You know, did Jesus masturbate? I don't know if anyone has even asked that question. He was a single guy that had to deal with his sexuality. We don't have information [from the Bible] about how he dealt with it other than we know he dealt with it perfectly."

Biblicism requires, among other things, that a clear scriptural precedent or teaching be provided for the Christian community to develop a strong moral opinion on a social problem or issue. Because the Bible provides no explicit mention of masturbation, authors often indicated that this *prevents* them from classifying masturbation as a clear moral threat. In his sex-education manual, Tim LaHaye affirmed, "Unfortunately, the Bible is silent on the subject; *therefore it is dangerous to be dogmatic.*"[18] Elsewhere, former megachurch pastor Mark Driscoll explains, "It must be noted that the Bible does not condemn [masturbation] outright. Though the practice is as old as the Scriptures, *the Bible's silence on the matter should cause us to avoid calling something a sin that God does not.*"[19] And pastor-author Tim Chester explains, "The Bible doesn't explicitly talk about masturbation. . . . *Because the Bible doesn't address masturbation explicitly, we should be cautious about giving a blanket condemnation.*"[20] Here, the clear implication of these quotes is that *because* the Bible does not give a clear teaching on masturbation, Christians should not condemn the practice unequivocally.

The lack of a clear biblical mandate against masturbation also prevents *consensus* among conservative Protestants. In their sex-education manual *How and When To Tell Your Kids About Sex* (2007), counselors Stan and Brenna Jones explain, "The Bible appears to be silent about masturbation. . . . It is not surprising, then, that Christians are quite divided over how to think about the morality of masturbation. One poll of laypeople and clergy by *Christianity Today* found that almost exactly one-third of each group reported that they believe masturbation is wrong, one-third believe it is not wrong, and one-third believe 'it depends.'"[21] Pastor and author Joshua Harris, famous for his evangelical classic *I Kissed Dating Goodbye*, issued a similar statement in his 2003 follow-up *Sex Is Not the Problem (Lust Is)*, "*Because* Scripture doesn't specifically name the act of masturbation, a heated debate has erupted among Christians, and there is an endless array of opinions on the issue. One Christian book will say it's wrong, another that it's perfectly fine. One expert will say it's healthy, another that it's destructive. There are even dozens of pro-masturbation and anti-masturbation Christian websites making their cases on the Internet."[22]

Indeed, in *Every Young Man's Battle* (2002), Arterburn and his coauthors acknowledged that the authors *themselves* were divided on the topic of masturbation: "Since God didn't address masturbation directly in Scripture, the questions can seem endless. Theologians will argue over this until Christ returns, *and maybe that's how it should be whenever Scripture is silent.* Even we coauthors have found it difficult to decide together what to label masturbation and where to draw the lines of sin."[23] Importantly, the authors suggest that Christian debate, rather than consensus, *should* be expected when the Bible has not given clear, definitive instruction on the topic. Biblicism requires that contemporary moral threats be connected to scriptural precedent, and the Bible's silence on masturbation means that conservative Protestants are unlikely to mobilize against it.

Conversely, conservative Protestant writers unequivocally reject pornography.[24] Mark and Grace Driscoll, for example, who argue that masturbation is sometimes morally permissible for Christians, explain: "The purpose for pornography is clearly lust. And throughout the Old and New Testaments, God repeatedly condemns—as a grievous evil—lust for anyone but your spouse."[25] Unlike masturbation, which is difficult to connect to explicit biblical teachings, the activity of *viewing* pornography is more easily connected to biblical prohibitions against looking at others "lustfully." This crucial distinction is one reason why conservative Protestants view these two issues so differently.

"Christianity Begins and Ends in the Heart"

Pietistic idealism emphasizes that beliefs and intentions are more important than actions.[26] For most conservative Protestants, and especially those of the reformed variety, one's physical actions—including everything from sexual behaviors to eating—are simply a manifestation of the condition of one's "heart," which is God's primary locus of concern. Conservative Protestant authors emphasize this point repeatedly. Christian counselor Steve Gallagher makes it clear: "The first thing that must be understood is that Christianity begins and ends in the heart. That is true because every action a person takes can ultimately be traced back to the heart."[27] A key distinction between the act of viewing pornography and the act of masturbating, on these grounds, is that the former is more clearly and directly connected with one's heart or intensions. Viewing pornography is tantamount to lust or sexually coveting someone that God has not given to you for that purpose.[28]

By contrast, because there is the *possibility* that one can masturbate without looking at sexual images and entertaining lustful thoughts, masturbation becomes morally ambiguous. One Southern Baptist pastor explained, "I agree with [Mark] Driscoll in that he says masturbation is not sin as long as you can do it without lusting. [For a married man away from his wife to masturbate], I don't think is sin, but as Driscoll says, it's flirting with sexual immorality, and therefore *could* be sin because of *that* commandment, not lust . . . Only the Spirit can teach us" (emphasis his). The issue for this pastor, like others I interviewed, is the lust in someone's heart. In theory, if a Christian can masturbate without lust, then the act is amoral. A number of lay conservative Protestant men I interviewed claimed that this was indeed the case for them. A graduate student in Oklahoma, for example, explained:

STUDENT: This may be hard to believe, but I trained myself to see [masturbating] as a bodily function. I mean, I trained myself to do it without fantasizing.
SAM: So, you can do it without lusting?
STUDENT: Yes.
SAM: So, what do you think about?
STUDENT: Well, now I think about my wife. Before I got married, I just trained myself to not masturbate if I was in a lustful state of mind. It was just for the sensation.

Similarly, another lay conservative Protestant man in Georgia explained that "My wife gave me some pictures of herself that I keep in a file on my computer—a well-hidden file, mind you [laughs]—so that I can take care of that myself (masturbate) whenever I feel tempted [to watch pornography]." Here again, the clear focus of this man and his wife is his heart or intentions. Masturbating to porn would be immoral, and hurtful to his wife, but masturbating to images of his wife is morally acceptable.[29]

Jared, a Southern Baptist computer programmer in Georgia, and his wife, Natalie, wrestled with infertility for years. They began undergoing testing and treatments to help. As part of that testing, Jared had to provide a semen sample, which required him to go into a private room at the doctor's office and masturbate into a cup. While pornographic videos and magazines are provided in these rooms to aid in the "collection process," Jared emphatically did not want to masturbate to pornography. So he and Natalie came up with a solution, "It was so awkward. [laughs] I had them take out all the magazines and movies. . . . Natalie gave me some pictures of her on my phone that I used, and I just made sure I deleted them as soon as I was done." By the standards of pietistic idealism, it would be difficult for conservative Protestants to categorize Jared's masturbation as sinful. Jared does not regularly masturbate, and the occasion of his masturbation in this case is not self-gratification but, rather, to make godly babies with his Christian wife; she is fully aware and supportive of his masturbation; and there is no extramarital lust involved since Natalie herself provided the visual stimuli. Only under the most rigidly legalistic interpretation of God's intentions for orgasmic sexual activity (e.g., "Every orgasm *must* happen inside a woman's vagina with the possibility of pregnancy") could Jared's actions be condemned here.

The centrality of pietistic idealism in distinguishing between pornography use and masturbation can clearly be seen in the way that that even those who believe masturbating to be immoral almost always justify their view on the basis of assumptions about Christians' hearts or God's intentions for sexuality, *not on the physical activity itself.* Tim Challies, for example, states plainly: "As God makes very clear in his word, sex and the issues surrounding it are fundamentally spiritual in nature. The temptations of pornography engage our minds and bodies in what is primarily a spiritual battle. This battle *includes* a physical component, but it is much *more* than that. Being tempted to masturbate is probably the most common illegitimate physical expression of this spiritual battle. . . . *The physical battle is not the core issue.* It's an outward expression of how well you have been fighting the inner, spiritual battle."[30] Similarly, Joshua Harris also argues that Christians should not masturbate on the grounds that it is a heart issue:

> Is masturbation a trivial issue that we need to stop worrying about so much? Or is it a big deal? I think it's both. . . . I think Christians make too big a deal of masturbation in that we obsess over the act and neglect the more important issues of the heart. No question, God is concerned with our actions, but He's even more interested in our motivations. . . . It's a mistake to make the act of masturbation the measure of our relationship with God. . . . The reason [masturbation] matters to God is not because it involves our genitals, but because it involves our hearts. And God is passionately committed to our hearts belonging completely to Him. . . . Masturbation isn't a filthy habit that makes people dirty. It only reveals the dirt that's already in our hearts. It's an indicator that we're feeding the wrong desires. That's why problems with lustful actions are symptoms of deeper heart problems.[31]

Practically speaking, if masturbation is connected in any way with lust or pornography, then it is clearly a sin. Authors and pastors stated this unequivocally. As pastor Tim Chester stated, "The fact that you use porn is a surefire sign that your masturbation is ungodly and unhealthy!"[32]

Along with a concern about the connection between masturbation and lust or fantasy, several pastors in my interviews added that masturbation was immoral because it was self-centered and they believe God intends sexuality to be self-giving. One Southern Baptist pastor in Alabama explained,

> I would say that [masturbation] is wrong because it promotes selfishness. To the single guy, I would say that he is not developing a good pattern of what marital sex should be, a giving to the other person, but instead is developing a self-focused mindset of personal orgasm and fulfillment. Plus, I'm not too sure he would be being totally honest in regards to his thoughts that he can do it without any lustful thoughts. But the self-centered sex would be my biggest concern. To the married guy I would pretty much say the same things in regards to him developing or feeding a self-focused view of sex.

He should learn self-control so that he can give his wife pleasure and not do things that would cause him to develop a habit of sexual self-centeredness.

While the pastor here does not point to any biblical passage to support the view that masturbation would be selfish, he concludes that his "biggest concern" was that masturbating would feed self-centeredness. Other pastors disagree with his point. One reformed Baptist pastor in Texas asked, "Sex is others-based, [but] who's to say that it's not another-focused to masturbate while your wife heals up from a miscarriage or pregnancy?" Others challenged the premise that masturbation can be done without lustful thoughts. "I call BS!" exclaimed one South Carolina pastor when I proposed that possibility.

Importantly, pietistic idealism led other pastors who discouraged masturbation to focus more concretely on heart issues rather than focusing on the physical act of masturbation itself. One pastor at a non-denominational Bible church in Pennsylvania, for example, explained,

> My practical counseling is always going to steer towards a holistic approach, rather than "Did you masturbate last week?" or "How many times in the last month?" The more important questions to me are about a person's heart and overall sexual health: Are you a slave to your sexual desires? Let's talk through why you think you are or aren't. If you can't control your desires, then there's a problem. Yes, masturbation is *probably* always wrong. But, as I alluded to before, I don't want to make too big of a deal out of this. If someone's life on the whole is clearly pointed towards Christ, then focusing on something like masturbation seems absurd to me. Sure, if there are patterns of clearly unhealthy sexual desires or behavior, then that needs to be addressed. But if a married dude jacks off thinking about his wife and it keeps him from looking at pornography or thinking about his secretary, then that's probably a good trade-off.

Here, the priority of pietistic idealism (ideas and beliefs in relation to God are paramount over bodily actions) is clearly articulated. Even though this pastor discourages masturbation, more important than questions about a person's habits is getting to the condition of their heart and whether they are serving sexual desires, as opposed to God himself. Also, the pastor sees masturbating to thoughts of one's wife as preferable to looking at pornography or fantasizing about another woman. An evangelical Anglican pastor followed similar reasoning. "The act of masturbation itself is sinful in the sense that it is disordered because you're using your body for something it isn't made for, like the guy rubbing himself with a pizza in [the movie] *Dodgeball*. However, it really is a lesser sin than masturbation coupled with lust." Thus, while biblicism precludes most conservative Protestant authors and pastors from dogmatically condemning masturbation itself as a sin, among those who do believe masturbation to be immoral, pietistic idealism sets the standard by which they make that evaluation.

Viewed through the interpretive prisms of biblicism and pietistic idealism, pornography is seen as a clear and unanimous moral threat. It can easily be connected to the Bible and intuitively involves the sin of "lust." Masturbation, by contrast, even though it is functionally related to pornography, has no clear biblical condemnation, nor can it be un-ambiguously connected to lust. Consequently, biblicism and pietistic idealism simultaneously engender a strong anti-porn consensus among conservative Protestants, on the one hand, and moral ambiguity and disagreement regarding masturbation, on the other.

But these influences are intrinsic to conservative Protestantism. What influence has the broader scientific and cultural shifts surrounding por-nography use and masturbation had on conservative Protestants' views? Quite a lot, actually.

"These Relaxed Standards Have Entered Christianity Through the Psychological Community"

While conservative Protestants are often insular in many respects, they are also quite mainstream in their cultural consumption and therefore greatly influenced by broader societal trends.[33] One impor-tant intellectual and cultural influence that has made inroads with conservative Protestants is popular psychology. Evangelical colleges like Wheaton and Biola and evangelical seminaries like Fuller have strong graduate programs in clinical and cognitive psychology. And while conservative Protestant leaders often lament the ways popular psychology has shaped Christian preaching and writing over the past few decades, its influence is undeniable. And nowhere is it more visible than in conservative Protestants' views regarding pornography and masturbation.

We saw earlier how conservative Protestant narratives had transitioned from concerns about moral purity to concerns about how regular pornography use could lead to personal, psychological harm. That transition coincided with a growing body of research among psychologists and other cognitive scientists connecting internet pornography with compulsivity and potentially deviant attitudes and behaviors.[34] Conservative Protestant books on pornography or sexual purity regularly cite empirical studies from the secular psychology or cognitive science communities highlighting pornography's long-term harm on "the brain."[35] Within the past decade, in fact, psychological research on pornography's purportedly addictive and destructive potential has been produced by conservative Protestants *themselves*. Most prominently, in his book *Wired for Intimacy: How Pornography Hijacks the Male Brain* (2009), William Struthers, an evangelical biopsychologist at Wheaton, contends that watching pornography "shapes and rewires" the neural circuitry of the male brain similar to the pattern observed in drug or gambling addicts.[36] Using the illustration of water carving out a trough through a concrete slab, Struthers explains:

> So it is with pornography in a man's brain. Because of the way the male brain is wired, it is prone to pick up on sexually relevant cues. These cues trigger arousal and a series of neurological, hormonal and neurochemical events are set into motion. Memories about how to respond to these cues are set off and the psychological, emotional and behavioral response begins. As the pattern of arousal and response continues, it deepens the neurological pathway making a trough. This neural system trough, along with neurotransmitters and hormones, are the underlying physical realities of a man's sexual experience. Each time that an unhealthy sexual pattern is repeated, a neurological, emotional and spiritual erosion carves out a channel that will eventually develop into a canyon from which there is no escape.[37]

Importantly, Struthers's discussion centers almost entirely on the influence of pornographic *images* on the male brain. Though he also believes masturbation is sinful, unhealthy, and addictive, he doesn't discuss masturbation at any length until three-quarters of the way through his book.

At the individual level, the influence of this larger "psychological harm" orientation toward pornography can be seen in the common self-diagnosis of "porn addiction" among conservative Protestant men. Yet, while psychological research on pornography's deleterious effects greatly increased the perceived social and personal threat of pornography in conservative Protestants' minds, such research also debunked longstanding myths about the supposed harms of masturbation. Indeed, a number of conservative Protestant authors explicitly connected Christians' growing moral ambivalence toward masturbation as stemming directly from secular psychology. In their best-selling manual on sex in Christian marriages, Tim and Beverley LaHaye wrote, "[H]umanistically oriented psychologists and psychiatrists . . . endorse [masturbation]. . . . Until about forty years ago, masturbation was regarded as harmful to one's health. . . . Now that medical science has proved that it is not harmful physically, popular opinion tends to accept it as a legitimate sexual function."[38] Counselor Steve Gallagher argues explicitly:

> Throughout most of Church history, Christian leaders considered any form of extra-marital sexuality to be sinful. Masturbation was rarely discussed openly. . . . Only during the past thirty years, as psychology has gained ever-increasing credibility within the Church, has it been suggested that masturbation is morally acceptable for a single person. . . . Seemingly, most of these relaxed [sexual] standards have entered Christianity through the psychological community.[39]

Each of these authors explains how the influence of secular or humanistic psychology has made many Christians see masturbation as harmless.

While psychological research from *outside* of conservative Protestantism was shaping conservative Protestants' views on masturbation, a number of conservative Protestant leaders who were *themselves* psychologists also had an impact. Many of the Christian authors who were the most accepting of masturbation (James Dobson, Clifford Penner, Steven Gerali, Stanton Jones, Douglas Weiss) were clinical psychologists by training. While these authors did not necessarily endorse masturbation, each offered more therapeutic interpretations of the practice, and each focused more explicitly on disarming the destructive guilt and shame often associated with it. Dobson, for example, wrote:

> It is my opinion that masturbation is not much of an issue with God. It's a normal part of adolescence which involves no one else. It does not cause disease, it does not produce babies, and Jesus did not mention it in the Bible. I'm not telling you to masturbate, and I hope you won't feel the need for it. But if you do, it is my opinion that you should not struggle with guilt over it. Why do I tell you this? Because I deal with so many Christian young people who are torn apart with guilt over masturbation; they want to stop and just can't. I would like to help you avoid that agony. [40]

Even among those authors and pastors who say masturbation is morally wrong, the concern over the way pathological guilt can intensify compulsive masturbation is a consistent theme.[41]

Pastors I interviewed expressed familiarity with psychological research on masturbation. For example, some were wary of habitual masturbation leading to compulsion or addiction. One pastor who affirmed that masturbation "like anything, could possibly be helpful or it can be really harmful" was cautious about the risk: "The thing about sexuality is it has such a hold in your brain in terms of chemistry. I think it's much easier to set up addictive patterns when it comes to sexuality than with food or alcohol. Your rewards center in your brain is so much more powerfully motivated. . . . But I'm just not sure." Another pastor in Georgia who also expressed ambivalence toward masturbation affirmed, on the one hand, "I think masturbation without the use of porn can be less [psychologically] damaging in multiple ways." However, he also cautioned, "My private opinion is that masturbation is just another way we avoid the pain of what God has given us or not given us. . . . I heard a therapist say once that you can be autonomous in masturbation, but sex with a real person is never autonomous."

Pastors often think through their own stance on masturbation in terms of the tools provided by psychological or counseling research on the topic. Taken together with data from conservative Protestant books on sexual purity, it is clear that the influence of psychology has shaped the differing responses to pornography and masturbation, with the former seen as harmful and addictive, and the latter being viewed as more innocuous.

Conclusion

What do their divergent views on masturbation and pornography teach us about conservative Protestants as a group? Conservative Protestants interpret social and moral issues through the interpretive prisms of biblicism and pietistic idealism. To the extent that a potential issue is understood as being explicitly addressed in the Bible and involves the "heart" of individual believers, conservative Protestants are more likely to perceive it as a black-and-white moral issue that merits a collective response. But to the extent no clear biblical mandate can be found on a subject, and it cannot be unequivocally related to the "heart" of believers, conservative Protestants generally avoid dispensing dogmatic moral condemnations against it and are more likely to view the issue as a personal matter between the individual and God.

Conservative Protestants' responses to pornography and mas-turbation also reveal their theology of the body—or, more accu-rately, their lack thereof. Pietistic idealism, which most conservative Protestants adhere to, emphasizes that what *really* matters to God is our "heart" (our intentions, values, desires, or allegiances) rather than our bodily actions. This emphasis is unmistakable in contemporary Christian teaching on masturbation. In fact, I would argue that pie-tistic idealism—and its flip side, a weak theology of the body—is one subcultural characteristic that makes conservative Protestants distinct from a number of other religious groups that place a strong emphasis on the body. Notably, at the heavily evangelical 2016 Set Free Global Summit that I referenced in the introduction, the plenary talk entitled "Theology of the Body" was given by a Catholic priest, Sean Kilcawley. Catholics are far more likely to stress the embodied nature of faith, obedience, and purity.[42]

Sociologist Dan Winchester has conducted a number of fascinating studies showing how converts to Islam or Eastern Orthodox
Christianity learn to more deeply internalize the moral teachings of
their own faiths by *first* performing religious rituals. Within these religious groups, Winchester shows that religious practices themselves
gradually transform the internal thought processes and feelings
of the believers. Practices come first; heart transformation comes
afterwards.[43]

Most conservative Protestants would have none of this, however.
"Christianity" as Steve Gallagher stresses, "begins and ends in the
heart." Obedience without proper motivation is empty formalism at
best, performative self-righteousness at worst.[44] As writers, pastors,
and laypeople continually highlight in this chapter, pornography is
evil because it involves the heart, and as (Christian) psychologists
have argued, it enslaves and corrupts the inner life of men and
women. Masturbation, on the other hand, is only sinful to the extent
that it affects the heart relationship with God in connection with lust
or it promotes selfishness, which would also be a heart issue. Genital
stimulation, however, is not primarily in view. Rather, a number of
authors, pastors, and lay individuals affirmed that if genital stimulation can be done in a way that is neither lustful nor compulsive, then
it is permissible.

3

Fleshly Lusts That War Against the Soul

When lust is pandered to, a habit is formed; when habit is not checked, it hardens into compulsion. These were like interlinking rings forming what I have described as a chain, and my harsh servitude used it to keep me under duress. A new will had begun to emerge in me, the will to worship you disinterestedly and enjoy you, O God, our only sure felicity; but it was not yet capable of surmounting that earlier will strengthened by inveterate custom. And so the two wills fought it out—the old and the new, the one carnal, the other spiritual—and in their struggle tore my soul apart.

—Augustine of Hippo (354–430 CE), *Confessions*, Book VIII

A Tale of Two Porn Users

David

Like many men who grew up before the age of wireless internet and smartphones, David, a life-long Georgia resident, first encountered pornography as a young teenager in the form of magazines and VHS tapes. "My friends all had dads or older brothers who had loaned or given them porn videos and so they would bring it over to my house and we'd watch it together. One of my friends also had *Playboys* his dad had given him and we looked at them at his house." Though he had discovered masturbation before porn, once he had his own stash of videos masturbating to porn became a near-daily habit. And while he certainly never wanted to be caught watching porn or masturbating, and never spoke about either with his parents, David told me, "It wasn't really something I felt guilty about back then."

David's feelings about his porn use changed when he "gave [his] life to Christ" in a college dorm room. After his conversion, David took advantage of every opportunity he had to grow deeper in his faith. He got involved in a local campus ministry, attended prayer meetings, and went on mission trips. Eventually, he began leading Bible studies and was recognized as a respected leader in his church. But while David quit swearing, dipping, drinking, and philandering, his pornography habit proved much harder to break. And now there was guilt. His repeated failures to quit pornography and masturbation first bothered David, then they exasperated him, and eventually they broke him. During what he describes as his low points, he would binge-watch internet pornography for hours, feeling completely defeated by his vice. Though he stayed religiously active, he was unable to stop watching porn, and he felt helpless.

David eventually carried his porn habit into marriage, and later, into parenthood. Though family and work have made his porn use less consistent, he still returns to it every week or so—usually for about fifteen minutes on his phone in the bathroom late at night or (on rarer occasions) when he has an hour alone at home. He has led his wife to believe that his "struggles" are completely in the past. Now, ten years into marriage, he feels that confessing his porn use to her would do more harm than good. David also described how his evangelical Presbyterian church, while "solid biblically," consists largely of older, upper-class persons who ostensibly either do not struggle with porn use or do not talk about it. Thus, he feels he has few options for support.

When I asked him what sort of porn he watched and whether the content had changed over time, he explained, "Pretty standard porn. I've never been interested in anything extreme at all. Some guys have had the experience that they've had to progressively move into more extreme stuff, but not me. My tastes have stayed about the same my whole life." Those tastes involve videos of strictly heterosexual sex, oral sex, and sometimes threesomes (the kind with two women, he specified). Even though David seems to have regulated his habit of masturbating to porn to about fifteen minutes a week, and his consumption patterns do not seem to be escalating in intensity owing to desensitization characteristic of those with a dependency or disorder, when I asked him about whether he would use the word "addiction" to describe his porn use, he replied,

> Absolutely. Totally addicted. Sometimes I've felt downright hope-less about my enslavement to pornography. I've looked at porn and masturbated in my office at work on multiple occasions, at my in-laws' [house], parents' house, on a plane, with my kids napping in the next room, you name it. I'm completely driven by the compul-sion; couldn't even dignify my behavior by calling it a "struggle." For long periods of time, I think I just resolved to get it over with quickly so I could feel like shit for a brief period of time, and then just move on with my day.

David's emotional state seemed somewhat matter-of-fact and de-tached throughout most of our conversation. It was not until the last set of questions in which I asked him how he felt pornography had affected his relationship with God that he became more emotional and began to choke up. After taking a moment to compose himself, he explained, his voice cracking,

> It's made me feel like a failure as a Christian. And someone who's a horrible hypocrite. There have been times when I've literally gotten up from a [devotional] time or prayer or given a Sunday school lesson or something and just looked at porn and masturbated. Or I've looked at porn and masturbated *before* I've given a Sunday school lesson on Sunday morning. What a freak! Whenever I finish, I come to my senses immediately and say, "What the fuck is wrong with you? God help me." But it's still there.

David's question to himself was not merely rhetorical. His inability to rid himself of porn had become an unresolved theological problem for him. In David's Calvinistic, reformed theology, and for most other conservative Protestants, those who have been born again by faith are supposed to have a new relationship to sin. Though they will never be perfect, their lives are supposed to be characterized by obedience to God. Conservative Protestants quote New Testament verses instructing believers that, "No one who lives in [Christ] keeps on sinning. No one who continues to sin has either seen Him or known Him" (1 John 3:6) and, "No one who is born of God will continue to sin, for God's seed remains in him; he cannot go on sinning because he has been born of God" (1 John 3:9).[1] Confronted with this teaching, recurrent sin in a professing Christian's life is a serious problem. And for many conservative Protestant men who habitually use pornography, there are grave concerns about the legitimacy of their own salvation. David described how he was theologically processing his inability to quit porn.

> I don't know if I doubt God's love for me. But I've wrestled with whether I can truly be a Christian and still continue on in this. I suppose it's some evidence of regeneration that I feel bad about it. But why can't I shake this? I've sometimes thought it was something like Paul's thorn in his flesh from 1st Corinthians 12, you know, he begged God to take it away, and God left it there to show Paul that God's grace was sufficient. So maybe God has let me wrestle with this to keep me humble and dependent on his grace? Or maybe it's just me and I'm a coward for not doing the hard thing. Maybe both. But I don't see why God would leave this thing in my life and punish my wife and kids for it.

By "punish [his] wife and kids," David was referring to the hiding and stolen intimacy he felt went along with his porn use.

Later, I asked David if he could sense himself backing away from his faith out of discouragement or turning down opportunities to serve in church because of his porn use. He answered in the affirmative, citing an example: "A few years ago I stopped taking opportunities to lead groups at church or disciple younger men because of where I am personally with porn and masturbation. I don't think I have much to offer in terms of spiritual maturity. And I'd really feel like a worthless hypocrite for teaching some young men about how to study the Bible and share their faith, when I'm regularly looking at pornography and masturbating. I certainly couldn't hold anyone else accountable. So yeah, I guess I have been turning down opportunities to live out my faith because of porn."

After our conversation, David told me he felt relieved. He had never really had an occasion to fully open up about his porn use to someone else—someone neither close to him nor a spiritual leader or peer—and so he found the experience cathartic. But his situation remained unchanged, practically speaking. He still feels beaten down because of his inability to fully eradicate pornography from his life. He is still unable to share this struggle with his wife or faith community. And he grapples with a desire to back away from religious participation in order to avoid the sting of hypocrisy.

Nick

Nick is similar to David in a number of ways. He is also from Georgia, white, college educated, in his early 30s, and has been partnered (not married) for the last six years. Also like David, Nick views porn about once a week. There have been times when porn use was more frequent, but he attributes the lower frequency these days to busyness at work and an active sex life with his partner. Even when he does view porn (usually on his home computer), Nick's tastes are for what he considers pretty vanilla, standard fare—usually heterosexual sex with either vaginal or oral penetration. He summarizes, "The things I dig [in porn] are the things I would encounter in a normal sexual experience."

Nick's evaluation of his own porn experience, however, differs considerably from David's, and much of this divergence lies in their different relationships to religion. David, a long-time conservative Protestant, has internalized an ethic that views *any* sexual activity outside of heterosexual marriage as immoral. Nick, who wavers between atheism and agnosticism, emphatically rejects such a sexual ethic as regressive—even hypocritical. When I asked him about his religious background, Nick explained, "There were attempts to *become* religious. That was because I had religious partners. So I made what I considered to be pretty strong attempts to do it, like go to church, and pray at meals, and try to feel like a personal relationship with God and pray and stuff like that. And I've tried that twice. But in the end, I was never doing that for me, and so I've been an atheist or agnostic my whole life, and I was never raised religious."

Nick went on to explain what he thought about religious perspectives on porn use, "I think religion suppresses natural human desires for sex. But even then, it doesn't stop them from doing sexual shit in the first place. [laughs] For example, my ex, who was fairly religious, that didn't stop her from having premarital sex with me and it hasn't for any women I've been with who claimed to be religious." Nick not only believes that religion is ineffective in curbing "sexual deviance," however religious people define it, but he feels that religion actually has a counteractive effect; it bottles up sexual desires and then causes frustrated religious people to act out sexually by viewing porn.

This does not mean that Nick embraces porn uncritically. In fact, he expressed considerable ambivalence on the topic. When I asked him about the morality of porn, for example, he explained, "I think there are two aspects of it. I have an opinion via morality about the *consumption* of pornography and the *production* of pornography" (emphasis his). On the production side, Nick expressed some concerns about the potential economic or social pressures placed on women to engage in sex work that they feel is degrading. "In the pornography industry, there are a lot of power dynamics between men and women. And most of these producers are men. And so the women getting involved in pornography, while there may be a contractual agreement for the performer, there is still a lot of pressure, you know. So from that end I think there are a lot of [moral] problems."

Regarding the *viewing* of pornography, however, Nick explained, "I don't think there's anything wrong morally. However, I do think it does screw with your psyche in a way that influences your family life, influences your dating life." Specifically, Nick worried that the consumption of certain kinds of pornography, such as violent porn, could stimulate violent sexual behavior in young men. He also expressed concern about men starting to develop unrealistic expectations of body image and sexual performance and then externalizing those expectations onto their romantic partner in harmful ways. Nick even feared that porn use might have some correlation with erectile dysfunction because male viewers may get used to the voyeuristic, third-party angle of the camera. Yet Nick did not consider porn use harmful per se—only certain types.

For instance, when I asked Nick about how he would advise young people regarding pornography use, he suggested, "Honestly, if someone wanted to consume porn, I would think it would be better to consume porn that's done from a POV [point of view] perspective, and also I think amateur porn would be better because you're not exposing yourself to [women at] the top 5%, right-tail of the bell curve [in terms of attractiveness]." This pattern, he felt, would help mitigate porn's potentially negative influence on one's relationships or sexual functioning. But he quickly reiterated, "So I don't think there's an intrinsic moral problem in the consumption of pornography, but it's all these other side effects that can occur."

As we concluded our interview, I asked Nick whether he had ever tried to stop using porn. "Absolutely," he answered, "because of what I've mentioned before, how I think it could be shaping my psyche. And obviously, in the endgame it's probably not going to help me, and the *last* thing I want is erectile dysfunction [laughs]." This prompted me to ask whether he thought pornography had harmed him in any way. He replied, "I do, but not to a severe degree. Hypothetically, I think that if I did not consume as much porn in my past I would not fantasize as much about other women besides my partner." But Nick was also quick to follow this by clarifying that his porn use did not bother him tremendously: "As far as feeling bad, the only feeling bad I have about [porn use] is thinking that I hope this doesn't affect my real world encounters [pauses briefly], but I know that it probably does."

The Social Meaning of Porn Makes the Difference

The clear contrast between David's and Nick's evaluations of their experiences with porn illustrates some central patterns I observed in my interviews. First, in all my conversations with conservative Protestants— men and women, pastors and laypeople—by far the most consistent trend is the relationship of pornography and porn-fueled masturbation to feelings of guilt, shame, and isolation from both their religious community and God. While David provides a particularly vivid example of how emotionally distressing this can be for conservative Protestants, I could fill several chapters with similar quotes. Moreover, this spiritual struggle with porn use, and its psychic consequences for conservative Protestant men and women, also represents the starkest contrast between the way conservative Protestants (like David) and those outside that subculture (like Nick) experience pornography. As Nick suspects, and as we will see later, porn use *can* negatively affect the intimate relationships of non-Christians and nominal or liberal Christians. In *some* heterosexual relationships, particularly at higher usage levels, porn can lead men to lose interest sexually in their spouse or make women feel insecure about themselves and resent their partner's porn use. These consequences are not specific to conservative Protestants. But those who are not conservative Protestants, unless they are holding on to what I would characterize as residual guilt from their earlier, more religious days, do not tend to wrestle with the private shame, discouragement, and self-loathing that conservative Protestants do.

Those feelings stem less from the *action* of viewing sexual images or masturbating to them than from what those actions *mean* for individuals and their community. David provides a prime example of this. Though he feels "totally addicted" to porn, his life does not fit the clinical pattern of addiction. Porn use is *not* destroying his life in practical ways. In all other areas of his life, in fact, David is a fairly well-ordered man. He is healthy, successful at work, an attentive husband, an involved father, and a valued leader in his church community. But for David and other conservative Protestant men and women, the recurrent moral incongruence of masturbating to porn, along with the attendant cover-up and deceit, creates within them the experience of profound dissonance, an internal conflict that is largely foreign to those outside their religious subculture. This incongruence, as we will see, holds consequences for conservative Protestants' mental health and even their faith.

Christian Sexual Exceptionalism

In orthodox Christian theology, life as a Christian is characterized by a struggle between two "natures"—the sinful nature (also called the "fallen nature" or "flesh") and the new nature (also called the "new heart" or "spirit"). The sinful nature, which is inherited from the biblical Adam and infects all humanity except for Jesus Christ, leads humans to rebel against God. After their conversion, however, Christians receive a new nature, which enables them to obey God's commands. Because Christian theology holds that believers still retain a sinful nature after their conversion, most conservative Protestants acknowledge that sin will always be part of a believer's life on earth. Yet Christians must strive for perfection by following the commands given in the Bible and the example of Jesus himself—even as perfection remains unattainable. The theological term "sanctification" refers to the lifelong process by which Christians, in cooperation with the Holy Spirit, bring more of their thoughts, intentions, and behavior into conformity with the commands of God and the example of Jesus.[2]

While sanctification is never completed in this life, in many conservative Protestant circles professing Christians who demonstrate a clear lack of concern with their sanctification—perhaps through willful, habitual sin—are often suspected to be false believers. As one popular systematic theology text cautions readers, "A consistent pattern of disobedience to Christ . . . is a warning signal that the person is probably not a true Christian inwardly, that there probably has been no genuine heart-faith from the beginning and no regenerating work of the Holy Spirit. . . . A long-term pattern of increasing disobedience to Christ should be taken as evidence to doubt that the person in question is really a Christian at all."[3]

But while the avoidance of all types of sin is a serious matter for conservative Protestants in general, in the United States they tend to be especially preoccupied with sexual sin. I call this tendency "sexual exceptionalism" because it takes sexual activities or desires conservative Protestants generally understand to be sin—e.g., adultery, premarital sex, homosexuality, lust, prostitution, pornography use—and singles them out as uniquely and especially corrupting for those who commit them. This tendency is captured by the evangelical satirist Joel Kilpatrick, who quips, "Every good evangelical knows that God has a much more difficult time forgiving sexual impurity than he does sins like gossip, judgmentalism, and neglecting the poor."[4] Biblical counselor and author of *Pornography: Slaying the Dragon*, David Powlison writes, "Sexual sins grab everyone's attention. They haunt the conscience and excite the gossip. They push other sins into the background. They go up on the on the marquee in red letters ten feet high."[5] Yet Powlison also acknowledges how conservative Protestants' preoccupation with sexual sin is a uniquely American phenomenon. He explains, "This characterization partly arises from tendencies within American Christian culture. Other Christian cultures may do their calculus of the conscience a bit differently. In Uganda, for example, *anger* is particularly shameful, the boogeyman sin that automatically disqualifies from ministry. But Ugandans view sexual immorality the way Americans view anger outbursts or gluttony. Such behaviors are sinful but aren't uniquely shocking or damning."[6]

Other conservative Protestant authors interpret the emphasis on sexuality as misguided. Best-selling author and columnist Philip Yancey, for instance, writes, "Jesus treated those who had fallen into sexual sins with compassion and forgiveness, and reserved his harshest words for the hidden sins of hypocrisy, pride, greed, and legalism. How is it that we who follow him use the word 'immoral' to signify sexual sins almost exclusively and reserve church discipline for those who fall sexually?"[7] And speaking to the topic of pornography use specifically, president of Barna Group David Kinnaman acknowledges, "We must recognize our tendency toward disproportionate bias when it comes to sexual ethics. The biblical standards on sexuality are unambiguous, particularly for evangelicals and conservative Catholics and Orthodox Christians, but somewhere along the way the focus on sexual morality became somewhat single-minded."[8]

Sexual exceptionalism manifests itself in a variety of ways. Pastors in prospering churches, for example, are seldom fired for being cocky, ambitious, and overbearing. In fact, such pastors are often celebrated as strong leaders, men of conviction.[9] But those pastors are quickly forced to resign for "moral failure" involving sexuality, even in situations not technically involving adultery.[10] Women in the church are unlikely to get bad reputations for being materialistic, having self-esteem issues, or not reading their Bibles, but as we will see later on, few things can shape a Christian woman's social identity like a known history of sexual promiscuity.[11]

Sexual sin is also unique because of the perception that it can corrupt even those who only hear about it. Male pastors, for example, may not have much trouble counseling a woman about her eating disorder, but numerous pastors have told me they would feel uncomfortable counseling women about their habitual porn or masturbation problems. Indeed, as I will show in the following chapter, for conservative Protestant women struggling with porn use, their lack of access to (almost always male) pastoral staff is often listed as a key reason they must struggle in silence. Additionally, we have already seen that conservative

Protestants are generally as connected to mainstream media as anyone else, but while conservative Protestants occasionally protest the violence in TV shows or movies, they are often far more vocal about the pervasive sex.[12] Noting this inconsistency, one Baptist pastor in Tennessee mused wryly, "How is it that you can get a group of deacons at your church to go to a movie where a thousand image-bearers are slaughtered on screen, and they don't give it a second thought, but if they see half a nipple [laughs], they're about ready to cut their body parts off so as not to fall into temptation!?"

Equating Porn Use with Sanctification

Many of the men I spoke with, adhering to sexual exceptionalism, seemed to measure their religious faith or sanctification almost solely by their success in resisting the temptation to watch pornography and masturbate. Jamarcus, for example, attends a predominantly white evangelical church in Oklahoma. He has watched pornography consistently for at least ten years, and recently he has been viewing it on his phone at work where he can take bathroom breaks to masturbate. This disturbs him tremendously. As he explained, "It makes me feel that if I could just get rid of this [porn habit], I could be one with God. I could be true. My relationship with God is going to be like my pastor, you know [laughs], it seems like his relationship with God is always like [snaps fingers], you know. Clicking." Other conservative Protestant men made similar statements, locating the entirety of their spiritual struggles within their sexual failures. An evangelical Presbyterian father in Illinois, for instance, recounted his off-and-on relationship with porn,

> I think, unfortunately, when I thought of sin I thought of pornography. That was like, you know, if there was a pie chart of the amount of time I thought about sin, it would be like 90% of it would be pornography and then some of it would be pride and anger, but it was like this gigantic thing [laughs]. And I would take communion and confess my sins and it would be like pornography, pornography, pornography. That was *the* thing. And I remember when I would go through stretches of a three or four months [without porn], and

I would go to communion and be like, what do I even confess now
[laughs]? And there was this big onion peel and all this other stuff
that I hadn't even dealt with because there was this big elephant in
the room that I can't see past.

In this instance, pornography virtually eclipsed all other areas of disobedience in this man's life to the point where, during periods of success
in not watching porn, he could not think of other sins to confess to
God. While he is certainly aware that there are other areas in his life
he wants to work on, pornography, in his words occupied 90% of his
attention.

One pastor in Tennessee beautifully described the contrast in
the patterns I observed regarding how conservative Protestant men
evaluated their experiences with pornography and how non-Christians
(or more nominal or liberal Christians) evaluated their experiences.

I think that with believers that one issue [porn use] can end up
shaping their entire identity. For instance, with believers you can say,
"How are you doing spiritually?" And many of them almost answer
purely based on how they're doing sexually. And so they've connected
how I'm doing in one small facet of my life with my entire sanctification. . . . But with unbelievers, I think there's a greater range of how
people are experiencing [pornography]. Like, some people think it's
great and no big deal, and that it's a normal part of life. And others
deal with shame and guilt. So I really think it's what shapes the conscience of the person more than anything.

As this pastor explains, conservative Protestants are more likely to define the "their entire identity," or the whole of their spiritual condition
in terms of porn use, which he acknowledges is a small aspect of their
lives. "Unbelievers" (or those who are not conservative Protestants), by
contrast, hold more diverse attitudes toward their porn experience since
they are not bound to a traditionalist Christian sexual ethic that singles
out porn use as supremely corrupting.

Sexual exceptionalism regarding porn in particular not only shapes
conservative Protestants as individuals but also in several ways is structured into the operation of many conservative Protestant congregations

and ministries. For example, a number of men and women I spoke with participated in "accountability groups," or what some called "fight clubs," where participants confess sin to one another and hold each other accountable for avoiding sinful thoughts and behaviors.[13] In many congregations and ministries, these groups are encouraged for *all* members. For men, these groups can revolve almost entirely around struggles with lust. When I asked one Baptist college student how much of the time in his group was spent talking about sexual sins, he replied:

> A lot of it. So usually we'll talk about what we've been reading, and then we'll talk about where we're feeling condemned. And then we'll take prayer requests. And so during [the condemnation] part of our conversation, which is definitely the biggest portion of the three chunks, [sexual sin] definitely dominates most of what we talk about, and that's really something that we've tried to get better about— like, let's talk about something else because it's not the only thing we're struggling with, you know? And so it almost becomes a group for the sin rather than a group for why we're really meeting, if that makes sense. We don't want to talk about, "Man, porn is tough," the whole time.

For this student's accountability group, the subject of where he and his fellow Christians are "feeling condemned" revolves almost exclusively around struggles with porn and gives little attention to growing in one's relationship with Christ.

The preoccupation with sexual purity can also be structured into personnel practices in conservative Protestant organizations. For example, I spoke with a leader of an evangelical collegiate ministry that has recently started requiring its campus ministers—men and women— to confess their porn use to their superiors. He added that repeated failures in this area of sexual purity (regardless of whether it is affecting others) would result in a loss of leadership opportunities and eventually termination.

Part of the reason conservative Protestants fixate on sexual sin, and masturbating to porn especially, is its premeditated, willful nature. Random instances of lust—perhaps clicking on a risky online advertisement or a sneaking a peak at a woman's chest—can almost be understood as involuntary reflex actions—what counselor David Powlison calls "no-effort sins."[14] Masturbating to porn, however, is deliberate. There is a degree of planning involved. Repeatedly engaging in these sorts of intentional sins can be more worrisome for conservative Protestants because of their theological commitments regarding sanctification. Christians are supposed to be set free from the power of sin, and thus they must pursue obedience, however imperfectly. Habitual, willful sin such as porn use could be a sign that one is not *truly* repentant—that is, not legitimately saved. In his exhortations on fighting lust, author and Baptist pastor John Piper warns readers gravely: "Jesus said, if you don't fight lust, you won't go to heaven. Not that saints will always succeed. The issue is that we resolve to fight, not that we succeed flawlessly. . . . [I]f we don't fight lust we lose our soul."[15] Similarly, in *Porn-Again Christian*, former megachurch pastor Mark Driscoll asserts, "Simply, any man who claims to be a Christian but lives in habitual, unrepentant sexual immorality is not fit for Christian friendship and community unless he repents, because he is defiling his friends and their church with his perversion. . . . God takes the sexual sins of his men so seriously that men who remain enslaved to sexual sin will die in their sins and wake up in the eternal torments of hell."[16]

Reflecting these very concerns, one college male who attends a nondenominational Bible church described his recurrent inner dialog:

> Every time it's anywhere near frequent, like, if it's more than once or twice a week, then I'm, like, "What are you doing? You're a porn addict." Like, obviously I'm not, but I'm just so hard on myself. So I'm, like, "You're an idiot, why do you suck at this?" And so I feel like if I consume porn, you're choosing that over God, because you know going in that you're about to sin, and you're, like, "Listen, Jesus, thanks for dying for me, but just one more time, like, probably again in a few days, is that all right?" Like, that just to me, yeah, you're going to be forgiven, but there's a point where it's habitual like that and there's—it's unrepentant. It doesn't matter if you repent every time, if you keep going back, I feel like that's unrepentant sin, so that's how I view it.

The young man is weary of taking God's forgiveness for granted by deliberately sinning with porn. Such behavior, he explains, gives him a reason to doubt his spiritual condition. Similarly, a married father of three in Illinois described how pornography, in that it is deliberate and calculated, was uniquely shameful and bothersome to him.

> I think for instance, when it comes to anger, when I'm at home and there's all this noise and no one is listening to me, and I'm, like, "Everyone get to bed!" and I'm frustrated. You know that's not acceptable, but it's, like, man, I just lost it for thirty seconds there. And for some reason, pornography seems different than that. I don't have a good answer why other than it's so calculated sometimes. There are times when I'm checking my email and I'm checking something else out and my mind just wanders. But there are other times where, I'm, like, you know, I've got nothing going on, I'm just going to stay home and indulge in [porn]. So right there I've decided. . . I don't ever decide I'm going to go home and yell at my kids [laughs]. I feel like that kind of calculated behavior that I can't stop is, like, I am *willfully* going against any kind of following Christ in this area. . . . I'm just so ashamed that I would know this going into it is wrong, and I'm just going to plow ahead even though I came up with this idea hours ago. So for some reason in my mind [porn is] unique in that way compared to sins that seem more reactionary, like, whoa, I just slipped, I shouldn't do that. For some reason I don't have the shame when I do pornography because it's that calculated.

The contrast between porn use and anger is instructive. It not only demonstrates sexual exceptionalism; it also reflects the underlying pietistic idealism that shapes how conservative Protestants often evaluate sins. The man experiences greater consternation over the porn use compared to lashing out at his kids because the porn use is carried out intentionally. And yet, no one else is directly affected by it. In losing his temper with his children, he is involving (perhaps even harming) other people with his behavior, but he does not feel the shame because it seems less intentional. The primary issue, then, is not whether others are harmed in the activity but rather, whether one's will remains consciously unbowed to God. It is a heart issue.

Whether or not it is consistent with orthodox Christian theology, the sexual exceptionalism of conservative Protestantism in the United States ultimately teaches that pornography and porn-fueled mastur- bation are a matter of Ultimate spiritual and social importance and therefore must be avoided. But the realities of their own sexual desires combined with the unlimited availability of porn often mean that many men will—intentionally and with some degree of regularity—consume porn. Many conservative Protestants, then, are forced to wrestle with a troublesome incongruence in their lives between the religious values they hold and their fleshly desires.

Porn Use, Moral Incongruence, and Mental Health

While relatively irreligious Americans like Nick may have few moral qualms with pornography use, research shows that regular porn viewing often creates guilt, shame, and mental distress in the lives of conserva- tive Protestants like David.[17] Economists Richard Patterson and Joseph Price have shown how committed, conservative Protestants may experi- ence what they call "psychic costs" from pornography use more severely than others. In a study of almost 30,000 American adults, they found that men and women who watched X-rated movies reported below- average levels of happiness, but that this association was most powerful for frequent churchgoers and those belonging to religious groups who held the strongest opposition to pornography use—namely, evangelical Protestants.[18]

Why does porn use seem to affect the subjective well-being of con- servative Protestants more powerfully than others? A growing body of research shows how the *meaning* of pornography use for religious per- sons negatively shapes their mental health and spiritual lives. Neither "pornography addiction" nor "sex addiction" are officially recognized as a disorder in the *DSM-5*.[19] And as we have already seen, religious persons are *not* more likely to use pornography than other Americans. In fact, studies consistently show they are less likely to do so, on av- erage.[20] And yet, studies show that religious Americans are more likely to consider themselves "addicted" to porn.[21] This trend was confirmed in my own conversations with conservative Protestants. It was not un- common, for example, for men to refer to themselves as "addicted," but report that in the past year they had viewed porn once, twice, or not at all. Mike is a Baptist college senior who describes himself as "addicted to pornography for a long time." During our conversation, he recounted that he had viewed pornography five times over the previous three years. When I asked him why he would consider himself addicted, Mike compared his experience to that of a friend participating in Alcoholics Anonymous (AA) who could not be around alcohol:

> I can't have the equivalent of one beer with pornography, if that makes sense. Like, I can't dabble. Just because I'm, like, incredibly weak in that sense. So I would say that I am a victim of addiction. You know, like, because, it's still a day-to-day battle. Like, naked women don't gross me out, by any means. Like, I'd look at someone naked right now [laughs], you know, what I mean? Like, I'm just sitting here talking to you and I'm, like, yeah, naked girls, that sounds really great [laughs]. And so it's just really, really tempting to me every day, and so I don't know that that is everyone's definition of addiction, but I would consider that an addiction.

While Mike has been fairly successful at minimizing his porn use, especially compared to the average college-age male, he is still harshly critical of his ability to resist temptation. He equates his craving for naked women, and his weakness in resisting that craving, to that of an alcoholic. And just as AA participants must admit that they are powerless over their addiction to alcohol, Mike cannot trust himself.

By comparison, in my conversations with men who were not conservative Protestants, not one labeled himself addicted to porn, even if he watched porn almost daily. Chad, for example, is a 22-year-old student who attended church growing up, but slowly became more agnostic in his late teenage years. When I asked Chad how often he watched pornography, he responded, "Like, five or six times a week." But when I asked him if he ever felt that porn had become an addiction or problem habit for him, he explained, "No. I mean, even though, like I said, I probably look at it most days in a week, I mean, it's probably, you know, fifteen minutes on those days. So it's not like it's this huge time commitment or anything that feels like it's taking away from anything. It's just a pretty short part of the day normally." Thus, for Chad, as for almost all my interviewees who were not conservative Protestants, the term "addiction" is reserved for life patterns that have become destructive. For most of them—and most conservative Protestants, in fact—porn use has not gotten to that extreme.

But beyond showing that religious people are more likely to consider themselves addicted to porn, research demonstrates how *perceptions* of porn addiction, rather than porn use itself, connects to someone's spiritual struggles. Numerous clinical psychology studies focusing on porn use among conservative Protestants have found that such groups often perceive that their pornography use has negatively influenced them spiritually. For instance, one study of undergraduates at an evangelical university found that among students who had used pornography, 43% of males and 20% of females felt that it worsened their relationship with God or Christ, and 20% of males and 9% of females felt using porn caused them to lose interest in spiritual things.[22] Another study of evangelical undergraduates found that students felt that viewing online porn hindered their spirituality and relationship with God. But was this due to the actual porn use? Mary Short and her coauthors propose that committed Christian students who use porn may experience a disorder called "scrupulosity" which is characterized by deep feelings of guilt for violating one's moral standards. It can impair social functioning, leading individuals to detach themselves from family or friends, including one's religious community.[23] Similarly, in a series of studies with college students and adults, Joshua Grubbs and his coauthors showed that whether one *perceived* him or herself to be addicted to pornography actually mattered more for predicting someone's religious or spiritual struggles than actual porn use. The spiritual harm of pornography for religious persons, in other words, comes not necessarily from the porn use itself but, rather, from the moral incongruence resulting in the mental stress religious persons feel—often manifesting itself in guilt, shame, and withdrawal—for violating their own deeply held moral values.[24]

My own work, along with that of professor Grubbs, has shown that moral incongruence can have still other consequences, including for mental health. In another set of studies, for example, Grubbs and his coauthors showed that both adults and college students who perceived that they were addicted to internet pornography, regardless of how often they actually viewed porn, were more likely to show symptoms of psychological distress by clinical standards. Importantly, they tested this association with the same people over time, which gives us greater reason to be believe the moral incongruence from porn use (measured by the belief that one is "addicted" to internet porn) leads to the psychological distress over time.[25] I sought to measure the effect of "moral incongruence" on mental health more directly by defining moral incongruence simply as the experience of viewing pornography when one believes that it is "always morally wrong." The results showed that viewing pornography does not cause a man to experience depression *unless* he believes viewing porn is always immoral. Moreover, like Grubbs and his coauthors, I found that this effect does not change as the frequency of porn use increases. Rather, the experience of morally rejecting pornography but viewing it anyway (however infrequently) led to depression for American men.[26]

Why does this matter for conservative Protestants? It matters because they are the most likely among all religious groups to experience moral incongruence. In one study, I found that more than 13% of Protestants who identified with either evangelical or other sectarian Protestant groups experienced "moral incongruence," related to porn—roughly twice as much as mainline Protestants, people of non-Christian religious faiths, and the religiously unaffiliated.[27] But these patterns hold true in more recent data as well. Figure 3.1 presents the percentage of respondents to the 2012 New Family Structures Study (NFSS) and 2014 Relationships in America (RIA) survey who said that viewing pornography was morally wrong, while also viewing it in the previous year. Almost identical to what I found in the previous study, between 13% (NFSS) and 15% (RIA) of Protestants who identify as "evangelical" or "fundamentalist" report violating their own moral views in pornography use. Importantly, in both surveys this is considerably higher than mainline/liberal Protestants, conservative Catholics, moderate/liberal Catholics, and the unaffiliated. Conservative Protestants, in other words, are the group most likely to experience moral incongruence, which can contribute to psychological distress.

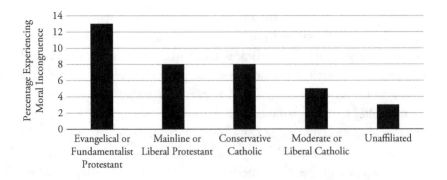

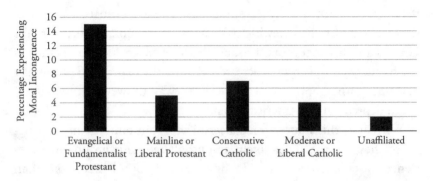

FIGURE 3.1 Percentage of Respondents Experiencing "Moral Incongruence" (Believing Porn Use Is Wrong, But Viewing It Anyway) Across Religious Tradition

Source: New Family Structures Study, 2012. (top panel)
Source: Relationships in America Survey, 2014. (bottom panel)

Moral Incongruence and Religious Participation

Moral incongruence can also help us understand how the meaning of porn use can shape conservative Protestants' attachment to religious faith and community. Researchers have long known that that religious commitment serves to deter participation in various forms of socially "deviant" behavior.[28] A number of studies, however, also suggest there are reciprocal effects, with deviant behaviors—and particularly those of the sexual nature—potentially leading men and women to detach themselves from religion over time.[29] In all these studies, scholars argue that individuals' attachment to religion may be weakened because of the mental stress that results from failing to reconcile discrepancies between one's sexual behavior and one's religious values and identity.[30]

The notion that conservative Christians, and conservative Protestants in particular, might withdraw from their faith in response to the moral incongruence (and the associated guilt and shame) they experience is entirely consistent with what I found in both the nationally representative data and my interviews. For conservative Protestants, more frequent pornography use tends to predict declines in religious participation over time.[31] Figure 3.2 shows the effect of pornography use on three different measures of religious commitment in the 2006 and 2012 Portraits of American Life Study. It controls for a variety of relevant sociodemographic characteristics, along with each measure of religious commitment. In other words, whatever relationship we see between earlier porn use and later religious commitment is not due to sociodemographic factors or how religious the respondent was to begin with. The trend lines clearly show that the more frequently conservative Protestants viewed porn earlier on corresponds to lower levels of religious commitment over time. Conservative Protestants who viewed porn more often reported higher levels of religious doubt, lower importance of God or spirituality, and lower rates of church attendance six years later.

We can see this same trend in three waves of the National Study of Youth and Religion (NSYR), collected in 2003, 2005, and 2007/2008. Figure 3.3 shows pornography's effect on church attendance, importance of faith, prayer frequency, closeness to God, and religious doubts for conservative Protestants ages 13 through 24.[32] Young Americans who viewed pornography more often at earlier waves reported lower levels of church attendance, importance of faith, prayer frequency, and closeness to God, and higher levels of religious doubt. But why is this the case?

My research suggests that the cause is the inner dissonance caused by moral incongruence. An almost universal refrain running throughout my interviews with conservative Protestants was that the guilt and shame they experienced from repeatedly failing to avoid pornography made them want to back away from religion. One man simply explained, "If I viewed pornography, I hide from God. I avoided talking to him." Another recalled, "If I had remaining guilt or shameful feelings from viewing porn, I would refrain from just about any activity that reminded

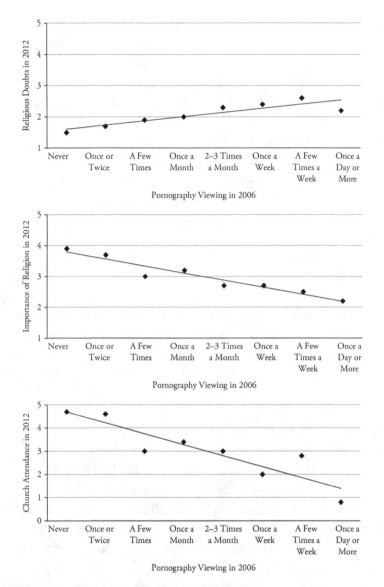

FIGURE 3.2 Predicted Values of Religiosity Measures at Wave 2 Across Values of Pornography Viewing Frequency at Wave 1 for Conservative Protestants

Note: Regression models controlled for Wave 1 religiosity measures, along with Wave 2 age, gender, marital status, parental status, education, household income, race, and region. Results are expressed as predicted values computed through ordinary least squares regression. All effects are statistically significant beyond the .001 level of significance. *Source*: Portraits of American Life Study, 2006 and 2012.

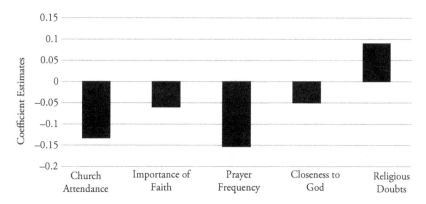

FIGURE 3.3 Coefficient Estimates for the Effect of Pornography Viewing Frequency on Religiosity Measures for Conservative Protestants
Note: Fixed effects models control for region, parent in the home, and age. Results are presented as coefficient estimates. All effects are statistically significant beyond the .05 level of significance.
Source: National Study of Youth and Religion, 2003, 2005, 2007/2008.

me of God." Some likened themselves to the biblical Adam, who hid in the bushes from God because he felt naked and ashamed (Genesis 3:10). One father who attends an evangelical community church in Georgia explained, "I think my natural tendency is to 'pull an Adam' and hide in the bushes [laughs]. I think porn's an insidious little thing that can happen often enough to break the fellowship [with God]. I don't find myself as eager to pray or even go to church."

For some, like this man, hiding from God meant they avoided religious practices that are usually consistent parts of their life. One father in Illinois recounted, "I felt too ashamed to pray and attend worship events and read the Bible when I was using porn." Derek, a college student in Oklahoma, explained, "Yeah, like, I always pray before I go to bed, and usually pornography viewing would occur at night for me. And so I would not want to pray because I was just ashamed. I knew, even when I didn't really know why, like, I knew that that's not what I was supposed to be doing, you know. And so it made me stray from like my religious practices, in a sense." Another college student named Jeremy expressed, "Because I feel bad [about porn use], I sometimes don't want to read the Bible because I know it's going to be right there. Or not go to church because then I feel [pauses, then laughs] it's kind of weird. Like, you know you did something wrong, so the place that you want to go, the place that you *need* to go is usually the place that you don't actually want to go. And so that's how it works." And still another explained, "When I see the Bible, I feel guilt and I'll try to avoid it. I'll, like, knowingly not look on my nightstand because I know the Bible's right there, and so I'll leave, and then I'm, like, you just *avoided the Bible*, like, that's how bad you're doing, that you have to not even look at the book, so that guilt" (emphasis his).

Guilt and shame over porn use compelled other men to withdraw from religious service. Damon, a college pastor in Oklahoma in his mid-twenties, described the practical consequences of porn use in the lives of young men in his ministry.

> Most of these guys [I counsel] really are ashamed—that's the overarching theme. [Sam: You mean shame in a good way or a bad way?] I think in a destructive way. Like Adam in the garden. "I need to hide. I'm unclean. I can't come to God. I need to get cleaned up and get my act together and then I can return to leading a Bible study." Even to be a missionary on campus. They think, "I need to handle my private stuff. Then I can return to leading our Bible studies or being a chaplain of my fraternity or whatever." So they feel this need to hide and withdraw totally.

This sentiment reflects the thinking of a number of conservative Protestant men and women I interviewed. Jamarcus, whom we met earlier, is a talented singer who used to regularly lead worship at his nondenominational evangelical congregation. But recently, he voluntarily stepped down from the worship team. He explained, "I have stopped a lot of . . . I get a lot of invitations to go places to sing and go perform and go do interviews and everything, and I don't do them, really, because of porn." When I asked why, he explained, "Yeah, too much conviction. It's hard for me to be in front of people like that. If everybody in the audience truly studied their Bible and they actually knew that we all sin and we all come short of the glory of God and everything. Nobody's perfect. If everybody had that mindset, and nobody ridiculed people. . . . But you know, when people be, like, no, man, you up there singing, dog, I know you. It's enough people that give the Christian religion a bad name."

The pattern of withdrawing from Christian community and service is not limited to men. One woman I spoke with, Stephanie, worked for an evangelical college ministry before she went back to graduate school. She described how she often saw women in her ministry who used porn remove themselves from leadership because of the guilt or shame, "Some of the women will shy away from leadership things—like, they will self-sabotage or sabotage their own opportunities to participate in leadership things. Whether they don't want [their sexual sin] to be found out, or they just don't feel qualified, but there is a lot of shame and guilt and that's one way that they respond by not really. . . . In some ways they feel like they can't get better, or they're not qualified anymore or they never will be. And they don't tell anyone but they also kind of remove themselves from other Christian environments."

The national data support this idea. Using data collected from the same people over time, we can see whether pornography viewing influences whether conservative Protestants serve in church leadership. Figure 3.4 illustrates the clear relationship. Even when we control for whether or not respondents had already served in leadership, church attendance, prayer frequency, beliefs about the Bible, and so on, the more frequently someone viewed pornography in 2006, the less likely he or she was to hold a leadership position or serve on a committee in the person's church in the following six years.

For Jamarcus, the decision to withdraw from church leadership was based on a perception that people in the congregation might judge him for his pornography use and a desire to avoid hurting Christianity's reputation. Other men talked about the perception of being judged. One Baptist student expressed:

Certain things like [porn use], I'd rather just fix on my own, or if I did get help, not with the church. Like, I would probably want it to be through something else. I just wouldn't feel comfortable doing it with the church when they constantly preach about not doing that and you still. . . . I just would feel hypocritical. And the thing is, a lot of the members would probably say, "Oh, we don't judge you; it's okay, we all have issues." But I would know in the back of their head,

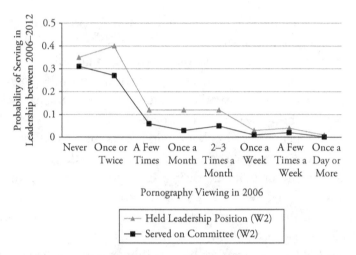

FIGURE 3.4 Predicted Probabilities of Serving in Leadership Between 2006 and 2012 Across Values of Pornography Viewing Frequency in 2006 for Conservative Protestants

Note: Regression models controlled for Wave 1 service in leadership, age, gender, marital status, parental status, education, race, region, household income, church attendance, prayer frequency, and beliefs about scripture. Results are expressed as predicted probabilities computed through binary logistic regression. All effects are statistically significant beyond the .05 level of significance.

Source: Portraits of American Life Study, 2006 and 2012.

they're judging you. So if I was to get help outside of just myself, I definitely would turn to other options besides church.

Another young man described feeling judged at church even when he consciously knew that no one else was aware of his struggle: "You'll be at church and you listen to the service, you know, and you're kind of sitting there and you know no one is *actually* judging you at all. They're just sitting there, but half the time it feels like they're actually, like, 'I can't believe you do that!' But you know that they don't actually know anything [laughs]. And so you know you need to go there because it'll help you, but you don't want to go there because you feel like you don't deserve to go there."

In more extreme cases, some conservative Protestants describe how repeated failure to quit pornography made them either lose interest in God or want to walk away from Christianity altogether. Shawn, a Baptist graduate student in Texas recounted,

> In some ways [porn use] eliminated any desire for a relationship with God. It was almost a zero-sum kind of thing, where the more of myself I gave to porn, the less interest, the less feeling like I could actually relate to God. So, it was largely a zero-sum kind of thing, I think. So, it was back and forth between, okay, I'm good, I'm a good Christian, I'm good with God, and, like, "Oh, I watched porn this week so it will be a little bit of time before I can get back with God."

Similarly, a student in Oklahoma told me, "[Porn use] just adds to the weight of things that you've already done in your life that you feel guilty about and it just compounds everything. So, it's just like, 'I'm not good enough for God' type of deal, 'I'm not good enough for his salvation through his Son,' and it just makes you kind of doubt if you should continue on this path of being a Christian or not."

A Presbyterian father in South Carolina described how his spiritual life suffers when he is consistently failing to avoid porn and masturbation, "During a really hard time, I think the prayer becomes kind of redundant as far as, like, 'God help me stop [watching porn], take this away, take this away, help me stop.' But then I feel like it doesn't happen. And not to say that God won't take it away, or can't take it away. He has reasons for that. But you know, [my prayer life] is definitely not as rich or consistent during those times." He went on to explain how his shame and the disappointment he believes God feels toward him sapped his motivation for spiritual things.

> I think the big thing with me in this is just shame and guilt. And I think it just plays into this idea that I have in my head that I'm a burden to everybody relationally. And that during this time, I just become a burden to God, too. It's, like, "Yeah, I love you. And you know, I died for you. But I really, I'm just tolerating you right now because I made a commitment to myself and I have to." So, I feel like I just feed into that lie when I'm in a season of struggle. And so it's just this big cycle and just makes the shame worse, makes the guilt

worse, makes me not want to spend time investing in my relationship with God, because I felt like I'm screwing it up.

Another man in Ohio had served as a church planter overseas for several years. He described how his discouragement over pornography became one of the key factors that contributed to his returning home from the mission field and even doubting his own faith.

> I went [overseas] to do church planting stuff, and after a couple of years, I was, like, "I don't know if I believe this anymore." And while I was [overseas], I struggled with pornography. And I think at that time I'm kind of going through a . . . I don't have a good Christian community, I'm trying to pursue God in this context, I'm struggling with pornography. And I don't think that was the only reason, but I think that was one of the big reasons, [the] big push in my walking the fence of faith to the side of, like, you know what? I'm struggling very hard in this, with Christianity in general and following God, and meanwhile I don't see any victory in [the area of porn]—I mean, is this real? I've got this pornography thing I'm beating myself over, and I don't want to deal with this anymore, so it'd be easier if I just didn't. And so there are a few reasons why I was sticking up my hand toward Christianity, and just being not interested and pushing it away. I think pornography is really one of them. That struggle of, okay, I'm reading here that, "How shall we sin anymore if Christ is in us?" And meanwhile I cannot shake this thing, and I have no idea what in the world to do about it.

Several of the men we have met described their acute mental distress at not knowing why God would leave this sin in their lives. While they are certainly aware that their pornography use is their decision, they have each felt overwhelmed and powerless to resist the temptation, desperate for God to grant them some "victory" in this area. For the Ohio man, habitual failure at overcoming his porn habit was "one of the big reasons" why he would question his faith ("I mean, is this real?").

These responses help explain how pornography use can lead to declines in religious commitment over time for conservative Protestants.

A fundamental observation of psychological research is that people long for cognitive consistency—a correspondence between their belief and their reality—and seek to avoid cognitive dissonance. The shame and internal discord many Christians feel at masturbating to porn leaves the option of either stopping the behavior (which proves far easier said than done) or pulling back from the source of those moral values—one's religious faith and community. Faced with the choice, many conservative Protestants eventually choose the latter.

Could Porn Coexist with (or Even Improve) Your Religious Life?

But withdrawing from religion is not the only possible response to habitual porn use. Some professing Christians I spoke with seemed content to maintain an active religious life while viewing pornography fairly regularly. These were virtually always either more liberal mainline Protestants or Catholics or persons who seemed to identify and affiliate with a conservative Protestant tradition while consciously rejecting the tradition's sexual ethic. A Methodist college student in Oklahoma, Brett, described his connection to religion this way: "Well, I'm a member of the Methodist church. I keep that membership based off of tradition, even though my family is not very religious at all. But I keep it just because I like the rituals. I like going to church." Brett explains that he subscribes to the Christian ethic of love and service, but largely rejects the teachings on sexual morality, which he calls "kind of ridiculous." He recently has pulled his pornography use back to "probably once every other week," out of respect for his girlfriend who does not like it. When I asked him if porn had ever influenced his religious faith, he replied,

> I think [porn and religion] are two separate spheres. But if it becomes a habit, if it becomes an addiction, then it's bad because then you can't really get rid of it. It's going to interfere with other parts of your life. You're not going to be able to love other people. You're not going to be able to do things to make yourself a viable member of society. You're not going to be able to do those kinds of things if it becomes an addiction. And so once it starts to interfere with other aspects of your life, then it's bad.

So for Brett—who is a fairly regular churchgoer, though not a conservative Protestant—his porn use and religious life are separate. But porn use *can* become a problem if it rises to the level of an addiction that keeps him from contributing to society. Other Christians in more liberal mainline traditions held similar views about their faith and pornography use, some expressing that perhaps God did not like porn use, but it was better than other sexual sins they could be committing. Curtis attends an African Methodist Episcopal congregation in Oklahoma City "at least once or twice a month," and prays, "at least once or twice a day." But he also views porn fairly consistently and occasionally goes to strip clubs. When I asked him if he found his porn use at odds with practicing his faith, he explained, "I don't think God has much of an opinion on it because it could be worse. I mean, I *could* be terrible. So it just doesn't bother me."

For conservative Protestants, however, there seems to be too much of a moral conflict to maintain an active spiritual life while habitually using pornography. But rather than withdraw from religion and God, some conservative Protestants felt porn drew them closer. They described how their religious practice became a way to compensate for failures in the realm of pornography, while others talked about coming to a place of repentance and then growing stronger in their faith, which they then attribute to their struggle with porn. For example, one female college student who grew up Pentecostal described her response to guilt over her sexual failure, "It almost made me, like, more religious—like, I needed to make up for it. Like, I felt really bad for a long time and prayed about it, went to church, asked for forgiveness for a really long time, read the Bible, looked up like stuff about it, and I, like, I've become more religious that way." Similarly, a male college student recounted, "[Porn] actually made me want to go to church even more because, like, I don't know, especially in high school, like freshman and sophomore year, whenever I viewed it, afterwards I feel like I would have to put on like a Christian station, like radio station or something like that, to kind of get me back."

But others described how struggling with pornography and eventually gaining more control over their use made them stronger in their faith. One Baptist man in Oklahoma explained, "With God, it's a constant push and pull. There's tension within your heart, if that's how you want to say it. I would pray that, you know, 'Lord, help me through this,' you know, 'guide me, just take this out of my life, but gosh I got to have it, but why did I just do that?' And so it's a constant battle. So I think it strengthened my relationship with God." And when I asked another young man if porn use inclined him to run away from God or toward God, he replied, "*To* God. Absolutely. I've never believed I've done too much for God to forgive me. Jesus died on the cross for our sins, past, present, and future. He's going to forgive you no matter what you've done. If you turn to him, he's going to take you into his arms, and so that's what I believe, and so it was always just a constant—the closer I get to God, the easier it will get. The closer I get to God, the easier it will get for me to just take [porn] out of my life."

For a number of conservative Protestant men, their eventual victory over porn not only became a source of spiritual strength but it also became a "testimony" that they would be encouraged to share at church or in other Christian groups in the hopes that it would inspire others.[33] This represents a flip side of sexual exceptionalism in that conservative Protestants who demonstrate mastery over sexual sin are encouraged to celebrate it in a way that Christians are not inclined to do with other sins like pride, anger, gossip, or gluttony.

Conclusion

Pornography use *is* shaping conservative Protestants' sense of self, mental health, and intimate relationships in powerful ways. Some of this—as Nick feared—may be due to the actual content and practice of pornography use itself. And to the extent that habitually viewing and masturbating to sexually explicit images can influence brain activity, sexual functioning, and relationship patterns, these effects are not limited to conservative Protestants. But much of the harm pornography does to conservative Protestants, particularly to their mental health and attachment to religious faith and community, is often less about the practice of watching pornography and more about the experience of willingly violating those moral values that are most sacred to oneself and one's community.

Certainly, Americans who are not conservative Protestants can also feel morally ambivalent, or even experience guilt or shame, as a result of regularly masturbating to porn. But as other scholars and my own re-search suggests, the conservative Protestant subculture uniquely stresses (even obsesses over, by their own reckoning) the scandal of sexual sin and its eternal consequences. Obedience to God is not expected to be perfect, but neither is it optional. Habitual, willful sin in a believer's life is a reason to doubt one's eternal standing before God, while sexual exceptionalism within the American Christian context amplifies the severity of pornography use. For conservative Protestants who fail to avoid porn, their moral incongruence is often accompanied by intense guilt and shame that can drive them away from religious community, practice, service, and even God himself. Alternatively, in some cases, habitual porn use becomes an impetus to throw oneself into religious activity and service in order to compensate. And consistent "victory" over porn can actually serve to strengthen Christian belief and identity and serve as an occasion to praise God's redemptive and sanctifying work publicly.

4

Every *Man's* Battle?

Nice girls are repulsed by porn-users. . . . Women who use pornography are usually well down the road to depravity.
— Tim LaHaye, *The Battle for the Family*, p. 180

The first time I heard about [porn] in a church setting, it was a Sunday school that focused mainly on men, their biology and potential weaknesses. It warned that all serial killers interviewed on the subject were addicted to hardcore porn. You can imagine how that made me feel as a 15-year-old female pornography addict, and I can tell you with certainty how it did not make me feel. It did not make me feel safe or welcome to speak out loud what I was struggling with in private. I only felt shame and a deep, growing reticence to ever inform anyone of my addiction because I felt certain that I was a freak and not "feminine" enough.
— Audrey Assad, *The Porn Phenomenon*, p. 59

GENDER—HERE I MEAN THE SYSTEM of attributes and expectations, privileges and penalties that societies tend to associate with being biologically male or female—inexorably shapes Americans' experiences with pornography. This is even truer for conservative Protestants. Thus far I have only selectively addressed gender dynamics, though not because I wish to minimize their significance. On the contrary, I concluded that a discussion of gender *as its own issue* deserves its own chapter.

While women—as conservative Protestants do in fact acknowledge occasionally—view pornography, they undeniably do so less frequently than (and somewhat differently from) men. *Some* of the gender differences in porn use ultimately reflect, at least in part, some biological "hardwiring" that distinguishes women from men. Both nature and nurture play a role in determining sexual behavior patterns across genders, and I'm comfortable saying that women and men, even when they do share similar goals in porn use, may also naturally (in a biological sense) respond to different cues and pursue different experiences.[1] That shouldn't be terribly controversial.

Much more interesting is how pornography's manifold influence in conservative Protestants' lives stem from the *meaning* they ascribe to it, and how other subcultural commitments, including beliefs about gender, shape that meaning. For conservative Protestants, gender's relationship to pornography, and sexuality more broadly, is *moral* in nature and infused with cosmic (even eternal) significance. For a man or woman to deviate from God's intended plan for sex is sin. But to violate God's prescribed roles and behaviors for men and women is also sin. In the realm of pornography use specifically, conservative Protestant women wrestle with a form of moral incongruence that is unique to them. Not only do they experience the guilt and shame of committing sexual sin but also they are forced to deal with the social challenges and intrapersonal turmoil of sinning against their gender—sinning "like a man." The "double shame" these women often experience poses a unique challenge while also, counterintuitively, serving to reaffirm men's God-ordained sexuality.

Complementarianism in Theory and in Practice

Conservative Protestants are, to varying degrees, essentialists when it comes to gender. They believe gender is *essential* in the dual sense that it is both nontrivial and intrinsic. More specifically, conservative Protestants tend to believe God created men and women to be fundamentally different, with different tendencies, drives, desires, and capacities. And these differences are essential because they are understood to be part of God's grand design from the inception of humanity, even before sin entered the world. From the creation story in Genesis 2:18, we read that God made Eve *for* Adam as a "helper suitable for him." In other words, conservative Protestants believe that

God, in some sense, had a very *practical* intent in making men and women different.[2] From the beginning, God intended women to be capable supporters for their spouses and men more generally. And this design determines the sorts of roles men and women embrace vis-à-vis one another, at least in the home and the church, if not the broader world.

But conservative Protestants also largely hold that God intended the differences between men and women, at least within the context of heterosexual marriage, to represent something cosmic and eternal—namely, the relationship between Christ and his Church. As the Apostle Paul explains in Ephesians 5:22–33, husbands are to represent Christ in his role as the loving authority over his bride, the church, while wives are to represent the Church itself as it joyfully submits to its husband, Christ. Thus, for many conservative Protestants, to push back against the various roles and characteristics the New Testament prescribes for men and women is to reject not only biblical teaching but also the gospel itself.[3] Conservative Protestants often call this view "complementarian." That is, they believe that the two genders—and they believe there are only two—complement one another because they are essentially different.[4]

Though, as I will show, the implications of complementarianism are important for understanding mainstream conservative Protestants' views regarding sexuality, three caveats are necessary to understand how this theology of gender often works out in practice. First, almost as often as they stress the essential differences between men and women, conservative Protestants stress their equality in value before God. Critical gender scholars may want to argue that because conservative Protestants believe certain leadership roles (elder and pastor being the most prominent) are exclusively for men, that necessarily means men are more valuable than women in that subculture. But this is not how conservative Protestants themselves see it or articulate it. Rather, they tend to believe, as the widely publicized declaration of conservative Protestant complementarianism, The Nashville Statement, declares: "WE AFFIRM that God created Adam and Eve, the first human beings, in his own image, equal before God as persons, and distinct as male and female. WE DENY that the divinely ordained differences between male and female render them unequal in dignity or worth."[5]

The second caveat is that conservative Protestants are fairly selective about which teachings in the New Testament about men's and women's roles are to be taken literally. Even the most fundamentalist Protestant churches rarely adhere to Paul's teaching that women should have their heads covered when they pray (1 Corinthians 11:4–5) or that "women should keep silent in the churches" (1 Corinthians 14:34–35). Pastors do not generally teach from the pulpit that wives "will be saved through childbearing" (1 Timothy 5:15), or that wives should call their husbands "master" (1 Peter 3:6). So even as conservative Protestant congregations still largely interpret New Testament passages to mean women cannot serve as elders or teaching pastors, and that women and men exercise different "complementary" roles in the family, their interpretation of numerous other New Testament passages on gender roles are likely far more influenced by contemporary egalitarian ideals than they acknowledge.

Related to this last point, the third caveat is that sociologists find that complementarianism is as much a symbolic language as an actual way of life. Most famously, sociologists Sally Gallagher and Christian Smith interviewed a representative sample of several hundred married evangelicals. They showed that while many formally subscribed to complementarian gender roles, in their day-to-day interactions most of these couples were functionally egalitarian. Women worked outside the home; they freely made decisions; they were not dutifully submitting to their husbands on a regular basis. Rather than functioning as strict complementarians, Gallagher and Smith observed, these couples were often employing complementarian language symbolically, as a way to identify themselves as "good, Bible-believing Christians."[6]

Even in conservative Protestant congregations themselves, leaders acknowledge that such congregations are often dominated numerically by women, and the church culture itself is often far more favorable to what society understands as characteristically "feminine" qualities (valuing relationships, sharing, comforting) than what society associates with patriarchal "masculinity."[7] And while some scholars have pointed to former megachurch pastor Mark Driscoll's hyper-masculine Christianity as an example of contemporary complementarianism, the fact that Driscoll's aggressive, authoritarian persona contributed to his own downfall should show that his brand of complementarianism is not the norm. In fact, many conservative Protestant commentators viewed it as a toxic extreme.[8]

None of the caveats I mention, however, should give the impression that complementarian ideals and teachings are empty rhetoric. Particularly when it comes to sexuality, complementarianism often shapes how conservative Protestants think about the natural tendencies of men and women. In their thinking, God designed men to be leaders and initiators. Women, by contrast, were designed to be helpers and responders. And the conservative Protestant subculture has ways to enforce these gender expectations. Men who abdicate their masculinity are rebuked and challenged in public statements, books, and parachurch organizations; from the pulpit; and in personal conversations to embody the characteristics appropriate to their God-given gender. Women, similarly, are discouraged, or prohibited outright, from taking on masculine roles involving leadership over men or aggression. And this all trickles down to how conservative Protestant men and women are expected to behave sexually.

Men Are Visual Sex Monsters, Women Lust After Relationships

Because, according to complementarian theology, God made men to be leaders and initiators, they are believed to have natural sexual agency. It is assumed that men, single or married, want sex and tend to pursue it for its own sake. More than this, men *should* pursue sexual intimacy; it is a characteristically masculine thing to do. Pastors and authors counsel single men to pursue early marriage, among other reasons, so that they can have sex.[9] And married men should pursue sex with their wives. Tim Challies, in his book *Sexual Detox*, argues that strengthening male leadership was God's intent in giving men stronger sexual desires than women. "God commands that men, husbands, be leaders. Men are to take the leading role while women are to follow. God intends that men take leadership even in sex, and, therefore, he gives men a greater desire for sex. This way, a man can lead his wife, taking the initiative."[10] As a corollary to this, it is generally assumed that, because God has designed men to pursue sex, sexual temptation is eminently "normal" for a man. While certainly not condoning lust, authors generally assume that almost all men lust after what they see, either in front of them or on a computer screen. As the authors of *Every Young Man's Battle* explain, "Why the prevalence of sexual sin among men? We got there naturally—simply by being male."[11] But as the above quotation from Challies also suggests, conservative Protestants believe that God made single or married women to be responders. Consequently, they have traditionally been thought of as less sexually oriented, or at least less interested in the physical act of sex. Rather, what women *really* desire, according to complementarian theology, are relationships and emotional connections. While this sort of thinking about men and women pervades conservative Protestant manuals on sexuality, it is particularly acute in those that are marketed explicitly toward women.

The *Every Man's Battle* series of books was enormously popular in the mid-2000s, with over four hundred thousand copies in their first two years after publication.[12] Despite this, Christian publishers were initially unwilling to take a chance on a counterpart volume marketed to women. Shannon Ethridge, author of *Every Woman's Battle*, recalled, "Time after time I heard [Christian] publishers say, 'Women don't deal with sexual issues enough that a book on that topic would really sell.' . . . I wondered how people could be so naïve as to think that sexual integrity is strictly a man's issue. Both men and women were created by God as sexual beings, weren't they?"[13] Interestingly, however, while Ethridge acknowledges that God made men and women to be sexual (and has since written books promoting sexual confidence and freedom for Christian wives[14]), she repeatedly returns to the complementarian narrative that men's and women's sexuality are *essentially* different by God's design.

> Men and women struggle in different ways when it comes to sexual integrity. While a man's battle begins with what he takes in through his eyes, a woman's begins with her heart and her thoughts. A man must guard his eyes to maintain sexual integrity, but *because God made women to be emotionally and mentally stimulated*, we must closely guard our hearts and minds as well as our bodies. While a man needs mental, emotional, and spiritual connection, his physical needs tend to be in the driver's seat and his other needs ride along

in the back. The reverse is true for women. If there is one particular need that drives us, it is certainly our emotional needs. That's why it's said that men give love to get sex and women give sex to get love. This isn't intended to be a bashing statement, *it's simply the way God made us.*[15]

And elsewhere in *Every Young Woman's Battle*, authors Ethridge and Arterburn make these God-given differences even more explicit. "*God wired* guys differently. They *are built* for visual stimulation. Their ultimate goal is physical intimacy. It's just *how they are made*. It's not that they don't value or want emotional bonding; many do. But it isn't their ultimate goal. On the other hand, you, as a female, *are built* for relational stimulation. Your ultimate goal is emotional bonding. It's just *how you're made*."[16] Ethridge wants to emphasize that both men and women wrestle with sexual temptation. But God "wired" men to be visual and driven primarily by their physical needs. They would naturally be drawn to porn. God made women, by contrast to be "emotionally and mentally stimulated," driven by their emotional needs. Sexual pleasure is not the end for a women—"women give sex to get love."

This assumption about male and female sexuality leads Ethridge to minimize the likelihood that women will be drawn to pornography. "The temptation to look at pornography can be overwhelming to a male, while females would much rather read the relational dialogue in a romance novel. Men want to look and touch, whereas women much prefer to talk and relate."[17] Elsewhere, Ethridge explains, "most women don't lust after men's bodies," and that those who do are "exceptions to this rule."[18] Certainly, in both *Every Woman's Battle* and *Every Young Woman's Battle*, the authors acknowledge that women *can* be stimulated visually and they share a number of stories from women who claim to be addicted to pornography and masturbation. Other Christian authors also acknowledge that women can be attracted to pornography, and even that this number may be increasing.[19] But the dominant narrative of these books is that healthy women tend to struggle with sexual purity in a way that is consistent with their God-given femininity, while others tend to struggle sexually in a way that is more manlike, and these are the exceptions—de facto deviants who transgress how "God made women to be."

But this assumption that "normal" Christian women are not attracted to visual pornography is becoming more difficult to square with reality, particularly among younger women. In the 1970s, around 26% of women ages 18 to 30 who affiliated with a "fundamentalist" Protestant denomination reported viewing an X-rated movie in the past year. In the 2010s, that percentage increased to 37%, well over a third. And in 2016 alone, that percentage reached its highest point yet at 49%. In other words, in 2016, roughly half of young women whom we could consider fundamentalist Protestants reported viewing porn in the previous year. By comparison, about 56% of conservative Protestant men reported viewing porn that same year, not even a statistically significant difference.[20] In a 2014 survey, nearly one quarter (23%) of women under 30 who self-identified as "evangelical" or "fundamentalist" Protestants reported that they had intentionally viewed pornography within the past month. And given that 44% of "fundamentalist" or "evangelical" women in that age group also report masturbating in a given month, it is likely that a large percentage of these women are consuming *visual* pornography as men are typically thought to—by themselves, to fuel masturbation.

Yet the dominant narrative that most Christian women, because of God's design, wouldn't be interested in porn not only persists but also is largely internalized by conservative Protestant women themselves, including those who sincerely struggle with the temptation to view pornography or other sexually explicit media like romance novels. Stephanie is a 26-year-old seminary student in Georgia who attends an evangelical nondenominational church. Throughout college and for a few years afterward, she worked for a well-known collegiate parachurch organization that specializes in evangelizing and mentoring college students. She now works part time at her church, leading women's ministries. When I asked her about the prevalence of porn use among women during her college ministry days and in her current church ministry, she became visibly impassioned, almost angry. She recounted,

In the churches I grew up we never talked about those kinds of things ever. I thought it was strange when I went to college and we would have "women's times" whether it was a leadership project or in discipleship groups I thought we'd be getting more serious about our faith and talking about our struggles. And I would hear "Well, this is what the guys are talking about. This is what accountability means to them." And, like, what the women would do would be honestly not anything compared to that. It was very surfacy. We'd talk about "identity." We'd talk about "beauty." We talk about struggles with how you look and acceptance and that sort of thing. We definitely don't talk about sexual issues. It's not very deep and it's very shallow. So when I would press into that and ask why it was always like "Well, women don't struggle with the same things." So, then I really started pushing on that a lot. Even now, people in this church ministry are more, like, "Yeah, the culture has changed and that's more prevalent." And I think that's true, but I also think that's not true. It's just that people are being more honest about it. Or they weren't dealing with it. And so now when I'm on staff people still say, "Yeah, some women deal with that but most don't. And so that's why we're not going to talk about it."

As Stephanie explains, and others affirmed frequently, men's corporate discussion times virtually always focus on some aspect of sexual purity, an area in which it is assumed virtually all Christian men struggle. Yet the women's discussions rarely touch on such issues because it is assumed that most women do not battle sexual temptation in the same way.

Yet pastors and writers are not completely unaware that an increasing number of conservative Protestant women are viewing pornography. One pastor in Tennessee affirmed, "From the women's ministry directors I've talked to, more younger women have struggled with the visual, but many women struggle with emotional pornography of romance novels and things like that." Another pastor in Ohio affirmed, "I've not heard too many stories first hand from women just because of the nature of confession, people want to confess to someone of the same gender, but I've heard far more second hand from women in our church that this is a significant issue for women, and there's research and another study I've read recently as well, and it's not just a male thing, and that's helped me see." And still another pastor in Texas shared something similar,

> Nowadays the deck may even be more stacked against women in terms of how I've seen things trending. [Sam: What do you mean by that?] The impression we get, over five to ten years ago as a pastor, and as internet search trends and counseling trends became more public, the impression you used to get is only men struggle with pornography and masturbation. And about that time we started to hear, like, whoa, while 90 percent of men [may struggle], we're all shocked to hear about ten years ago like 30% of women struggle, and about five years ago, we're hearing 50% of women. All that to say, nowadays, I haven't seen a recent study, but if I happened to read a study it wouldn't surprise me if the struggle was now just as common in women as men.

Yet despite this growing recognition that more conservative Protestant women are viewing pornography, ministries and authors are still slow or unwilling to address it, largely because it is inconsistent with their underlying complementation ideology. Stephanie mused: "It's kinda hard for me to put my finger on. I don't really understand why other people who are like older leaders who've already been in ministry . . . [pause] it kinda feels like people aren't okay with admitting that, that women struggle with those things, too. It's like they're committed to saying, 'Well, men are like this and women are like this and this kinda violates the paradigm I have in my mind that women can't enjoy sexual experiences like this or turned on by that kind of thing [pornography].'"[21]

The notion that conservative Protestant men consume more pornography and other sexual media (outside of romance novels, at least) than conservative Protestant women is not a point worth debating. While research suggests that women do tend to underreport their porn use more often than men owing to social desirability bias (an obvious example of how gendered stigma around sexual behavior precludes women from discussing it candidly), it is still a virtual certainty that men, conservative Protestant or otherwise, view porn more often.[22] Nor do I wish to debate that men tend to pursue and consume sexually explicit media for different reasons than women, which is also likely true to some degree.[23] What my interview data suggest, rather, is the deeply rooted perception that pornography is a male problem, combined with complementarian expectations about gender, causes conservative Protestant women to be doubly punished, internally and socially, for their porn use, while conservative Protestant men, oddly enough, are affirmed in a way by that same gender system.

"I Struggle with a Dude Thing"

Conservative Protestant women seldom confess to viewing pornography. While I had no trouble at all recruiting men, conservative Protestant or otherwise, to participate in my interviews (along with a good number of irreligious women), conservative Protestant women seemed far less interested in opening up about their pornography use. Often I had to provide alternatives: one of my female research assistants would conduct the interview, for example, or I would provide an open-ended anonymous survey that women could fill out online. Among the few conservative Protestant women willing to discuss her own porn use, McKenna, a 21-year-old Baptist college student, remarked on the discomfort women feel discussing issues like pornography and masturbation. "Honestly, [pornography's] not something Christian women, or women at all, really talk about. Like, I feel men are more open. Like, lots of men watch porn, so why not talk about it? I feel like women don't really talk about it, so I don't really have a general feel for what other women experience because women just don't like; it's not something we talk about." When I asked her to explain why she felt that this might be the case, she pointed out the obvious gender discrepancy regarding women and sexuality in general.

> It's almost like taboo. Almost like the double standard of where it's okay for men to have lots of sexual partners but if women have lots of sexual partners, like, they're considered a whore. So I feel like it kind of goes along those lines, like what I don't understand why it's like that, but it's just kind of taboo for women to like to watch porn by themselves almost. Like, if you're with a boyfriend, I feel like it's not

a big deal. Like, that's happened. But to just like watch it yourself, it's, like, kind of unheard of.

The "double standard" McKenna identifies here boils down to men being socially free to be sexual beings, pursuing sex and exercising sexual agency, while women are afforded no such freedom. Illustrating this point further, McKenna also explains that—in general, not necessarily for conservative Protestants—women's porn use is more socially acceptable if they are viewing it with a boyfriend, while for women to view porn by themselves, for their own pleasure, is an aberration. The clear implication here, again, is that according to pervasive gender expectations, a woman's sexual interest and pleasure are wrapped up in her man's. For a woman to pursue sexual pleasure in isolation, *like a man*, is taboo. For this reason, women who have experiences with explicit sexual media, and especially conservative Protestant women, understandably don't want to talk about it.

Though conservative Protestant ministers and authors recognize that some Christian women do view pornography, they also recognize that such women are highly reticent to confess this or seek pastoral help the way men do. Interestingly enough, most also recognize why this is the case. Max, a Southern Baptist pastor in Tennessee, affirmed: "I think there's a gender double standard which is one of the things I'm . . . I read a lot of things on the internet, like 15 to 25% of women struggle with visual pornography, but I would say that it's extremely rare for a woman to confess that." When I asked Max why, he explained, "Typically the level of shame dealing with that [sin] . . . there's just so many more stigmas associated with *women* confessing something like that than with a man" (emphasis his). I asked Max to highlight why he thought that might be the case; he answered:

I just think there's a massive gender disconnect where, if it's a man, for a man to be sexually interested or vigorous would be something that would validate his manhood at some level. Even in the secular world! For a woman to be that way, even in this day and age, you get more "slut" than "enlightened." People are going to call you more promiscuous. Promiscuity with a woman is still far more frowned upon than promiscuity with a man, from a social perspective. *And I think that's probably vastly amplified in the church* [emphasis added].

Here, Max puts his finger on a way the gender dynamic among conservative Protestants influences men's and women's experiences in drastically different ways. For a man, Max explains, being sexually interested actually validates his God-given, masculine sex drives. Though he is expressing it in a sinful way, his sexual desire is viewed as normative, and, therefore, morally good. But for women, being interested in sex, as evidenced by their viewing pornography, associates them with promiscuity, the stigma for which Max feels is "vastly amplified in the church." Max went on to explain that even the emphasis on sexual purity more broadly among conservative Protestants—what I have called sexual exceptionalism—is gendered and reflects inordinate values within the church. "We sort of have this idol of [female] virginity. And I think it is an idol. Of course, God has sexual precepts that he calls us to act upon and we're called to be obedient to that. But in many ways I feel like the whole concept of virginity has been made an idol by the church and I think it's affected a ton of people in the church."

Other leaders recognized the gender double standard and how this inhibited women from opening up about their temptations or experiences with pornography. Stephanie, for example, recalled her experiences with women who wanted to come on staff with her collegiate parachurch ministry:

For a girl who does want to talk about [sexual temptation with porn], she's coming up against leadership from people who are going to say from upfront in mixed groups, if you're having a relationships talk or something like that, they're going to say from up front, "Well, this probably doesn't apply to the women." So, it's going to be really hard to bring it up if someone has already said that from up front. And then if girls do bring it up, they really are treated differently. Like, that they've got *serious* issues they need to deal with. They're going to be put in a different category. So, it's really hard for them to be honest about it because they've already seen people be treated differently because she was honest about that [emphasis hers].

Like Max, Stephanie recognizes the greater social stigma associated with being a woman and confessing her porn use to others, being perceived as having "serious issues," and being "put in a different category" from women who struggle with ostensibly normal temptations. Comparing this to men's experiences, Stephanie explained, "And girls don't even realize . . . I had a staff girl last year tell me, 'I want to talk to you about this, but people have told me if this is a struggle for you, then you can't be on staff.' And I was, like, 'Well, that's not true because if that were true, then a lot of *guys* we work with probably wouldn't be on staff!' " (emphasis hers). Apparently it had been communicated to this young woman, either implicitly or explicitly, that she would be fired for viewing pornography. Whether this double standard was real or perceived, this female staffer's perception that she would get fired for confessing her porn use made her reticent to confess it, even as Stephanie pointed out the obvious truth that firing someone for porn use would lead to a large number of men leaving staff.

But gender does not only differentially affect the social perceptions of women who view porn. They also experience internalized shame associated with violating the expectations of their gender. Chris is 33-year-old pastor of a church plant in Georgia. Acknowledging that women rarely confess to viewing pornography, Chris explains:

> Any men's retreat or men's Bible study, it's kind of assumed that this topic will be brought up, and women hear that and they feel even more shame, like, "I struggle with a dude thing." Where's the women's Bible study that this topic will be addressed? So, to the degree that it's associated as a specifically men's issue, I think they feel ostracized, like, "I'm the only one who struggles with this. This isn't a normal women thing." Which may be true percentage wise, but for the women who do struggle with it, I think they feel more isolated. Like, "Should I go to the men's recovery group?" So, they feel more shamed, more paralyzed, and don't even know the next steps that they should take.

The elevated distress among conservative Protestant women who view porn, as Chris expresses so clearly, stems not only from the porn use itself but also from the fact that it is a characteristically male sin and thus makes them abnormal, not as Christians but *as women*. It is the gender contradiction that leads to them feeling, in Chris's words, ostracized, isolated, ashamed, and paralyzed.[24]

Bringing attention to this issue from another angle, Christian recording artist Audrey Assad, who describes herself as having gone through a long battle with "pornography addiction" as a teenager, has made it a priority at her concerts to address the issue of sexual shame and isolation for women, particularly those using pornography. She has also given a number of online talks devoted to these issues and contributed a section to Barna Group's 2016 book *The Porn Phenomenon*. In her public lecture for the evangelical gathering Q Ideas (TED talks for Christians) in 2016, Assad summarized her experience growing up: "My whole young life I was instructed that men have pornography problems, not women. . . . The church's silence on this isolated and perpetuated the problem. I found myself trapped and alone in a shame cycle that daily impacted my health, mentally, emotionally, physically, and spiritually."[25] Elaborating on the disparity between facts and assumptions about women's porn use, in her interview with Barna Group, Assad explains:

I think gender stereotypes run rampant inside Christianity. Femininity is traditionally associated with things like purity and modesty. Because of these stereotypes and how deeply they are ingrained in the church, women do not feel free to confess or speak publicly about lust, sexual addictions, pornography, masturbation, or anything of the sort. This perpetuates a cycle of shame and bondage and silence for the women who are affected, and in turn reinforces the erroneous idea that women do not struggle with things like this—the idea that it's a "guy problem" remains the status quo because women do not feel safe to speak—they feel they will not be seen as feminine or womanly. Christian teaching in youth ministry has barely shifted in all these years to reflect what the newest studies show. Young girls go to retreats and camps all over this country and hear that pornography addiction is an issue that affects men. Again, this reinforces the idea in their minds that they cannot tell anyone about their struggles with pornography, and perpetuates the cycle of shame and bondage and silence.[26]

Similarly, in her online talk, Assad recalled her personal experiences with pornography, and her reticence to open up:

> I had no intention of seeking out pornography, but pornography found me when I was 15 years old. Within days I was compulsively viewing it. Often several times in a 24-hour period. Each night I prayed fervently for deliverance. I cried hot tears of shame. And I hated myself because I could not stop. Unfortunately, the topic of sexuality, perhaps especially pornography, and perhaps most of all, as it pertains to women, is stigmatized in many church communities. Even in the one place that we would usually go for help in our struggles we feel our honest conversations and confessions may in fact be unwelcome. . . . One year, my Sunday school teachers announced that we were going to begin a series on pornography addiction, which was considered to be very edgy. And I felt relieved, I thought, "Maybe someone's going to give me something I could use to get out of this." But it was immediately posited and stated that pornography is strictly a male issue, which isolated me immediately. Furthermore, the study laid out a strong correlative relationship between pornography addiction and serial killing. And I connected those dots. I have an anxious personality, so not only did I feel like a freak of nature for being a girl who looked at porn, but I began to worry that my addiction signified something sinister about who I was, something fundamentally broken. And I was terrified. And as I looked around me at 16 years old I came to the conclusion that vulnerability simply was not an option.[27]

Like Chris, Assad attributes Christian women's (and her own) shame, bondage, and silence about pornography use to pervasive stereotypes about Christian gender identity, and the perception that confessors will be judged, not for their porn use but for violating gender norms. This led her to claim, toward the end of her interview with Barna, "I have undergone more therapy because of my sexual baggage from fundamentalist Christianity than because of pornography addiction."[28]

Interestingly, while the dominant narratives about women not struggling with sexual, and particularly visual, temptation could exacerbate the shame and guilt these women feel, for some it could also be strategically used to mitigate social (or perhaps internal) disapproval. When I asked Stephanie about how prevalent pornography use was among the women she worked with in the church, she explained: "Probably more than most people think. They read romance novels and/or watch sex scenes on TV under the guise of they want to be relevant to unbelievers or their friends they are ministering to. Or that it doesn't affect them. . . . That's one of the big things is that women often say it doesn't affect them in the same way [as men]; it doesn't cause them to stumble."

Other sociologists have also observed the narrative among conservative Protestant women that pornography does not affect them the way it does men, which allows these women to rationalize, to themselves and others, viewing material that would be too tempting for a Christian man. In Kelsy Burke's research among conservative Protestants who run websites to enhance Christians' sexual experiences (providing toys or new techniques), she quotes a woman, Holly: "I think guys are much more visually stimulated, so I go through (sexually explicit) catalogues and attend shows. . . . Women, being less likely to be tempted by visual stimulus, have the upper hand when it comes to finding resources/products for sex lives."[29] Indeed, Burke shows that simply being a woman, and thus being perceived as somewhat impervious to visual sexual temptation, was often enough to qualify creators of Christian sexuality websites as being the "right kind of Christian" for that job.

Yet more often, it seems that because of complementarian ideals of femininity, masculinity, and sexuality in combination with dominant gender stereotypes, conservative Protestant men's porn use, while not necessarily approved of, is normalized and therefore, openly discussed. Conservative Protestant women's porn use, by contrast, is particularly isolating, primarily because it is a man's sin. Conservative Protestants interpretations of a closely related issue, solo masturbation, also reveals the double standard of complementarian gender expectations.

The Kind of Masturbation That's *Always* Wrong (When Women Do It)

In Chapter 2, I showed how masturbation, though functionally related to pornography, is far less stigmatized in conservative Protestantism.

This is primarily because of conservative Protestants' commitments to biblicism (needing explicit biblical teaching on a subject to develop a strong moral condemnation) and pietistic idealism (the heart matters more than the body). But readers are likely aware that the quotes from pastors and authors are all specific to men. This is because masturbation is primarily a morally ambiguous issue when men do it. Authors tend to be unequivocal in condemning masturbation when single women are involved. The authors of *Every Young Man's Battle* disagreed with each other about whether to call masturbation a sin, because of the lack of explicit biblical teaching on the subject.[30] But in *Every Woman's Battle*, masturbation is rejected unambiguously. Shannon Ethridge argues: "The most popular argument in favor of self-gratification is, 'The Bible does not expressly forbid it.' Let's be honest. When women masturbate, they don't think pure thoughts, and the Bible is very clear about that issue (see Philippians 4:8). We don't entertain thoughts that are pure, noble, or praiseworthy when we engage in self-gratification."[31]

Notably, neither Ethridge nor other authors who make such allowances for men acknowledge the possibility that married women might masturbate to thoughts of their husband, or the possibility that single women might masturbate without lustful thoughts. The tremendous irony here is that research suggests women, compared to men, are more likely to *actually* be able to accomplish just that—that is, masturbate without necessarily having overtly sexual thoughts that would constitute sinful lust for conservative Protestants. Experimental studies have shown that while men tend to be psychologically aroused whenever they are physically aroused, women can more easily be physically aroused (as evidenced by things like vaginal lubrication and even orgasm) even while they are not psychologically aroused.[32] In their systematic review of 132 studies from 1969 to 2007, psychologist Meredith Chivers and her colleagues found that while there was a strong correlation between men's psychological and physical sexual arousal, for women this correlation was weak.[33] McKenna, whom we met earlier, confirmed that masturbation for her didn't have to involve lustful thoughts: "I've had an orgasm on a bicycle!" she explained. "It was just the sensation. I could masturbate and not think of anything at all. It just feels good."

And women's masturbation would likely be far more detached from pornography than men, on average. Readers will recall that conservative Protestant women seemed to masturbate far more often relative to their porn use compared to conservative Protestant men, suggesting that conservative Protestant women would be less likely to violate the "looking lustfully" standard during masturbation. My interviews confirmed this as well. One women's pastor at a church in South Carolina recalled her conversations with college women about their sexuality: "There were a lot more women who were engaging in masturbation, and it might not be because they were watching pornography. Like, I think that's a little different for women; they don't really have to watch something to participate in that. So other girls were in a different category. They weren't watching pornography, but [masturbation] was a pretty consistent habit in their lives."

Why the double standard? Some of this may simply be due to the fact that conservative Protestant men are more likely to masturbate than conservative Protestant women. Conservative Protestant men may simply be giving themselves a pass here, possibly to avoid what some consider to be unnecessary guilt, as numerous authors explained.[34] Indeed, men may even be considered unmasculine for *not* masturbating at some point.

But beneath even this, the gender double standard regarding masturbation points to an underlying assumption about men's implied sexual agency as opposed to women's assumed lack of sexual agency. We can see this assumption in one of the top arguments authors give for women not masturbating—namely, that it will rob their *husbands* of sexual satisfaction. Speaking to married women in particular, Ethridge explains: "Most husbands find pleasure and satisfaction in bringing their wives to orgasm. If you typically find sexual release through masturbation, you may rob your husband of this pleasure by insisting that he allow you to 'help him.'"[35] Certainly, authors and pastors appeal to God's intention of shared sexuality as a reason for men not masturbating, but it's not because a husband's masturbating denies his wife sexual pleasure. Rather, those appeals are couched in terms of pietistic idealism—masturbating is wrong because it makes you selfish, not because you are denying your wife the sexual pleasure she gets from pleasing you.

Breaking with this trend, one pastor thought masturbation could be permissible for Christian women, but under different circumstances than for men. Adam, an evangelical Presbyterian pastor in California shared that: "I read a pastor say a long time ago that masturbation is okay for a single guy, but never for a married guy. Because single guys, especially if they've been single for a while, might need that release. And married guys shouldn't need to masturbate, and shouldn't masturbate because they have a wife. But for women, it's the opposite. Single women shouldn't masturbate because, for them, [lust is] just not as big of an issue. But married women probably should masturbate because that way they'll know what actually feels good and they can teach their husbands."[36] While allowing that Christian women can masturbate, this quote actually affirms two of the assumptions prevalent among those who forbid masturbation for Christian women. First, there is the assumption that single men, being sexual beings, might need to masturbate if they don't have other alternatives. Single women, by contrast, are assumed to not desire a sexual release—at least not to the extent that their male counterparts do. We see the second assumption in the reasoning for married Christian women to masturbate. Why should they do it? Because they probably don't have a good handle on what feels good physically, and they'll want to teach their husbands so that they'll know what they're doing. Thus, even in the rarer instances where conservative Protestants allow for women masturbating, the gendering of their assumptions point to women's assumed lack of sexual agency and the primacy of her husband's.

Does Gender Trump Heteronormativity in Discussing Sexual Temptation?

Complementarianism theologies of sex assume heterosexuality.[37] Women who view porn, and thus sin "like a man," are doubly sinning by violating God's design for women—namely, that they should be sexual responders who, deep down, long for emotional connections, not physical pleasure. But in virtually all my interviews, as well as porn-recovery and sexuality manuals for conservative Protestants, the assumption is heterosexual lust. What about conservative Protestant men and women who not only sin sexually with pornography but also sin with homosexual porn? One might expect that because same-sex attraction is a deeply stigmatizing sin for conservative Protestants, men might be just as reticent to open up about patterns of porn use involving homosexual material as women are regarding porn in general. But this was not the case. Interestingly, the same gendered patterns persisted, with conservative Protestant men being far more likely to open up about viewing pornography—even if it was homosexual pornography —than their female counterparts.

This was illustrated in one men's meeting I attended at a reformed Baptist church in Oklahoma. The meeting included a panel discussion with a Q&A, in which four men sat on a stage and shared their own experiences with pornography use and how they had overcome it. Two were heterosexual, one a pastor, the other a lay leader; the other two were seminary students who both said they were wrestling with same-sex attraction. Each discussed his experiences with pornography, patterns of use, and what he did to prevent further recurrences. There were few meaningful differences between them other than two of them having expressed that their temptation came from homosexual porn. While the issue of homosexual attraction was obviously salient enough for the leaders of the event to address it and intentionally select two men who wrestled with their sexuality in that way, the most salient issue was pornographic lust, and *that* issue (the porn)—not whether the content was heterosexual or homosexual—was what united the speakers and the other men in the audience. This suggests that, for conservative Protestant men, there may be an operative assumption that the temptation to lust visually is a normal struggle, and both heterosexual and homosexual lust fall into the same category ("lust") rather than being two completely different kinds of sins.

This is certainly not to diminish how much homosexuality is stigmatized among conservative Protestants. In fact, several conservative Protestant authors use the possibility of "becoming homosexual" to discourage conservative Protestant men from viewing pornography. This was a repeated refrain of Tim LaHaye who claimed, "We have seen rising levels of . . . homosexuality . . . in America because of the spread of pornography,"[38] Elsewhere, in a breathtaking example of fallacious reasoning and speculation, LaHaye asserted, "Most of the homosexuals I know indulged in [fantasy and] masturbation early and frequently.

This seems to be a crucial step in adopting a homosexual lifestyle. As frequent masturbators, they learn to associate their genitals with sexual pleasure. This association can overcome heterosexual leanings and destroy a natural attraction toward females. Masturbating and fantasizing can divert a child from normal sexual desires and serve as a catalyst that will provide him with a mental attitude favorable to homosexuality."[39] While more recent authors are not so explicit, a majority warn that pornography and porn-fueled masturbation virtually always escalate into more deviant sexual behavior, using language that often implies potentially homosexual behavior.[40]

Other pastors and authors propose that porn use and masturbation are inherently homosexual behaviors because they do not involve a woman. Rodney, a pastor in South Carolina, mused, "Here's a thought. Masturbating is actually a homosexual act. Think about it. A dude touches your penis and you have an orgasm." While Mark Driscoll does not categorically denounce masturbation as sinful, he argues: "masturbation can be a form of homosexuality because it is a sexual act that does not involve a woman. . . . Any man who [masturbates] without his wife in the room is bordering on homosexual activity, particularly if he's watching himself in a mirror and being turned on by his own body."[41] Clearly, the dreaded thought of engaging in homosexual activity—or worse, *being* homosexual—is seen as a potential motivator to discourage porn use and masturbation.

But that does not seem to discourage men from talking about the temptation to view gay porn. While it was admittedly uncommon in my interviews for conservative Protestant men to discuss being tempted by homosexual porn (likely a combination of both small sample size and that men with same-sex attraction may select out of conservative Protestantism altogether), the subject did come up. For example, one evangelical Presbyterian college student in Georgia told me that he was attracted to gay "transvestite porn"—in particular, in which actors who were anatomically male performed sex acts while dressed as women. And still another Baptist college student in Oklahoma, who said his parents were "very fundamentalist and very homophobic," explained that he had found himself from an early age admiring the physiques of male athletes and fitness models, and later began viewing gay porn. Both these men expressed that they were in conversation with their pastors about their temptations and affirmed that these counseling relationships were a valuable source of support for them.

Conservative Protestant women, by contrast, never disclosed viewing lesbian porn, or even heterosexual porn in which they were attracted to females in the scenes. And only one women's minister, Stephanie, had ever interacted with a young woman on staff with their college ministry who had confessed to wrestling with homosexual desires. Interestingly, however, Stephanie proposed that the issue of women's porn use and homosexuality were both closely related in that conservative Protestant women felt unable to open up about either:

> When I was a student, one of my really good friends—we were in Bible study together—and two other girls that I was discipling, and just out of nowhere they started dating women. And just last year, we had a staff girl who was let go because she started dating a female student. And all I was told was that there was physical intimacy between her and another girl student in our ministry. And I think that that and the porn issue are linked—if we could talk more about "your personal issues," you know, "What are you dealing with, temptation wise?" then my perception is that some women wouldn't go so far down those roads—if they'd been talking about it way before then. But it's so hard to talk about.

Putting aside the issue of whether conversations with these young women would have actually kept them from developing lesbian relationships, Stephanie's larger point is instructive. She does not seem to view homosexual temptation as somehow separate from women's struggles with pornography use and lust. Rather, she feels that both the issue of homosexual temptation and the temptation to view pornography are related, in that conservative Protestant women lack the opportunity to process their thoughts and experiences and/or feel discouraged from ever doing so. Thus, while the issue of homosexuality remains highly controversial for conservative Protestants, complementarian gender expectations and dynamics seem to be the more salient factor preventing women from discussing these topics openly and instead internalizing their shame, while men have the opportunity to speak candidly with other men and seek support.

A Lack of Resources

That conservative Protestant women do not open up about their pornography use is not only because of their unwillingness to do so. Many
would, in fact, love to talk with someone about it. But such women
have few people to talk to who are equipped to help. Most of the male
pastors I interviewed said that they had rarely counseled a woman about
her pornography use, likely in part because these women would be uncomfortable discussing their sexual sins with a man. But many pastors
themselves would find this arrangement problematic. One woman
who volunteers for her church explained that whenever the subject of
women's sexual temptations comes up in staff meetings, "There's just
always been a lot of pushback because a lot of the guys aren't comfortable talking about those things. And they don't feel like they want to
be polluted by hearing about what some women struggle with sexually
so they don't even want to hear about it." This obviously disadvantages
women who are tempted sexually. Their male counterparts can more
easily access support because counselors are almost always men. The
gender dynamics of complementarian church leadership create a situation in which women do not have qualified counselors to speak with.

But even if the church has women on staff with whom other women
can speak, there is no guarantee that such staff would be qualified to give
advice on issues related to pornography. Max, for example, explained
that in his church, "There are a lot of women's ministry leaders that
aren't equipped to understand the nature of addiction or the nature
of how people change; and so, I think that not only are there not safe
spaces but many of the women I've had to counsel alongside of—I've
spent a lot of time counseling with them [on] how to even approach the
subject, because they had no clue. [It's] simply because it's not something they struggle with or it's not something they've known anyone
that's struggled with it." Compared to men, for whom problematic
sexual fantasies and pornography use are a perpetual topic of discussion, women in ministry are simply less apt to encounter the situation and thus less able to effectively walk women through it. Similarly,
Stephanie affirmed, "That's always bothered me, that it seemed like
[women] didn't have any help from older women or, like, anyone they
were working with, because a lot of older women (on staff) don't feel

like they have personal experience with that kind of thing, so they can't offer any help." But the problem is not just a lack of experience working with women with these sorts of temptations. As Stephanie explains, the very pursuit of training to help women in these areas can result in push-back because of gender expectations:

> In my experience, we have had women [for whom] that's their role, and I don't know exactly why it doesn't work. Maybe it's a lack of training or a lack of convictions about that kind of thing. But we definitely haven't had a lot of women who have felt that that's their responsibility—to talk to women about these things [lust and por-nography]. So, I guess that's a lack of training. And that's why I'm going to seminary. But even in that—my going to seminary—there's a lot of cultural pushback, like . . . "Women don't need to do that." And it's, like, really obvious that we do. We've got issues that no one knows how to deal with because we don't have the training.

So, even as Stephanie seeks training to help other women who are striving toward sexual purity, which she sees as a tremendous need, she perceives skepticism that women would need those sorts of counseling resources.

Conservative Protestant women also lack access to other kinds of re-sources. For example, Stephanie points out that her collegiate ministry purchased accountability software for all the male staff, but not the female staff. "During staff meetings, where we have a lot of staff and it's not fun, . . . I try to bring that up. You've heard of Covenant Eyes? Well, we've always had that for men, and I've said, you know, 'I think we need to have that for the women, too.' It seems like that should just be a standard for anyone who works with us. Just because you didn't know it was an issue, doesn't mean it's not."

As Stephanie states, an obviously helpful way to address both the challenge of pornography temptation and the elevated shame associ-ated with gendered expectations of sexuality would be to simply remove the gender stereotype from the decision to purchase accountability software for the campus staff. Related to this, conservative Protestant women were hindered by the lack of materials that speak to the growing prevalence of those women who are tempted with porn. Some have addressed this challenge by simply using *men's* resources. For example, a church volunteer who counsels women through sexual issues explained:

> I wish there was more material out there just to get women talking about it. I've tried some things because I think it's important and women respond to it. So, like, one book I've used, we tried to read *Every Woman's Battle*. But sometimes with some girls we read *Every Man's Battle*, because *Every Woman's Battle* isn't always helpful. And, like, a lot of Christian women's books that I read are difficult because they'll sort of paint Christian women one way, and so all the women who feel like they don't relate to that will feel like they're doing something wrong or that there's something wrong with them. Or, that it isn't helpful. And because there's not a lot, like, on this issue. That would be my hope—that more women would write about more women's issues.

Just as the heightened distress and isolation that conservative Protestant women feel about their porn use stems from pervasive gender expectations and judgments, concerned interviewees and authors also said that countering this trend required addressing directly the gender double standard. Audrey Assad said simply, "I would love to see pornography addiction destigmatized and stripped of any unnecessary stereotyping in terms of gender."[42]

Stephanie identified a counseling pastor at her church whom she felt had been particularly helpful to women struggling with pornography use: "We have a pastor at our church who is a counseling pastor. . . . I've had staff girls who have talked to him and they're comfortable talking to him about those issues." I asked her to elaborate on why he was particularly helpful for women seeking counseling. She replied, "I think it's because he will put it on the table. I think when leadership, male or female, when they can put those things on the table and not say 'men are like this and women are like this,' that women will talk about it. Especially women who are struggling with these things. And if they want to see change in their lives, they'll talk about it. But they have to feel like it's okay to talk about those things." Here, Stephanie stresses that Christian women who are tempted by pornography do, in fact, desperately want to talk about their struggles. And she identifies this pastor's ability to help women with his willingness to not make porn use a male or female issue, but simply to "put it on the table."

Conclusion

American women in general—not just those in patriarchal, complementarian subcultures like mainstream conservative Protestantism—experience a double standard when it comes to their sexuality. But as one pastor, Max, affirmed earlier, this gender double standard is "vastly amplified in the church." Regarding porn use in particular, we have seen that complementarian expectations surrounding women's God-given sexual nature add another layer of moral incongruence for women. Viewing visual pornography is a characteristically "masculine" thing to do, and thus, women who are sexually aroused by such material and are tempted to pursue it experience both the social and the internal stigma of sinning "like a man." Indeed, a number of interviewees suggested that it is the violation of gender norms in particular, not merely pornography use itself, that prevents women from opening up about their temptation.

Conversely, while habitual pornography use is certainly stigmatizing for conservative Protestant men, it is also consistent with complementarian gender expectations. In this way, again, as Max explained, for a man to struggle with porn use may "validate his manhood at some level." When it is categorically assumed that men are designed by God to be visually aroused, and therefore wrestle with temptation to lust at what they see, confessing that you struggle with porn use can amount to confessing that you are simply a "normal" man. In this way, the unique gender dynamics within mainstream conservative Protestant communities creates a situation in which women who view pornography feel particularly beaten down and isolated, while men, though still feeling guilty because of sexual sin, can access social resources to feel supported and affirmed.

5

Till Porn Do Us Part?

I didn't like [my husband's porn use] at first, but I guess I don't really care now. As long as it's kept on the down low and I don't know about it, I really don't care. It's not cheating, in my book. It's a natural instinct that Christians really try to harp on, and it's just really not my biggest concern.

—Julia, Methodist

About two years into marriage, I ended up confessing to her again that I was still struggling [with porn every three to six months]. And she was clearly shocked, totally appalled. I remember that conversation like it was yesterday, and that was five and a half years ago, almost. She basically said [long pause]: "This is serious. If this keeps happening, I don't know if our marriage will last."

—Martin, evangelical Presbyterian

"NO WAY!" LUCAS RESPONDED. "She'd divorce me!" The men in the group said nothing at first. If one of the others, perhaps Mike or Chris, had said the same thing, everyone else would have immediately shared a laugh. But it was clear that Lucas wasn't joking. "How do you know she'd divorce you, Lucas?" Mike asked in a tone that was serious yet still a bit incredulous. "Because we've talked about it, and she *said* she would," Lucas explained. "She said: 'If I ever caught you looking at porn, I'd totally divorce you.' So, no. There's no way I'm telling her."

All the men in the focus group were conservative Protestants who had been part of the same church for the last few years. Several had voluntarily confessed to their wives that they had been watching porn and masturbating. Others had been caught. They had all experienced considerable pain as a result, as had their wives.[1]

Mike went first. "She was extremely pissed," he explained. After several years of marriage, Mike, a father of two girls, had confessed to his wife that he had been masturbating to pornography several times a month. Mike's wife, Gwen, had become a committed Christian later in life, and during her college years she had been sexually active. Some of her boyfriends had used pornography. Though she demanded that Mike find accountability and take proactive steps to ensure that he would avoid future temptation, Gwen's response was not as drastic as others' wives had been. While a number of conservative Protestant women from "more sheltered backgrounds," as one pastor put it, "think [that] because you looked at porn, you're almost some kind of pedophile," Gwen didn't see Mike's pornography use as a "perversion." She knew that it was common among men. But she was still shocked and angered by it, and she had expected more from her husband, who had served in leadership positions at several of their churches.

Chris had been caught. Not in the act, but after the fact. Before they had kids, Chris's wife, who (according to Chris) is prone to jealousy and suspicion (perhaps not without justification), had privately searched his internet history and found the websites he had visited. He came home from work to find his bags packed and on the front porch. Attached to one of his bags, his wife had left a note explaining that she had discovered his pornography use, that she was hurt, and that she did not want him to come inside. Instead, she wanted him to stay at a hotel for a few days while he figured out what really mattered to him and how he could get this sin out of his life. "She didn't use the D-word or anything," he explained, "But the packed bags was a pretty clear signal." A warning shot of sorts. Still others, like Lucas, a soon-to-be father, hadn't been caught and were too terrified of the consequences to tell their wives.

As I heard these stories, I thought back to a conversation I had had just a month earlier. I was at a conference presenting my research on pornography use among conservative Protestants. I showed survey data indicating that 60 to 70% of American men ages 18 to 30 reported watching porn in the past year, and that this number was only slightly lower for conservative Protestant men (50–60%). After the presentation, a group of female graduate students came up to chat about the findings. One of them, who had recently gotten married, looked unconvinced and asked lightheartedly, "I want to know *who* are these 30% of men who were *not* looking at pornography?"

I asked her what she meant, and she explained, "Well, I don't think I've ever actually met a man who didn't look at pornography at least sometimes." The other young ladies quickly nodded in agreement. They all seemed to assume that most of those in the 30% must be lying, and the ones who truly were not occasionally watching porn were outliers. Conservative Protestants, as we have seen, would likely agree with these young sociologists that more men regularly watch pornography than honestly report it on surveys. But their shock was informative. While not necessarily irreligious, none had ever been a conservative Protestant herself and neither were their spouses. To them, men—even married ones—watching pornography is normal, even expected, behavior. Along with this, they did not see porn use as a significant moral problem, even for their husbands or partners.

All these examples are a bit extreme—polar ends of a spectrum, really. And there are certainly exceptions. A number of conservative Protestant men and women I interviewed, for example, were quite understanding, gracious, and (permit me the antiquated term) longsuffering with one another about struggles with pornography use. And while some interviewees recalled those initial discussions as achingly awkward and upsetting, others, as we will see, described it as a positive turning point in their marriages. By contrast, in some of my interviews with women who were not particularly religious, the knowledge of their partner's or spouse's pornography use was incredibly hurtful, and it became an occasion for later conflict and breakup. Just because someone is not a conservative Protestant doesn't mean the person thinks pornography use is *a*moral, let alone thinks it's okay for their own spouse or partner to regularly look at porn.

Yet, the examples I have just described are indicative of a clear trend I have observed in research examining the connection between pornography use and committed relationships. Simply put, whereas pornography use (not always, but *on average*) seems to have a deleterious influence on the quality and stability of romantic and family relationships, these effects are far worse for conservative Protestants than for other Americans.

Marriage (Usually) Goes Worse with Porn

The majority of research examining the connection between pornography use and committed relationship outcomes can be summarized as follows: pornography use is almost always associated with lower relationship quality for men; for women, it all depends. Nothing about that statement should be controversial. To be sure, there is tremendous controversy when the discussion turns to *causation*. But regarding *correlation*, there is little debate. Indeed, the finding that men (and sometimes, but not always, women) who use pornography tend to report lower relationship quality is one of the most consistent findings in all pornography research.[2] That association also happens to be quite stable over time.

Rather than survey the dozens of studies that support these claims, let's consider a simple analysis that looks at whether a married American uses pornography at all, and the likelihood that the person reports being very happy in his or her marriage. Table 5.1 presents the

TABLE 5.1 Percentage of Married Americans Who Indicate Being "Very Happy" in Their Marriage, Related to Whether They Viewed Pornography

Years	Full Sample			Men			Women		
	No Porn	Viewed Porn	% Diff.	No Porn	Viewed Porn	% Diff.	No Porn	Viewed Porn	% Diff.
1970s	68	60.2	−7.8	70.3	61.5	-8.8	66	58.5	-7.5
1980s	65.6	60.2	−5.4	68.8	60.6	-8.2	63.1	59.7	-3.4
1990s	65.3	61.6	−3.7	69.3	60.0	-9.3	62	63.9	+1.9
2000s	62.3	56.7	−5.6	67.1	56.5	-10.6	58.6	56.9	-1.7
2010s	63.6	54.6	−9	66.3	56.7	-9.6	61.5	50.3	-11.5
1973–2016	65.1	59.2	−5.9	68.6	59.3	-9.3	62.4	59	-3.4

Note: Porn users are significantly different from abstainers for all decades except for women in the 1990s and 2000s.
Source: General Social Surveys, 1973–2016.

percentages of married Americans who indicate they are "very happy" in their marriage by whether or not they report viewing pornography. While these percentages do not tell us anything about the causal direction of the relationship (what causes what), they can give us a general idea of whether married porn users differ from abstainers in terms of their reported marital happiness.

As shown in table 5.1, the trends are clear and consistent. For the full sample, as well as for married men considered separately, those who view pornography are less likely to report being "very happy" in their marriage. For married women, those who viewed porn in the 1970s, 1980s, and 2010s are also less likely to report being "very happy" in their marriage compared to abstainers. In the 1990s and 2000s, these differences were not statistically significant. And while the percentage differences in table 5.1 are not particularly stark, they remain statistically significant, even when controlling for other factors like age, years of education, race, parental status, and worship attendance.[3] More important, the trend is clear: whichever direction the "causal arrow" is pointing (porn use leading to low marital quality or low marital quality leading to porn use), married Americans who view pornography tend to report lower marital happiness.[4]

But surely marital quality is more complex than a single-item survey measure? What do we see in surveys that use a variety of measures of marital quality—and, for that matter, better measures of pornography use? Table 5.2 shows the correlations between pornography use and various relationship outcomes for married persons on the whole, and married men and women separately. Plus signs (+) indicate a statistically significant positive correlation; minus signs (–) mean a statistically significant negative correlation; and "NS" means the correlation is "not significant" by conventional standards (for actual numbers, see appendix table B.4).

Despite some variation in statistical significance across genders (possibly due to sample size when men and women are split), the trends shown in table 5.2 are quite clear: more frequent pornography use is either associated with negative marital outcomes, or it is not associated at all. By contrast, porn use is *never* linked with positive marital outcomes.

But *why* do we find these persistent associations? This is where we start to wade into the ideologically charged debates over pornography.

TABLE 5.2 Bivariate Correlations Between Porn Frequency in the Past Year and Relationship Outcomes for the Full Sample and Across Gender

2006 PALS	Full Sample	Men	Women
How often spouse expressed affection in past year	NS	NS	NS
How often spouse compliments you for the work you do	NS	–	–
How often spouse performs acts of kindness	NS	NS	–
How often insults or harshly criticizes	+	NS	NS
How often spouse hits or slaps	+	NS	NS
How happy with relationship	–	–	–
How satisfied with affection received from spouse	–	–	NS
How satisfied with sex life with spouse	–	–	NS
How satisfied with decision-making	–	–	–
Believes spouse has cheated	+	+	NS
Respondent cheated	+	+	+
Experienced marital separation	+	NS	+

2012 NFSS	Full Sample	Men	Women
Ever thought about leaving your spouse?	NS	NS	NS
Have you and your spouse talked about separating?	NS	NS	NS
How often have you thought your relationship is in trouble?	+	+	+
How often have you and your spouse discussed ending the relationship?	+	+	+
How often have you broken up and then got back together?	+	+	+
Agree/Disagree: we have a good relationship.	–	NS	–
Agree/Disagree: our relationship is very healthy.	–	–	–
Agree/Disagree: our relationship is strong.	–	NS	–
Agree/Disagree: my relationship makes me happy.	–	NS	–
Agree/Disagree: I feel like part of a team with partner.	–	NS	–
Agree/Disagree: our relationship is pretty much perfect.	–	–	–
Marital Happiness Scale (1 = worst, 10 = best)	NS	NS	NS

(continued)

TABLE 5.2 Continued

2014 RIA	Full Sample	Men	Women
Ever thought about leaving your spouse?	+	+	+
Have you and your spouse talked about separating?	+	+	+
Respondent cheated sexually	+	+	+
Experienced physical violence in current marriage?	+	+	+
Marital Happiness Scale (1 = worst, 10 = best)	−	−	−

Note: − negatively correlated and statistically significant at .05 level; + positively correlated and statistically significant at .05 level; NS not statistically significant. PALS = Portraits of American Life Study; NFSS = New Family Structures Study; RIA = Relationships in America Survey.

While just about everyone has to agree that pornography use is associated with poorer relationship quality (and particularly for men), people have strong opinions about which direction the causal arrow is pointing. Historically, the dominant assumption has been that pornography use is somehow damaging to committed romantic relationships. Others argue that pornography isn't necessarily harmful, but that frustrated men and women turn to pornography and masturbation because something is missing in their romantic relationship. While this is likely true to some extent, studies based on experimental, longitudinal, and qualitative data suggest that pornography use itself likely affects committed romantic relationships.[5] It can do this through two primary mechanisms.

First, pornography use can shape the cognitive lenses through which viewers interpret their social lives. Pornography use might consciously or unconsciously shape viewers' expectations about body image and sexual behavior in ways that leave them disappointed with their spouse or partner. This might explain why men's romantic relationships are often more negatively affected by pornography use than women's— that is, men are viewing it more often and are therefore more likely to internalize its messages.[6] Moreover, studies find that viewers are more likely to apply sexual scripts from pornography when those scripts resonate with messages they have already acquired from the broader society. Having been exposed to dominant messages about sexuality, beauty, and masculinity in society at large, men would arguably be more in-clined to apply pornography's standards to their own relationships.[7]

Second, pornography use can negatively influence romantic relationships when couples have strong disagreements about whether to use pornography and how much is too much. Some studies show that couples who either use pornography together or at least openly communicate about it are better off than those in which only one partner (most often the man in heterosexual couples) is viewing pornography in isolation.[8] Qualitative studies have also shown that women, especially if they hold strongly negative opinions of pornography, can be deeply hurt by their male partner's pornography use, often viewing it as a sort of betrayal or cheating.[9]

But again, the negative association between pornography use and relationship outcomes likely goes both ways. Qualitative interviews suggest that frustrated partners or spouses do indeed seek out pornography as a source of release or escape.[10] In reality, the relationship between pornography use and poorer relationship quality is likely cyclical. Whichever comes first, it is possible that pornography use can erode romantic relationships through various mechanisms, which in turn likely drives partners or spouses to use pornography out of frustration, and the cycle goes on.[11] But are there other factors at play here? Some emerging work suggests that whatever negative association exists between pornography use and relationship outcome, it is significantly worse for Americans who are more conventionally religious—and particularly for conservative Protestants.

Being a Committed, Conservative Christian Makes It Worse

For decades, studies have shown that pornography use and poorer relationship quality tend to go together. But only within the past few years have studies begun to look specifically at conservative and committed Christians. One of the first such studies, by economists Kirk Doran and Joseph Price, showed that married Americans who viewed pornography tended to report lower marital happiness, but that this association was particularly strong for those who attended church weekly or more. The authors explained this finding by suggesting that pornography use may have greater "social costs" for those who are more embedded in a reli-gious community that stigmatizes pornography use.[12]

Other data have confirmed and expanded on this idea. For example, one of the most consistent findings linking pornography use to rela-tionship outcomes is that men who view pornography more often tend to report lower sexual satisfaction.[13] Along with my coauthor Andrew Whitehead, I tested whether this association may be worse for com-mitted and theologically conservative Christian men. We controlled for how frequently someone is having sex and whether the person is in a romantic relationship, with the goal of mitigating the possibility that both porn use and sexual dissatisfaction are the result of too little sex. Sure enough, while pornography use predicts lower sexual satisfaction for men (as expected), we found that this association is significantly stronger for those men who attend church more frequently and who hold a higher opinion of the Bible.[14]

What about those who in particular identify as conservative Protestants? While pornography use is associated with lower marital happiness for Americans in general (table 5.1), the strength of this asso-ciation is stronger for conservative Protestants (figure 5.1). Conservative Protestant men and women who *do not* report watching pornography are more likely to be "very happy" in their marriage compared to other Americans, but conservative Protestants who *do* view porn report lower marital happiness compared to others. Indeed, the difference in happi-ness between porn users and abstainers is more than twice as large for conservative Protestants as for other Americans.

But why is this the case? Is this just about religious guilt? In part, yes. As we have seen, committed Christians, and conservative Protestants in particular, who use pornography are often gripped with guilt and shame that colors their outlook on life and their relationships. And it's likely that in those studies, being a committed Christian is basically a proxy for being morally opposed to pornography use. To show this more clearly, I refer to a longitudinal study I conducted that found married porn users reported lower relationship quality as their porn viewing increased—but *only* if they explicitly felt that viewing pornog-raphy was morally wrong. For married porn users who did not morally object to pornography use, their marital quality was essentially unaf-fected by their viewing frequency.[15] This would suggest that the moral

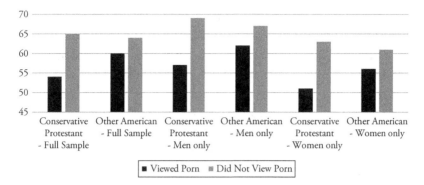

FIGURE 5.1 Predicted Percentage of Married Americans Being "Very Happy" in Their Marriage, Across Porn Use and Conservative Protestant Identification

Note: Results from logistic regression predicting "very happy" in marriage. Here, "conservative Protestant" is defined as "evangelical" according to Steensland et al. (2000), but using Protestant "fundamentalist" yields same results (see appendix B). Controls are included for year of survey, age, gender, race, number of children, worship attendance, and years of education. Triple interactions showed no significant gender interaction.
Source: General Social Surveys, 1973–2016.

incongruence from porn use, and the guilt and shame that accompanies it, is likely an important factor shaping the marital experiences of conservative Protestant couples. Illustrating this thought process, Brett, a Baptist pastor in Texas said of the men he counsels: "When you feel that shame and you feel dirty, I mean it's tough to even look in a mirror, much less to look in someone's else's eyes, much less to look in a *spouse's* eyes, and feel anything but fake and dirty; and so the weight of that with God and the weight of that with a spouse—it's so devastating to think about."

But there is likely another factor at work. A married person's porn use may influence his or her relationship outcomes because of the *spouse's* religious beliefs and commitment. Having a spouse who is more religious consistently intensifies the negative association between pornography viewing and marital quality. A recent study of mine showed that, for those Americans who affirmed their spouse to be extremely religious, more frequent pornography use was a stronger indicator of lower marital satisfaction, not just in general but also on specific aspects like sex life, decision-making, and the amount of affection one received. Moreover, these associations held across different measures of spousal religiosity, such as whether they attended church more often, prayed more often, read their sacred Scriptures more often, or personally reported that religion was more important to them.[16] Simply put, being married to a spouse for whom pornography use is highly problematic makes whatever negative influence pornography use would have on the relationship notably worse. This could be partly because of the guilt or shame connected with porn use. Pastor Brett went on to explain that:

> I find that [to be the case], even with those [husbands] who are the most versed in understanding that, "If we confess our sins, God is faithful to forgive our sins." Even those who have *spouses* who understand that, and don't make it a personal thing—they understand that, you know, "This is way more about him than it is about me." So, even in the more mature, or even in the response of the spouse, those [husbands] who'd have an easier time confessing those things to that spouse . . . for the spouse [doing the] confessing, that shame and guilt is really thick.

In other words, even for those married to more spiritually mature and understanding spouses, the moral incongruence experienced through porn use could cause significant emotional distress. But as we will see, conservative Protestant spouses (wives, almost exclusively) often intensify these negative feelings in the way they respond to their husbands' porn use.

Most of the quantitative studies I've cited are based on cross-sectional data, so we don't know in which direction the causal arrow moves. Perhaps relationship troubles make conservative Protestants more likely to seek out porn than it does other Americans. But that seems particularly unlikely in this case. Because pornography use is so unambiguously condemned by conservative Protestants (even among those who view it), it seems unlikely that those who are experiencing relationship troubles are more likely to turn to pornography use. What makes more sense is that watching porn when you are a conservative Protestant who is married to another conservative Protestant simply has more negative repercussions on the quality of your relationship than it would for Americans who do not hold such strong moral opposition to porn.

Beyond measures of marital quality, we see that pornography use also has stronger ramifications for the longevity of conservative Protestant marriages. When divorced Americans were asked in a survey why they wanted a divorce, very few men (and no conservative Protestant men) chose "spouse's pornography use." But a small percentage of women did, and a strongly disproportionate number of these respondents are conservative Protestants. As figure 5.2 shows, among women who had been divorced, those who identified as "evangelical" Protestants were more than twice as likely as other women in the survey to indicate they wanted a divorce because of their husband's pornography use.[17]

Part of this difference could be due to conservative Christian women feeling a need to publicly signal their moral innocence. In the New Testament, Jesus provides only one justifiable basis for divorce—namely, *porneia*, or "sexual immorality" (Matthew 5:32,

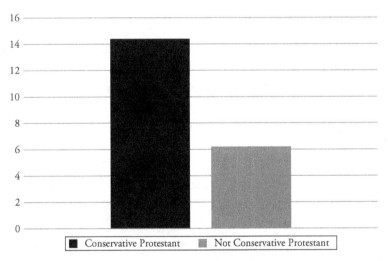

FIGURE 5.2 Predicted Percentage of American Women Who Wanted a Divorce Because of Their Spouse's Pornography Use

Note: Models control for age, educational attainment, race, parental status, and worship attendance. "Conservative Protestant" refers to those who identified as "evangelical" Protestants.
Source: Relationships in America Survey, 2014.

19:9). Divorces often happen for a variety of interrelated reasons, but conservative Protestant women may feel social pressure to stress their husbands' porn use, in particular, as a way of designating their divorce as righteous in God's eyes. But my interviews suggest that married conservative Protestant women genuinely seem to draw a harder line than other married women when it comes to pornography—one that holds out divorce as a possible option if their spouse doesn't get control of his pornography use. Before we hear from conservative Protestants themselves, however, we will listen to those who often interpret and experience pornography in their relationships in a different way.

"It's Great," "No Big Deal," or "Not Wrong, but Wrong for Me"

Julia is a recently married woman in her mid-twenties. A health and science major in college, she now works for a local gym as a personal trainer. She grew up in the Methodist Church and still considers her faith "extremely important" to her. When I asked her how she felt about pornography, she explained, "I was raised to think it was a super sin. I'm not a proponent by any means, but I also don't think you'll go to hell for watching it." While she did not necessarily find pornography appealing ("I don't really understand how it turns someone on."), she indicated that she has had boyfriends who used pornography and her husband occasionally watches it. I asked her to tell me about how she felt about her past boyfriends' porn use. She responded:

> Growing up with it being a super sin I had to, like, talk myself through the fact that a good majority of boys do use it and that if I make that a hard-and-fast rule of [its] being absolutely not allowed, I would probably end up with them lying to me and getting my feelings hurt. I had one boyfriend who told me the two biggest lies boys tell is, "I don't do that" [and] "I never would with you." I remember being pretty upset with that at the time, but at this point I have come to terms with it because I really just think that it's not my hill I want to die on. I have also heard that it's actually good for guys and girls to regularly get off, so I guess—why not?

Though Julia doesn't necessarily like porn, and seems to have faint religious reservations about it, she adopted a more pragmatic approach: men *will* look at pornography and she can either get used to the idea or be lied to. When I asked her about her husband's porn use, she again took a more pragmatic perspective: "I didn't like it at first, but I guess I don't really care now. As long as it's kept on the down low and I don't know about it I really don't care. It's not cheating, in my book. It's a natural instinct that Christians really try to harp on and it's just really not my biggest concern."

While she's not a conservative Protestant, Julia's Christian background in some ways still orients her feelings about pornography, making her initially uneasy with the idea. But her initial discomfort with porn is in no way limited to women with religious backgrounds. Karen, who refers to herself as an atheist, recalls negative feelings surrounding her boyfriends' pornography use as a teenager, "In my relationships in high school I felt like I was inadequate or not as sexy as the women they were watching. It made me feel jealous." But much of this she attributes to her own insecurities and lack of conversation about the issue. When I asked about her current boyfriend, she explained, "We have had open conversations about [his porn use]. I think it stems from a day when I was really sick and asleep. I woke up and couldn't find him, so I went into the computer room and he was masturbating to porn. I felt the shame and jealousy I felt before, but then it became funny and opened up a dialogue about it later on." Catching her boyfriend in the act, though troubling at first, had the positive effect of fostering clear communication.

Another young woman who was nominally religious, Lydia, said that her boyfriend's porn use wasn't a big deal for her so long as it wasn't dysfunctional. "My boyfriend watches porn occasionally, but he explained that it is a biological necessity for boys to masturbate and porn helps, and I don't really mind his use of porn as long as it's not excessive and not addictive." Another woman was similarly indifferent: "Yeah, [my previous boyfriend] watched porn. I wasn't mad. It was just something I didn't understand, but it didn't affect our sexual life."

Other men and women indicated that they preferred to be open about their pornography use, seeing it as improving their sex life as a couple. "It offered different ways to spice up the intimacy in our relationship," shared Craig, a manager at an Oklahoma City music store in his late twenties. Similarly, Sarah felt that her being able to talk with her boyfriend about his porn use has helped bond them. "I don't watch porn as much [as he does], but when I learned my boyfriend was watching porn, I feel like it made our relationship stronger. We were able to discuss our likes and dislikes in porn and in bed more openly, without fear of criticism."

Others went even further, suggesting that it was essential for their porn use to be mutually participatory. One college student explained that he felt his porn use had not negatively influenced any of his romantic relationships, but that "I don't stay with partners who won't watch porn with me." Another man, Jacob, in his mid-thirties and a father of two, will only watch pornography if his wife is with him. Though his wife has no moral objection to watching pornography, she would interpret any private pornography use on Jacob's part as a form of extramarital sexuality and prefer that she be the one to satisfy him sexually. Here's how Jacob explained the arrangement:

SAM: How did you broach the topic of pornography use with your wife?

JACOB: With my wife now, she's really open-minded. I think it just popped up and we were talking about the things we liked during sex, and I think I said, "Wait let me just show you." And so I pulled it up and I think that was the first time we watched porn together.

SAM: And does she enjoy watching it herself? Like, does that turn her on? Or how does she experience that?

JACOB: She enjoys me getting horny, watching the porn. I don't think she enjoys watching porn herself, but she enjoys watching me watch the porn.

SAM: So, what if you guys are apart for a time? Is it okay for you to watch porn by yourself?

JACOB: No, I don't think it would [be okay], and I know my wife wouldn't like that. I think she wouldn't have any problem if I watched it with her, but I don't think she would like it if I watch it by myself.

SAM: Why not?

JACOB: I think she sees it as a form of cheating. I think she sees it as, you know, if you need to get off or if you need to get something out of your system sexually just come to me and we can take care of it or we can talk about it. So yeah, I don't think she would like me doing that. She hasn't said that explicitly, but she's a lawyer (laughs) and she has a way with words. She made it pretty clear. I can read between the lines [laughs].

Jacob's wife apparently does not have a problem with his being turned on by watching other women have sex, so long as it is done in the context of their own sexual relationship. In fact, Jacob explained that it is usually his wife who initiates the use of porn in their sex life: "I mean, we have two kids and sometimes you're tired, and she's like, 'Hey, it's been a couple of days and we should have sex. Do you need to watch something or are we good?' Or, when she wants to have sex and I'm tired, most of the time she's like, 'Okay, let's watch something together so we can both get into the mood.'" Interestingly, however, Jacob's wife felt that his watching porn by himself would be a form of cheating. Rather, she'd prefer he come to her to "get off," even if porn is the thing that initially gets him aroused.

By contrast, one married man I spoke with, Andrew, did not feel morally comfortable masturbating to porn because of his Catholic background. But his wife wished he did, so that she would not feel full responsibility to satisfy his sexual needs. Andrew mused, "I don't know if this is strange or not, but I think my biases against porn and mas- turbation are occasionally frustrating for my wife, who would prefer I 'take care of myself' instead of obligating her to have sex on those days [when] she is not feeling sexy."

Though spicing up one's sex life is often the motivation behind couples' viewing porn, others found just the experience of watching porn together so uncomfortable and ridiculous that the act itself increased intimacy. One man in his mid-twenties had used pornog- raphy "several times in several relationships," he explained. "I am usu- ally the one to initiate. It is not a regular thing, but something done on occasion to change things up. And it's only influenced my relationships in a positive way. Even if the viewing doesn't excite one or both of us sexually, we always at least get a laugh out of it and commend ourselves for trying." I asked if he could give me an example, and he recalled, "My college girlfriend and I were going through a dry spell, and [we] wandered into a sex shop. She picked [up] a video and thought it would be fun to watch it together. It ended up being a cheesy instructional video with a lot of women using strap-ons on men [laughs]. We had a really good laugh."

Similarly, a woman in her mid-thirties who only occasionally watched porn with her live-in boyfriend expressed that the intimacy came from the shared humor: "My partner and I rarely watch porn together for sexual reasons. But we *have* watched porn together. We might watch it together once every few months for the purposes of foreplay. I always initiate. Now, our regular habit with porn is to play obnoxiously loud porn, with lots of fake moaning, screaming, and ridiculous dirty talk at each other. It acts as an inside joke between the two of us."

While most of the stories from men and women who were not conservative Protestants were either positive or indifferent regarding how porn use had influenced their committed relationships, this was certainly not the case for everyone. As some of the previous comments suggest, several men and women encountered trouble in their relationships because of jealousy. One woman simply explained, "We had a lot of fights about him viewing it." In one rather different situation, a young woman had been regularly watching pornography with boyfriends and was asked to stop by her most recent boyfriend. "[Porn] has helped enhance the sex life of most of my relationships. In one relationship it was a problem because my partner felt that I was cheating on him."

Most of the time, however, it was men whose girlfriends or spouses felt jealous or did not want to do the sorts of things men had seen in pornography. One man in his mid-twenties explained, "When I watched regular porn videos, I would ask my girlfriend at the time to try what I've watched. My girlfriend now isn't pleased with me watching it for that reason." Another man, when asked about whether pornography use had influenced his marriage, acknowledged, "Yeah, it has. It has caused problems by creating arguments and us questioning each other's loyalty, and most of all our attractiveness to each other." Similar comments suggested that women felt insecure about their partner's or husband's pornography use, as if they were not enough: "My partner had an addiction, and it affected our intimate activity. It made me feel less worthy." Another mentioned that her partner's porn use made her feel like their sex had become impersonal. "He started wanting to act out things in porn, and it was obvious and I felt objectified. I got angry and cried, and it became a hot-button issue that we avoided talking about. And since that happened, we stopped being intimate nearly as often."

Yet even though a number of interviewees felt porn use had hurt their relationship, and women felt jealous, or insecure, or objectified, none of them expressed that they felt porn itself was inherently immoral or harmful. Rather, the morality of porn use centered on what it meant to them and their relationship specifically. Conservative Protestant couples, however, operate under entirely different interpretations of porn use.

When Pornography Use = Adultery and Betrayal

Earlier, I explained how conservative Protestants not only subscribe to sexual exceptionalism—believing sexual sin to be among the most corrupting and shameful of all sins—but, because of pietistic idealism, are also prone to expand definitions of sexual sin beyond *behavioral* violations to *heart-level* violations. Jesus' own words lend themselves to this interpretation. In Matthew 5:27–28, Jesus states: "You have heard that it was said, 'You shall not commit adultery.' But I say to you that everyone who looks at a woman with lustful intent has already committed adultery with her in his heart." Conservative Protestant authors and pastors usually acknowledge the hyperbole in Jesus' words here and view him as trying to emphasize both the gravity and the interiority of sin. (In the verses after this, Jesus tells his listeners to gouge out their eyes and cut off their arms lest their whole body be thrown into hell; and a few verses earlier, he compares being angry with one's brother to murder.) Lay conservative Protestants, however, often speak of pornography use—being a prime example of "looking with lustful intent"—as a form of adultery. Luke Gilkerson, former educational resource manager with Covenant Eyes, argues, "[P]orn use is breaking a vow—either implicitly or explicitly—made to one's spouse. This is because marriage is, in part, about sexual exclusivity; it is about 'forsaking all others.' . . . If your husband (or wife) is engrossed in porn, you are right to feel like this is cheating. He is defrauding you of something that should be your exclusive domain. You are not a prude for thinking this. You just take your vows seriously, as everyone should."[18]

Gerald, an evangelical Presbyterian father of three from South Carolina, explained his wife's devastation over his own pornography use: "Earlier on in our marriage, I struggled with [porn], and my wife caught me. And it was like the most shameful thing in the world. I mean in her eyes, it's the same as—it's not the same, but it sort of is the same as—adultery, in her eyes. And in some cases, some people would say that it is. If that's how she wants to define it, she has that right. So it was a very painful experience for her and a humbling experience for me." While Gerald, who has a degree in Biblical Studies, hints that he believes pornography use is not technically adultery, he believes that his wife has a right to see it that way.

Because pornography use is so consistently viewed as a form of sexual betrayal and infidelity in the conservative Protestant community, wives are not only caught off-guard by their husbands' pornography use but also can seem almost as devastated as they would be if they had discovered an affair with someone else. The most consistent narrative, in fact, when conservative Protestant women publish books, blog posts, and lectures on pornography use, is how to deal with the revelation of their husbands' "affair" with porn. A sampling of titles include "Shattered: A Letter to Wives After the Betrayal of Pornography,"[19] "Betrayal Trauma: The Side of Porn Use No One Talks About,"[20] and "Tough Love for Your Unrepentant, Porn-Using Husband."[21] Contributors to the *Every Man's Battle* series wrote three different books to help marriages recover from a *husband's* porn use—two for women. Each of these three books speaks about pornography use and having a physical affair with another woman as virtually interchangeable.[22]

Because of the linking of porn use with infidelity, in fact, a common question for organizations like Focus on the Family, or groups like Covenant Eyes or Pure Life Ministries, is whether pornography use constitutes grounds for divorce.[23] In a Q&A forum for Focus on the Family, one wife asked, "Would it be fair to say that my spouse's use of pornography amounts to the same thing as marital infidelity? Here's why I ask. Jesus said that to look with lust is to commit adultery in your heart (Matthew 5:27–28). My husband's porn addiction is a huge problem in itself, but what I really want to know at this point is whether I can cite it as valid grounds for divorce (Matthew

5:32)?"[24] A number of commentators, including a Focus on the Family counselor, preferred to champion marriage as a relationship worth fighting for, rather than to advocate divorce.[25] Other writers, however, like Luke Gilkerson for Covenant Eyes, felt that persistent and unrepentant porn use would be grounds for divorce, viewing the act of watching pornography as essentially participating in the "entertainment wing of prostitution."[26]

While all the conservative Protestant men I interviewed viewed their pornography use as sinful and knew it hurt their wives, none saw it as adultery and certainly not to the extent of justifying divorce. Most, in fact, wished their wives wouldn't take it so personally. Chuck is a Baptist father of two in Texas. While not currently a pastor, he has served in leadership roles at several churches. In his counseling experience with Christian couples, he felt that wives often misconstrue what pornography and masturbation *mean* to their husbands, perceiving the situation in rigidly binary terms. For example, when husbands confess their pornography use, Chuck explained, "Their wife doesn't understand, and thinks 'You don't know me, love me, or even like me at all.' And the man would say, 'That's not right!' And he certainly wouldn't believe that." Most Christian men who view pornography, Chuck believes, don't have a *love* relationship with pornography, and it doesn't have to mean more than a fleshly attraction to the images and activity. But Christian wives, he believes, are prone to read it as an affair. He recalled his own wife's reaction when he confessed his struggles. "I remember the first time pornography was a conversation between me and my wife, and she was like 'Wow, you're the most godless, adultery-minded.' And it's like, no, it's not that deeply rooted. This is a strong, but very flesh-level, not a heart-level, flesh-level temptation. Just because I stumbled in this doesn't mean I want to go support the porn industry and that I want that kind of experience. Fortunately, it doesn't have to mean all that."

Other men shared similar stories. Alex, a pastor in Georgia, explained, "I've seen women sort of be control freaks on this. I had one friend who was engaged to a girl and he told her one time he struggled with [porn] and she wanted weekly reports from him. And she felt totally justified in that. [Porn use] just feels more personal and violating to [Christian] women. And it's not, it's not that personal. I wish it was, it might be easier to solve. But it's a heart, gospel issue." Not only does Alex believe this woman's response to the revelation of her fiancé's porn use is extreme but he feels it is indicative of a common misunderstanding Christian women have about their man's porn use—namely, that they can't seem to realize "it's not that personal."

Talking to conservative Protestant wives about their husbands' porn use affirms some of these feelings and complicates others. Rebecca is a married mother of three from Oklahoma. She and her family attend an evangelical Bible church where her husband, Steve, is a deacon and elder-in-training. As a couple, they have worked through Steve's own struggles with pornography, and Rebecca was happy to discuss that process and her feelings throughout that experience. Recalling how she learned about his continued porn use, she explained: "I knew there was some pornography use in the past. We 'discussed' it while we were engaged, and he told me he had 'struggled with it in the past,' which led me to assume that he no longer struggled with it. At the time, he was happy for me to be misled, as he was using pornography regularly in secret." Rebecca ultimately found a long list of pornographic websites on Steve's search history while, she made sure to note, "I was pregnant with our second child," emphasizing both the caddishness of Steve's behavior and the fact that this wasn't the prime time for marital sex. She confronted him about the porn, and he came clean.

I asked Rebecca to recount her thoughts when she discovered Steve's porn use, and she immediately described feelings of sexual betrayal: "I was extremely surprised and hurt that he had been hiding the information for the previous three years. I felt very betrayed, because I thought we openly discussed all things and felt immediately less secure in our own sexual intimacy. I felt like he had willingly, intentionally, deceptively brought sexual images and experiences of other women into our marriage." And she added: "It made me doubt that he had any kind of specific sexual desire for me."

Consistent with what we've seen so far, Rebecca viewed Steve's porn use as a form of adultery, bringing sexual images of other women into their bedroom, and made her doubt his sexual attraction to her. She opened up further about what specifically she hated about Steve's porn use:

I think it's wholeheartedly selfish. For a Christian, I think that makes it especially ugly. When I got married, I committed to give of myself completely for my spouse, forsaking all others. I take that vow very seriously, you know, and expect my spouse to as well. I preserved my own sexuality for him, forsaking all others, prior to and since our marriage. I mean, all of my sexual experiences have been with him, within the bounds of our marital relationship, so I think it's especially distasteful to me that he would choose to ignite, encourage, or expend any sexual energy outside our marriage. I'm always willing to satisfy any sexual desire he has, and I've communicated that to him. So, when he then chooses to view images of other women for the purpose of self-gratification, I see it as an affront to me personally. It shows that what he wants isn't found in me, or that he's too lazy to let me participate in his sexual activity.

Here, the interpretation of porn use as adultery and betrayal is clear. Rebecca compares Steve's infidelity with porn to her virginity before marriage. She saved herself for him sexually, so it is a very personal insult for him to "expend sexual energy outside [their] marriage" with pornography. Importantly, Rebecca also notes that from a professing Christian man, that sort of sexual selfishness in porn use is particularly offensive.

But beyond the actual porn use, Rebecca felt just as upset about the deception and hiding: "I felt [Steve's continued porn use] showed that he hadn't trusted me because he didn't confide in me about his struggle. That hurt about as much as the actual porn use. And [it] shook my trust in him, since he knew I'd interpreted his answers to previous questions to mean he no longer used porn or struggled with lust." While conservative Protestant women do seem to employ a more expanded definition of "sexual fidelity" by including things like fantasy and lust, and they draw a harder line regarding those activities for their spouses, the feelings of betrayal are also closely tied to the act of deception. As we will see, along with outright selfishness, this deception can stem from real or perceived concerns about the consequences if these men ever opened up about their porn use.

For Better or For Worse?

The association between porn use and marital problems does not go only in a single direction. Just as porn use can lead to marital conflict and strife, particularly for conservative Protestants, marital challenges can make pornography use more attractive or, in some cases, more difficult to avoid. This is somewhat paradoxical in that conservative Protestant husbands often emphasize to their spouses that their porn use is not about their wives or indicative of their marital happiness. Chuck and Alex both said as much. And wives reported hearing this, as well. Rebecca, for example, shared that, "[Steve] assures me that he is happy with our sex, and that his porn use isn't related to me. I have to take his word on that, since I don't really understand what drives him to use it."

Paradoxically, however, several husbands described how marriage actually made their struggle with pornography worse. Martin, for example, described how the frustrations involved in marriage could lead to him seeking out porn as a comfort: "[My porn use] actually got worse in marriage. Because marriage didn't end up being that Holy Grail that I thought it would be. I mean, fighting with the person you're supposed to be more in love with than anybody else was a real downer. And I guess pornography became my refuge. And so it actually got worse that first year of marriage, not better." Martin doesn't blame his wife, but feels he turned to pornography as a means of coping with disappointment over unmet expectations.

In other cases, conservative Protestant men found that, contrary to the popular narrative that marriage would satisfy their sexual desires, marriage intensified those desires. Daniel, a former pastor in Texas, explained: "I didn't really get into pornography until I was married. Before I got married, I was a Christian and I lived like a monk with other Christian roommates, with no access to the internet or smartphone. And I didn't talk to other girls hardly at all. But when I got married, I basically had this naked lady walking around my house all the time. But we're not having sex all the time. So it kinda made it worse." Daniel went on to describe how being married also prevented him from dealing more aggressively with his pornography use than he would have as a single man: "Even in the early 2000s, getting pornography either meant you had a laptop or desktop computer with internet access in your room, or you had to access it somewhere else like at school or through dirty magazines or watching some raunchy VHS, you know. Once we had internet in our house in seminary, I had unfettered access to all the porn I could handle and I sort of went nuts."

Even while interactions between husbands and wives over the issue of porn use were often very difficult, some couples described those conversations as the best thing that could have happened to their marriage. Rebecca's initial reaction to discovering Steve's porn use reflected her deeply felt perception of his behavior as an "affront" and a "betrayal." She recalled: "I was too shaken up to talk about it when he first confessed. I ended up writing a letter to him the next day trying to capture my feelings of betrayal. The news of his porn use really impacted my own sexual desire for him, making me far less interested in engaging in sex altogether." Despite this, however, when I asked Rebecca about whether Steve's porn use had had a lasting impact on their marriage, she was enthusiastically optimistic: "It definitely has! Speaking from our marriage today, now seven years in, I would say we now have a stronger marriage. There's definitely better communication and opportunity to practice our marriage vows, laying the groundwork for other, harder things that are likely to come."

To be sure, Rebecca acknowledges residual feelings of hurt, but she very much saw the current challenges with Steve's temptations as opportunities for her to grow personally and for them to grow as a couple:

> It isn't easy to know that he prefers a different type of body type than mine, or that he still periodically seeks out sexual fulfillment from a source other than me, or that there are things he would rather think about a stranger than share with his wife, so I have to be extra diligent about talking to him about my hope for his fidelity whenever he or I is away, but at the same time, I see the value in growing with each other in this. Since I learned about [his porn use], I'm certainly better informed, I ask better questions, I can express my own feelings with more clarity, can forgive more easily, I feel better equipped to talk to our son and daughters about their own sexuality. I've seen my husband strive to serve me by doing the hard thing of confessing to

me regularly, asking for forgiveness and trying to please me in his imperfect sexual fidelity. What more could I ask for?

Another wife and mother, Caitlyn, who attends an Evangelical Free congregation in Texas, seemed particularly embittered about her husband's porn use throughout the interview, tending to emphasize his deceit and using familiar language of betrayal and adultery. "I was shocked and hurt, mainly because it was going on for so long and I had no idea. I don't like the idea of him finding sexual pleasure using something outside the intimacy of our marriage. I should be the only one sharing sexual experiences with my spouse." And yet, like Rebecca, Caitlyn was largely positive in thinking about the long-term repercussions of them working through that experience:

The Lord has granted [my spouse] much freedom in this area so a lot of healing has happened in our marriage since the confession. Prior to his confession, when the pornography use was at its highest, our marriage was really struggling, especially in the area of [sexual] intimacy. We'd have continual fights about sex. Since the pornography struggle has come out in the open we're able to have better communication concerning intimacy. There are still days when I wonder if the pornography use is still there and I question myself being an adequate enough sexual partner for [him]. So it's impacted our marriage for good but also has had some pretty severe consequences. . . . But the Lord has done an amazing work in my spouse and is continually restoring the years the locusts have eaten.

Several husbands also described the positive long-term consequences of their initially painful discussions about porn use. Two years into their marriage, Martin was occasionally returning to pornography about "once every three to six months." Though infrequent, Martin felt he needed to confess his porn use to Amy. He recalls:

She was clearly shocked, totally appalled. I remember that conversation like it was yesterday, and that was five and a half years ago almost. She basically said [long pause], "This is serious. If this keeps happening, I don't know if our marriage will last." I mean, you say a lot of things you don't necessarily mean in conversations, and she never explicitly threatened divorce if I didn't [stop], but I think she meant "I don't know if our marriage will last because I'll never be enough and I won't be able to live up to that. You'll never be satisfied. And we may last for five or ten years, but [porn] will continue to eat away at the core of our marriage until one day we'll likely get divorced." And I was like, . . . she just used the D word, man. She just talked about divorce and we're just under a year of being married, and I thought, "I can't even contemplate being divorced and why that would happen, and you're saying it's *that* serious."

Rocked by this statement from his wife, Martin was forced to get serious about his on-again-off-again pornography habit and begun to take more deliberate actions to avoid future missteps in this area:

That was the first time somebody forced me, and God used someone to force me to see this is a big deal. And so at that point, I sort of came up with a battle plan. And she required me to, but I got Covenant Eyes on the computer, and got a good enforcer (accountability partner). Cuz, you've got to have a good enforcer with Covenant Eyes; cuz, otherwise it's worthless. But I did that and really started trying to be broken about it. And that's when I started to see pornography as bigger than just videos and images and masturbation, but I saw it as this systemic strain in the culture all around us that is trying to get us to that ethical point, because they're trying to sell us on something. That's when the light sort of clicked on. . . . And that's when the back was broken is when somebody said, "This has to be seriously dealt with or else, serious consequences happen in life because of this."

Gerald described the initial confrontation with his wife as being beneficial to their marriage in the end. When I asked him whether he thought Tina's initial response to his porn use was helpful or harmful, he immediately said, "It wasn't harmful at all. It was more of 'Wow, I'm hurt.'" When I asked him to elaborate on what came about in their relationship as a result of that conversation, Gerald explained:

> You know, we had to work through it and we had to put up some boundaries and that kind of stuff, but it was one of the best things that could have happened because it forced us to face our depravity, and mine and hers as well. Because we tend to demonize certain sins more than others and it forced us to come to Jesus and realize that we can't forgive until we realize we've been forgiven by you. And just because my sins are different doesn't mean they're any worse than her sins. And I've shared that with couples and we've even talked about that in front of our church.

Gerald's comments about his sins not necessarily being worse than hers is significant because the general perception among conservative Protestant wives seemed to be that his sins *are* worse than hers, whatever they may be. A Presbyterian pastor in Georgia, Alex, has counseled a number of couples through pornography use. After our initial interview, Alex actually called me back because he wanted to get something off his chest when it came to the response of conservative Protestant wives to their husband's pornography use. He explained:

> I'm of the opinion that Christian women who are married need a massive rebuke. I think the way women handle [their husband's porn use] is almost more problematic than men going to it. It's like a codependent relationship. If a man is battling something like that . . . it's like the one person you can't talk to is your spouse, not because they're ill-equipped but because they will explode and dump the shame. And it's like no one will say this, but "Women, don't you understand the way you're handling this is driving your husband deeper into this? And all the while you get to play this victim card." And that is a massive narrative that no one wants to . . . it's the elephant in the room.

What does Alex mean by saying Christian wives' responses could drive their husbands' deeper into pornography? On the face of it, this sounds like a husband blaming his wife for his own inappropriate and hurtful behavior. Still, a practical example of how Alex's description might play out can be seen in Daniel's experiences. Daniel's descriptions of the depth of his struggle were among the most graphic in my interviews.

While most of the conservative Protestant men I spoke with had experienced some success in reducing their pornography use, and most viewed pornography quite infrequently compared to the average man, Daniel has experienced repeated failures in his attempts to stop masturbating to pornography and was still doing so regularly.

DANIEL: At some points I was masturbating twice a day to pornography while my wife was away. If she was gone for a longer period of time, like on a trip or something like that, I would masturbate so often that I rubbed myself raw at times.

SAM: How would that affect your marriage?

DANIEL: The way it would affect my marriage is that I really wouldn't be that motivated to have sex with my spouse because I was jerking off so much on my own. If she wanted to have sex, I basically had to get myself into it because there wasn't any drive left for that. Even within the past couple of years, I know my wife is going to want to be physically intimate, but I've already looked at porn and don't have a lot of motivation, so I'll look at porn in the bathroom to get going and then I'll be ready to be physical with her. . . . At times, I've justified this situation by telling myself that "She's tired and doesn't really get that much out of sex anyway and I don't want to give her one more obligation to tend to. So it's just best if she thinks I don't need sex that much." I knew this was all wrong, but I didn't really want to stop enough.

What Daniel describes was echoed by others. While Daniel doesn't necessarily think that his pornography use has shaped his sexual expectations, his regular masturbation habit sapped whatever sexual motivation he had. It is also important to note that Daniel recognizes the ways he has tried to rationalize his behavior, and he himself feels the fault ultimately lies with him. When I asked Daniel about his conversations with his wife, Rachel, over the matter, he explained:

She eventually found out. I think she'd been suspecting that I'd been watching porn and masturbating and asked me directly. Looking back, I don't know why I fessed up to it, but I did and it all came out. I told her I'd been looking at porn for years. She was hurt and outraged. She didn't speak to me for several days and we weren't intimate for weeks, probably. I didn't look at porn or masturbate for a while because I felt so crappy about myself. But eventually that wore off and I just started looking at porn and masturbating again. And that pattern has basically stayed with me throughout the remainder of our marriage.

While men like Martin who confessed their porn use, or Gerald who was caught, recall their wives' responses as being a positive step toward stopping the habit, Daniel recalls Rachel's response as so deeply traumatic, and the experience for himself so mortifying, that it makes him unsure of whether he should have confessed at all. Indeed, Daniel thinks that learning about his porn use was so upsetting for Rachel that she has been reluctant to ever ask him about it again. "Sometimes I think she still suspects that I've been looking at porn, but I think she was hurt so bad by the first time it all came out that she doesn't dare press in further. And I don't want her to. She freaked out so bad the first time, I don't know how she'd respond if she knew how often I've looked at porn and masturbated in the past year."

Whether Daniel is right or wrong about how Rachel feels, his fear over her response and what that might mean for their marriage is greater than his willpower to stop using pornography. Thus, Daniel makes the observation:

One of the many downsides about keeping my porn habit hidden from my wife is that I can't take really drastic steps to stop it. She would know something's up. I can't join a recovery group at church. Cuz she'd ask why I need it all of a sudden. And appearances are sort of a big thing for her, too, so she might be embarrassed that her husband is going to the "porn recovery" group when she'd rather everyone else at church think the porn stuff is all behind me. No one wants to be the wife of a known porn addict. And I can't ask her to get rid of Internet access or change the computer passwords or take my smartphone away. She'd know I'd been looking at porn and want to dig deeper until she knew the truth. I've been hiding it from her for so long that's it's actually one of the things that keeps the cycle going.

Daniel blames himself for the situation he is in. He is the one who has kept his porn habit hidden for years, oftentimes justifying it while being unwilling to stop. But Daniel's description of his catch-22 here reveals a predicament that conservative Protestant couples confront more than others. Daniel's habitual porn use is a problem that he is deeply ashamed of. And his attempts at stopping on his own have failed repeatedly. But because the first interaction with Rachel over his pornography use was so wounding for them both, Daniel feels he must continue to hide his habit and fight it on his own, lest he be discovered and their marriage rocked.

The first time Daniel confessed his pornography use to Rachel, she could think of nothing else to call him but "a coward." Those reading Daniel's account of his struggle with porn use in marriage may agree with Rachel's judgment. But Daniel's internal conflict, as well as his marital conflict, over the issue of pornography marks the marriages of conservative Protestant men and women more than those of other Americans. In my interviews with men and women who were not conservative Protestants, a number expressed concern or hurt regarding their partner's pornography use. Some, like Jacob's wife, perhaps, even see it as a form of cheating. But few if any of those conflicts or hurts stemmed from a deep-seated rejection of pornography itself as inherently immoral and a personal betrayal on par with a physical affair.

Couples who are not conservative Protestants also seemed more apt to talk about their feelings so they could work through the conflict and consider whether porn use is a problem and when it might be appropriate. For conservative Protestant couples, however, there is no such discussion about the "appropriate" uses of pornography. There's no "working through" as if there could be a compromise with porn somehow "under certain circumstances." There is discovery; then, there is wounding and conflict. Sometimes there is redemption. But, as Daniel's case suggests, there is also a greater likelihood of hiding and lying that can lead to both shame and inner turmoil for the viewer and insecurity and isolation for their spouse.

Conclusion

Committed romantic relationships *tend to* be worse with porn. But couples of all religious or irreligious persuasions now live in a world where the majority of men (and increasingly women) have viewed pornography with some regularity, and thus, each couple must now negotiate what that behavior means for them. Conflict over that issue is not limited to conservative Protestants—not by a long shot. But both quantitative data and my interviews suggest that, for conservative Protestants, porn use comes with none of the possible benefits described by some—only heightened drawbacks.

Some research suggests that couples who view erotic movies together as a part of lovemaking may actually experience benefits in their sex lives, particularly women who might learn more about what they like.[27] And a number of my interviews with men and women who are not conservative Protestants affirmed this possibility. While such couples also needed to negotiate their feelings about porn and respect each other's wishes and boundaries, porn did not seem to be a serious point of conflict, and many felt that it *improved* their sex lives. But this is not a possibility for conservative Protestants, for whom the idea of mutual porn use is a complete nonstarter. (Which also means that, unlike Jacob who committed to only view pornography when it was with his wife, conservative Protestant porn use will almost always be hidden.)

Despite providing opportunities for the relational redemption that Rebecca, Caitlyn, Martin, and Gerald described, there are no *immediate* positive effects of porn use for conservative Protestant couples as there might be for others. Related to this, the potentially negative consequences of porn use for such relationships tend to be amplified for conservative Protestants, owing to moral incongruence and sexual exceptionalism, leading to greater inner strife and relational conflict. Simply put, porn use rarely (though occasionally) seems to help committed romantic relationships, but it is wholly toxic for conservative Protestants.

6

So Help Me God (or Whatever Works)

So there's your battle plan. That's it. Nothing more, nothing less. Setting up defense perimeters and choosing not to sin. You'll have freedom from sexual impurity as soon as those defense perimeters are in place.

—Stephen Arterburn, Fred Stoeker, with Mike Yorkey,
Every Man's Battle, p. 105

Some of you [can turn away from pornography] by constructing walls of legalism and forcing themselves to live within those boundaries. . . . I can't encourage that approach with any enthusiasm. . . . [Y]ou must ultimately find freedom through the Word of God. We need to fight sin with God's truth; we need to replace lies we want to believe with what God says is true.

—Tim Challies, *Sexual Detox*, p. 81

CONSERVATIVE PROTESTANTS, I HAVE ARGUED, by and large no longer hold out hope that they can keep pornography out of their nation and communities. It's in their churches and their homes. For a growing number, it occupies their smartphones and their minds. Consequently, one of the most remarkable institutional developments over the past few decades within conservative Protestantism has been what I call the "purity industrial complex" that has emerged to help Christians battle pornography in their daily lives.[1] This includes innumerable books on the subject of sexual purity and on porn specifically; multimillion-dollar accountability software and internet filter companies; national conferences; multimedia series for small groups; and even much of the impetus for participation in larger church-based recovery groups.[2]

Given the vastness of these resources, a thorough treatment of "porn recovery" among conservative Protestants could fill a book of its own. But if we take a broader view, what emerges is a tension between pragmatism, on the one hand, and pietistic idealism and biblicism, on the other. Though conservative Protestants are known for their emphasis on the latter, as we will see, their quest for sexual purity often depends on the former.[3]

A purely pragmatic approach would focus on the behavior itself, and would suggest that one should do whatever "works" to help avoid unhealthy behaviors. Such an approach also assumes that there need be no higher motive; the simple fact that one wants to eliminate certain negative thoughts and behaviors is enough. Wanting to stop lusting or masturbating to pornography, for instance, requires no deeper rationale, and the tools at my disposal are nearly limitless. If some author or pastor suggests that getting into an accountability group, installing software on my computer, memorizing Bible verses, taking my bedroom door off its hinges, or exchanging my smartphone for a flip phone will help break my habitual porn use, then I can simply see what works for me. Whether the practices or techniques I apply are taken directly from the Bible or a psychologist, the point is that I get results. Lastly, a pragmatic approach can allow for slow progress and incremental victories. If what matters is eliminating negative behaviors, then any progress is good. Pragmatism, as should be clear, is a foundation for secular behavioral therapies.

Pietistic idealism, on the other hand, says it's not enough to simply *do* the right thing or to *not do* the wrong thing. Behaviors like porn use are not simply bad habits of good people; they are outward manifestations of the sin and idolatry in one's heart. Consequently, there is no bargaining, there is no "tapering down"—only repentance. The deeper spiritual issue of sin is paramount. Beneath this is the belief that God focuses more on the interiority and motives (e.g., *why* someone does or doesn't view porn) than the actions themselves; and God himself, his glory and initiating grace offered in Christ, are the truly proper motives for personal transformation. More than this, true moral purity must not only emerge from a right heart but also pietistic idealism takes it a priori that a right heart *will be* morally pure. Tackle the heart first and behaviors will inevitably follow—not the other way around.

To pietistic idealism add biblicism, and not only must personal transformation happen for the right reasons but it also must be accomplished in the right way, as God has prescribed, according to the Bible. Extra-biblical "techniques" for defeating sinful thoughts and behaviors—say, from secular psychology or therapies—may be helpful in the short term, but they are insufficient and may even be contrary to "biblical" teaching.

Conservative Protestant approaches to quitting pornography tend to split along these lines. One camp, which was dominant in the mid-1990s and early 2000s, is influenced by contemporary psychological-therapeutic—and ultimately pragmatic—approaches to addiction recovery. They tend to take Christian values as given and thus offer a variety of "tools" or "steps" or "principles" that believers can selectively apply to break destructive cycles of pornography use. Another camp, which has in the past decade become dominant, embraces a view that locates life change within beliefs and values almost exclusively. Operating at the more extreme ends of pietistic idealism and biblicism, supporters of this approach argue that setting believers free from pornography consumption requires changing their beliefs and values first, then supposing that actions will inevitably follow. While many of these authors and pastors do advocate certain practical strategies to "throw off" the sin of pornography use, some do not suggest practical steps at all; in fact, they view an emphasis on behaviors themselves to be wrongheaded. Instead, they emphasize believing right things and valuing right things as the only "real" way to defeat the sins of lust and pornography use.

But which perspective best describes how conservative Protestants actually aim to stop using pornography in their day-to-day lives? The contemporary emphasis on one perspective over the other differs across levels of authority within conservative Protestantism, and reveals a divergence between what sociologists call "formal" and "operative" understandings within social groups.[4] Thought leaders at the top espouse one set of "formal" ideals and goals, while men and women at the bottom of the hierarchy often embrace a different "operative" approach when it comes to getting the job done.

How does this play out specifically in the case of conservative Protestants and porn recovery? Figure 6.1 illustrates a spectrum of

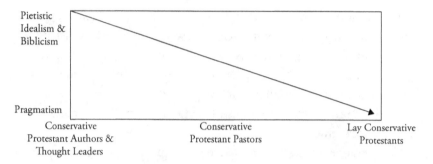

FIGURE 6.1 Pietistic Idealism and Biblicism vs. Pragmatism Across Leadership Hierarchy Within

adherence to a pietistic idealist/biblicist or pragmatic approaches across levels of authority. Contemporary conservative Protestant authors and thought leaders—who I argue are increasingly from more reformed camps—often advocate a staunchly biblicist and pietistic-idealist approach to defeating sexual sin, emphasizing the primacy of heart transformation, repentance, and faith in God's Word and the gospel over and above extra-biblical "techniques," "strategies," or "disciplines." Grassroots pastors in these traditions, however, ostensibly embrace those perspectives, but they often advocate more therapeutic and pragmatic strategies for success. And practically none of the laity describes anything like a change in beliefs or values that contributes to their discontinuing pornography use. Rather, most seem to approach quitting porn pragmatically, using something of a toolbox of strategies that are bounced around, with the most effective strategies being personal accountability and setting physical boundaries for electronic devices.

In other words, while a growing number of (reformed) conservative Protestant authors insist that defeating the sin of pornography *must* start with beliefs and values, most conservative Protestants in my interviews tended to find success with methods suggesting that it would be more "effective" to target more basic psychological drives (seeking approval, avoiding embarrassment) and physiological drives (avoiding visual cues, short-circuiting cycles of reward-seeking behavior).

But we need to step back for a moment. Let us consider how an ongoing debate within conservative Protestantism helps us better

understand the seemingly disparate philosophies and approaches to
porn recovery.

Competing Models of Counseling Within Conservative Protestantism

It bears repeating once again that conservative Protestantism (or even
a more coherent subculture like "evangelicalism") is not monolithic.
Conservative Protestant traditions, denominations, and congregations,
and even believers within the same congregation, differ on a variety of
theological and moral issues. Some disagreements that are quite well
known include disputes over Calvinism vs. Armenianism (over the degree to which God determines who will be eternally saved); cessationism
vs. continuationism (over whether miraculous gifts of the Holy Spirit
have ceased for modern Christians); and various debates over baptism
(sprinkling or dunking? infants or believers?). One recent debate that
is less well known centers on the extent to which principles from secular psychology may be integrated with the Bible in order to counsel
believers toward sanctification and improved mental health. On this
issue, conservative Protestant teachers and pastors often fall along a
continuum, represented in Figure 6.2.[5]

At the far left end of the spectrum, there is the view that psychology
and the Bible represent different "levels of explanation" for the various
problems humans face. The Bible deals with the spiritual aspects of
peoples' lives while psychology deals with mental and cognitive aspects
that the Bible does not address. This view, then, holds that there needn't
be any tension between psychology and the Bible. This approach is the
least likely to be embraced by actual conservative Protestant pastors,
authors, and counselors, but it is common among academic Christian

Most Open to Psychology				Least Open to Psychology
Different Levels of Explanation Approach	Integration Approach	Christian Psychology Approach	Transformational Approach	Biblical Counseling Approach

FIGURE 6.2 Spectrum of Openness to Integrating Secular Psychology in
Counseling

psychologists. It allows them to publish empirical research without having to consider whether it supports or contradicts something taught in the Bible.

The "integration" approach is a more mainstream philosophy among actual Christian counselors and is taught explicitly at various conservative Protestant universities and seminaries. While this approach views both the Bible and psychology as addressing human brokenness, integrationists are willing to acknowledge that secular psychology, viewed as a form of "general revelation" from God, can contribute helpful insights and techniques that can be integrated with God's "special revelation" in the Bible. The "Christian psychology" and "transformational" approaches are quite similar in that, compared to integrationists, they adopt a more critical approach to the underlying secular assumptions of modern psychology, and they advocate an approach to counseling that (1) grounds human problems in spiritual fallenness; and (2) avoids distinctions between the mind and the spirit but sees the two as closely related, and thus, requiring a holistic redemption process. Both approaches also draw on insights about human nature from psychology and Christian philosophers, though always viewed through the lens of biblical teaching.

The approach that is the most critical of secular psychology, and is now becoming the most widely accepted, is the "biblical counseling" approach. Originally articulated by Westminster Theological Seminary professor Jay Adams, biblical counseling has become tremendously influential, corresponding largely to the growing popularity of reformed theology within mainstream evangelicalism. It is the approach embraced by influential pastors, authors, and thought leaders like John MacArthur, John Piper, Russell Moore, Mark Dever, Al Mohler, Matt Chandler, and Tim Keller; organizations like The Gospel Coalition and Acts 29 Network; and large swaths of the evangelical Presbyterian (PCA denomination) and reformed Southern Baptist communities. The biblical counseling approach holds that the Bible contains all of God's revealed will and, by implication, everything a Christian needs to counsel a fellow believer.[6] Thus, biblical counseling advocates tend to be highly skeptical of secular psychology as rooted in fundamentally unbiblical presuppositions and, consequently, aimed at achieving fundamentally unchristian goals using unchristian methods. While biblical counselors *do* acknowledge that there are disorders rooted in physiological problems (thus requiring psychiatric care), they see these instances as rather rare and tend to emphasize how virtually all nonphysiological disorders or problems—including anxiety, eating disorders, obsessive-compulsive disorder, many forms of depression, and sexuality problems—are ultimately the result of sin in a believer's life. Thus, the biblical counseling strategy must involve confronting the believer by pointing out how he or she is sinning, and admonishing the individual to repent and apply the Bible to that specific situation.

If the biblical counseling approach sounds familiar at this point, it should. It represents a clear example of the biblicism and pietistic idealism that I have described in previous chapters. Understood in this way, the debate over integrated versus biblical counseling can be understood as a debate over the extent to which the spiritual maintains primacy over the physical. Biblical counseling emerges directly from pietistic idealism and biblicism. To the extent one believes that human beings' deepest need is to be in the right relationship with God, and that every wrong behavior can ultimately be traced back to our rebellion or lack of faith, and to the extent that one believes the Bible contains God's all-sufficient instruction for everything Christians need this side of Heaven, then secular psychology has little to offer—indeed, its primary contribution is falsehood.

Predictably, then, proponents of biblical counseling are the most strident in their opposition to alternative Christian counseling philosophies, viewing them as dangerously secular.[7] Certainly, those who hold a more integrationist stance resent the notion that their counseling philosophy is anything but biblical in an ultimate sense. But to the growing and vocal numbers of biblical counseling proponents, the very willingness to integrate teachings and techniques from secular psychology implicitly denies the sufficiency of Scripture and the primacy of the spiritual; instead, it elevates the physical or behavioral. This is ultimately the axis on which the counseling debate within conservative Protestantism turns.

These debates play out in conservative Protestant manuals on pornography use. While many of these books do provide plenty of reasons *why* Christians should quit using pornography, they are written primarily to counsel believers on *how* to avoid or, in a growing majority of cases, how to stop looking at pornography and masturbating to it. This makes these manuals—written *by* conservative Protestants *for* other conservative Protestants—a particularly important source for understanding what conservative Protestants think. By comparing these messages with the accounts of pastors and lay conservative Protestants, we can see whether what happens in books matters on the ground.

Pornography Use as a Bad Habit

In his counsel to adolescent men, Bob Gresh illustrates the pragmatic approach, "Winning the game of sexual integrity requires a game plan—a set of strategies you live by each day. [God's] not going to do it for you. It takes time, discipline, pain, and sweat. You will toil and ache. You will feel yourself stretched beyond your comfort zone."[8] God wants sexual integrity for his followers, according to Gresh, but obtaining it requires that Christians take responsibility for their decisions. "How do you become pure? Chuck Swindoll says that every action either makes or unmakes character. By making right choices (or living righteously) even in the face of temptation like that evil dude Lust, you actually are afforded the great opportunity to develop purity. As you face the lust and make right choices to deny it and let Christ rid you of it, it is transformed into the Christlike character of purity."[9] Thus, the battle against lust is fought by individual Christians making the right decisions, which over time helps them forge a godly character. More than this, Gresh suggests that Christians ought to develop sets of guidelines for themselves to live by. Anticipating that some might consider a system of guidelines as a form of legalism, Gresh explains:

> Am I suggesting that we have a list of rules to follow? Yes, actually, I am. I have a list that I follow and you should have one too. Is that legalism? No. Legalism is . . . forcing your own personal preferences on others and acting like they are biblical commandments. . . . Legalism . . . no! Strong heart-motivated guidelines for your life . . . yes! If you have them, you will be molded into what God desires for you to be. Great men do not occur spontaneously. . . . They are produced only after submitting themselves to a disciplined lifestyle.[10]

Gresh suggests that men of high moral character are forged *by* their moral discipline. While acknowledging that the guidelines should be "heart-motivated," the philosophy underlying Gresh's advice views sexual impurity as primarily a physiological habit or compulsion that is most effectively addressed by developing better habits.

Those with more explicit counseling training like Stephen Arterburn and Fred Stoeker offer similar advice to young men, framing the fight against pornography and lust in behavioral terms. They summarize their strategy: "To accomplish [sexuality purity], you need to build three perimeters of defense in your life: 1. You need to build a line of defense with your eyes. 2. You need to build a line of defense in your mind. 3. You need to build a line of defense in your heart. . . . So there's your battle plan. That's it—nothing more, nothing less. As soon as you set up the perimeters, you'll have freedom from sexual impurity."[11]

For these authors, freedom from sexual sin is essentially a formula, a series of proactive defense systems that will guide what men are seeing (notably, this was listed first), what men let their minds dwell on, and how they honor the women in their lives by not making them objects of lust. They recommend that young men develop a habit they call "bouncing the eyes," in which they refuse to let their eyes dwell on what might be an object of temptation. Ultimately, the authors conclude: "Do you want to know the truth? Impurity is a habit. . . . So how do you break the bad habit of locking on to every rack and tush that swivels your way? You simply replace it with a new and better habit."[12]

Other evangelical writers who are themselves professional counselors or psychologists offer similar sorts of advice that tends to focus on the power of learned behaviors and bad habits. Psychologist Douglass Weiss, who is a featured speaker at the 2017 Breaking Free Virtual Summit sponsored by Covenant Eyes (a follow-up to the 2016 Set Free Summit) recommends developing a practice called keeping a "lust log." He explains:

This is simply a piece of paper you keep in your pocket. Each time you lust or objectify a woman, put a mark on that paper. Check in daily for one hundred days with your accountability partner as to how you are doing. Some competitive friends even make the man with the highest score pay for the lunch of the low-scoring man each week. You'll be amazed at how quickly you can stop lusting when there is free food on the line! *If you are still doubtful, it may be that you do not understand that lust is a learned, intentional behavior. Because that is true, it is possible to unlearn lust and choose not to allow it.*[13]

Weiss's last two sentences are key. Lust is simply learned behavior. And Christians can unlearn it and gain power over it by making good decisions, fighting bad habits with better habits.

This view of lust, pornography use, and masturbation as largely physical can also be seen in the concessions writers and teachers often make in order to help readers break these habits in their lives. Many conservative Protestant writers, particularly of the reformed variety, believe you must quit pornography cold turkey. One does not "taper down" when it comes to sin. If pornography use offends God, then it must be stopped immediately.[14] However, those that are more influenced by psychological interpretations of pornography and masturbation as "addictions" take a more pragmatic approach. For example, Stephen Arterburn and his coauthors agree that cold turkey would be ideal, but for pragmatic reasons, since they feel it is the best method of dealing with visual lust: "In overcoming some addictions, the addictive source can be gradually reduced. For others, the best method is cold turkey. What works best with sexual impurity? Answer: going cold turkey. You cannot just taper down . . . cold turkey is the way to go. You should shut off the spigot by totally starving your eyes of all things sensual."[15]

Elsewhere, however, they suggest that masturbating *less* would be a necessary step in the right direction: "The standard is no masturbation. . . . Truth is truth, there aren't two standards. But there may also be more than one way to get there. Some of you may be able to get victory over masturbation right away. Some of you, however, may not get to 'none' unless you first achieve the standard of less masturbation than you're practicing now. The standard of less may help you bring your habit under control until the real standard of none becomes achievable."[16] Here, the emphasis is not on *spiritual* change that leads to freedom from pornography but, rather, simply making conscious decisions to bring a sinful habit "under control."[17]

This perspective on how to conquer lust and pornography use are rooted in a broadly evangelical, integrated, and ultimately pragmatic approach to personal change. In this view, habitual sexual sin is certainly spiritual, but it is also a physical habit that operates like an addiction, and thus, it can be addressed using the tools and techniques of psychology: addressing problem habits, setting boundaries, and tapering down if necessary. However, conservative Protestant writers from a solidly reformed perspective advocate a completely different approach.

Pornography Use as a Lack of Belief in the Gospel and God's Word

A growing majority of conservative Protestant manuals on pornography use and sexual sin are written from a biblical counseling perspective. Grounded in biblicism and pietistic idealism, these manuals consistently call pornography use a sin that stems from a person's inordinate beliefs and desires. These writers also maintain that believing the "truth" about God and valuing God above all else (1) necessarily precede changing one's sinful behavior; and (2) *must* be the primary weapons in fighting sexual sin.

As quoted earlier, Tim Challies argues: "As God makes very clear in his word, sex and the issues surrounding it are fundamentally spiritual in nature. The temptations of pornography engage our minds and bodies in what is primarily a spiritual battle."[18] And spiritual battles are a matter of cosmic, eternal importance. One of the most striking features of this type of anti-pornography literature is the perceived gravity of the stakes. Readers are reminded that *eternity* is on the line. Those who fail to take lust seriously by fighting against pornography use should be afraid. A leading proponent of biblical counseling, Heath Lambert, issues a solemn warning: "The words [of Paul] are clear: if you are sexually immoral you will not inherit the kingdom of God. All those who look at pornography have only a fearful expectation of condemnation."[19]

A related theme is escalation—namely, that pornography use, like all sin, will only get worse until it consumes everything in a person's life. While some warnings stress eternal damnation, this line of reasoning focuses on the this-worldly consequences. Tim Challies explains:

The first message of this book . . . is that you must see what porn is doing to your heart. You must recognize that the corruption of pornography is real and, despite the convenient and self-indulgent little lies we tell ourselves, that corruption is only going to get worse. The sin underlying the consumption of pornography will not stop escalating until it cripples your marriage, or until you die, or until you get too old and weak to care about sex. The only difference for single guys? The sin won't stop escalating until it destroys any hope you will ever get married.[20]

But the primary concern of these books is not telling people why they shouldn't use pornography but, rather, showing them how they can be transformed. Accordingly, the most prominent theme in these manuals is heart transformation, which can only be accomplished by believing the truth of the Bible, and it must be the primary factor in conquering the sin of pornography use. As Baptist pastor John Piper explains, "So what should I do [to fight lust]? Some people would say, 'Remember God's command to be holy (1 Peter 1:16), and exercise your will to obey because he is God!' But something crucial is missing from this advice. . . . The challenge before us in our fight against lust is not merely to do what God says because he is God, but to desire what God says because he is glorious. The challenge is not merely to *pursue* right-eousness, but to *prefer* righteousness."[21] In his book *You Can Change* (2010), pastor Tim Chester makes explicit this emphasis on heart trans-formation over behaviors, disciplines, or activities. He writes:

> [H]oliness always starts in the heart. The essence of holiness is not new behavior, activity, or disciplines. Holiness is new affections, new desires, and new motives that then lead to new behavior. . . . Many people change their behavior, but their motives and desires are still wrong; so their new behavior is no more pleasing to God than their old behavior. [22]
>
> Where does sin come from? From within. Out of men's hearts. From inside. According to the Bible, *the source of all human behavior and emotions is the heart.* . . . *Heart* is shorthand for our thinking and desires. The root cause of my behavior is *always* my heart. What we see is behavior and emotions, and it's easy to focus on changing

behavior and emotions. But lasting change is achieved only by tackling their source—the heart.[23]

Even if one's behavior itself seems righteous, Chester argues, doing it for the wrong reasons is just as offensive to God. And changing behavior will not solve the problem when the root lies deeper. Any approach to conquering pornography use that does not start with the heart will ultimately fail.[24]

Those who take a more practical approach, these authors argue, are destined to fail because they rely on human activities rather than on God's sovereign, sanctifying work. Chester writes: "It is God himself who sanctifies us. Other therapies can modify behavior. . . . But only God can bring true and lasting change. And that's because only God can change our hearts. . . . Jesus does what legalism can never do: he gives us a new heart and a new spirit. Without this inner transformation, we can never please God. People aren't changed by therapy or analysis—not even biblical analysis. They are changed by God. God is in the business of change."[25]

But precisely how are Christians changed? While the counseling approaches articulated by Gresh, Weiss, and the *Every Man's Battle* authors stress certain "disciplines" and practical strategies that create distance between men and their porn use, Chester is skeptical. The language of "disciplines," he argues, "can make Christian growth seem like an achievement on our part." Instead, he insists, "In reality, it's God who changes us through his grace. The only true spiritual disciplines in the Christian life are faith and repentance, actions that direct our attention to God's gracious activity."[26] In other words, Christians are transformed by the same formula that made them Christians to begin with: repent and believe the gospel. Chester explains: "We sin because we do not trust God and do not worship God. Our struggles reveal our hearts. . . . There is a twofold problem in the heart: what we think or trust and what we desire or worship. Sin happens when we don't trust God above everything . . . and when we don't desire God above everything. Sin happens when we believe lies about God instead of God's Word and when we worship idols instead of worship God. . . . The answer is faith and repentance."[27] This is the prescribed therapy: repent and trust in God.[28]

Does disciplining oneself and employing strategies to avoid porn have a place in recovery? These authors say it does, but it must always be a limited one. As Chester explains, "Not sowing to the sinful nature means avoiding situations in which our sinful desires will be provoked. We can't change ourselves simply by avoiding temptation: change must begin within our hearts. But avoiding temptation does have a role to play. It's never the whole solution, but it's part of the solution."[29] Similarly, Heath Lambert, in *Finally Free*, also qualifies his promotion of "strategies" or "steps" to avoiding pornography, emphasizing the power of the gospel: "no strategy to combat sin can bring profound and lasting change if it is disconnected from the power of Jesus. Strategies are important, but they must flow from the gospel."[30]

So on the one hand, Christians are encouraged to believe the truth of the gospel. That will provide the only sufficient (in a moral sense) motivation to avoid sexual sin. But what are the most important practical steps one can take? Some authors suggest basically nothing other than meditating on the truths of the Bible. Tim Challies, for example, explains: "How is [freedom from porn] accomplished? No one has ever devised a better method for overcoming sin than that which God articulated through Paul. Standing firm in the gospel and relying on the grace and power of God to make our efforts effective, we must put off that which is of the flesh and in its place put on that which is of the Spirit."[31] How exactly does one "put off" the flesh and "put on" the Spirit? Primarily by believing God's promises, Challies says:

Instead of ignoring your sin, you need to be about the daily business of killing it. . . . God has given you the Bible so you can do just that. Through the Bible we are able to borrow God's eyes, see the world as he sees it, and know what to do about it. . . . For me, a handful of Scripture passages became foundational to my understanding of sex, and empowered my self-control . . . these passages were instrumental means of grace to me in my determination not to succumb to the allure of pornography. . . . These verses, though an eclectic collection, challenged me deeply. More than that, they reset my mind. I memorized them, pondered them, called them to mind, and lived by them. Over time, they detoxified my soul. Any desire to pursue sinful lust melted away. I know this was a work of God because he worked it through his Word, just as he says he will.[32]

It's that simple. For Challies, lust and temptation to look at pornography were "melted away" by memorizing and believing Bible verses. Challies insists that Christians *will* obtain victory over pornography if they commit the Bible to heart and use it to transform their thinking. Conversely, while he acknowledges that Christians may benefit from outside help in the form of accountability, he is wary of any practical substitutes for what only the Bible can accomplish.

> Some men can turn away from pornography by an act of will. If that's you, then great: go for it. Some can do it by constructing walls of legalism and forcing themselves to live in those boundaries. This approach trades the sinful self-focus of pornography for the sinful self-reliance of legalism, so I can't encourage that approach with any enthusiasm. Many men, probably most, need outside help—a form of accountability that emphasizes encouragement and honesty, and rejects condemnation and legalism. So whether this is a battle you fight with God, or with God plus brothers in Christ, you must ultimately find freedom through the Word of God. We need to fight sin with God's truth; we need to replace the lies we want to believe with what God says is true . . . go to the Bible and find there both the foundation for purity and the wisdom that can help you moment-by-moment.[33]

This underscores the dual commitment to pietistic idealism and biblicism. Genuine freedom from pornography and other sexual sin *must* start with heart transformation. It cannot start with disciplines, practices, steps, boundaries, or other behavioral techniques, for such is the dead-end road of legalism. But how is this philosophy applied by pastors working in the trenches with those seeking freedom from pornography?

How Conservative Protestant Pastors Counsel Regarding Pornography

In my interviews with pastors, I intentionally left my questions about counseling men and women who were struggling with pornography as open-ended as possible. Most often, in fact, that part of the conversation began with no more than my asking, "So when you're talking to men and women in your church who are struggling with pornography, what's your counsel there? Take me through the process." I kept these questions nonspecific because I was interested in what perspectives and strategies they would seek to emphasize over others. Their responses constituted at least a third of my conversations with these pastors, the vast majority of whom were younger and had their theologies shaped by neo-Calvinist influences, including those I have cited here. Despite this, the most consistent theme that emerged was a surprisingly pragmatic, behavioral emphasis, even among those who ostensibly stressed the centrality of the gospel in bringing about lasting heart change.

Several of the pastors led by emphasizing the need for heart transformation and gospel truth. A Baptist church planter in Georgia, Chris explained that he tries to stress the theological side of things before he gets to the practical:

> [The practical things are] what I was told to do in college, just get better and do practical stuff, and it didn't work. So, I took the door off my dorm room and I found ways to access porn. And I don't want to create Pharisees like, "I'm super holy, I took my door off," when in reality you're struggling with it and you're just a guy without a door. So, there's a fear of fake holiness, and that's a short-term solution. Like when you get married, you can't take your door off, so we need to develop some self-control and some wisdom and some patience. And maybe it's easier to take your door off, but that doesn't require anything of you. So, if you understand your standing in Christ and how that alleviates shame, that'll help you for fifty years, but getting a flip phone is a short-term deal.

Like biblical counseling proponents, Chris differentiates between what he feels are short-term (practical) solutions and long-term (spiritual) solutions. But Chris also recognizes the need for behavioral change, just in the proper order. "And you know, behavior modification isn't a bad deal; it's a necessary deal, but it seems like if you read Ephesians and Colossians, it seems like Paul was more interested in establishing the identity, and then the actions would reflect the identity—not vice versa. Focusing on the actions first could become a works-righteousness thing." Chris's references to "Pharisees" in the longer quote and "works righteousness" in this last one underscore the priority that one's motivations be pure.

Also consistent with the biblical counseling approach, Matthew, pastor at a nondenominational church in Oklahoma, tried to focus on pornography use as a reflection of deeper "idols" in the Christian life. He saw his role as helping men diagnose which idol was causing the problem of pornography use to manifest itself:

> I'll ask, [Timothy] Keller has the four idols that I always think through: approval, control, comfort, and power. I think maybe Keller took it from David Powlison. Thinking through what's the deeper issue behind why you're doing this. You're given a God-given desire for the opposite sex and you've gone beyond the bounds. This is a wayward sexual desire, but why? I think control is a big deal, approval; and I'll share for me—there was a season, it was the first time of my life feeling severe disapproval when I was struggling with pornography. So, it's showing them it's not just, "I'm a dude, I have these desires, and I shouldn't be doing this with these desires." It's so much deeper than that. So, [it's] trying to get underneath why they're doing this from more of an idolatry standpoint. What are you not getting that you're using this as medication—like you would food, or exercise, or Netflix consumption? What are you escaping? Usually that'll spit out something about their life, where I can speak the gospel.

When I asked Matthew to explain what he meant by "speak the gospel" to these men, he explained: "Where is Jesus the answer? Not to sound cliché, but where does Jesus and their identity in him confront this sin and the idolatry beneath it? And for a lot of guys, that's eye-opening. And I usually save all that stuff to the very end. Jesus has given you approval. There's no need to escape. You're a failure and that's good news." Porn use is the symptom of the disease of sinful idolatry; the prescription is believing in Jesus and what the gospel means for them. But Matthew specified that he usually saves his diagnostics about idols and application of the gospel to the very end of their conversation. As we will see, he actually precedes this with a discussion of practical steps to be taken.

Like those in the biblical counseling camp, pastors emphasized the issue of "sin" and stressed that men need to understand their pornography use as not just unhealthy but also offensive to God. Blane, a Baptist pastor in Texas, explained:

> The really important part is going back to the individual coming and confessing and wanting to stop. After a period of time, after I've had conversations with them, I can tell more often than not where they are in regards to the conviction and seriousness of the sin. I think that's really important, because if someone's to that point where they see the seriousness of the sin and they have that deep guilt, that's where I will apply the gospel really heavily. If someone just got caught and there isn't this true repentance, then I will more or less turn up the seriousness of the sin—let's just say "the law"—to let them see the seriousness of the sin where the gospel can be applied. If someone isn't truly convicted, seeing their sin as a sin against God, they may get a little freedom, but they're going back to it.

The key here, Blane argues, is that unless individuals recognize their porn use as sin, there can be no true change in the person's life.

But even within the initial emphasis on theological truths, one could still see a commitment to the pragmatic goal of quitting pornography. Chris explained:

> So, first we talk about the gospel, not about this particular area (pornography use). [I remind them] "You're hidden with Christ. God doesn't see your shortcomings; he sees Christ. God is totally aware of your sin; you're not successfully hiding. God's still proud of you and loves you." *Then, if that can alleviate some of the shame, then we get into some of the practical stuff*—of, you know, put [accountability

software] on your computer, or maybe you need to get rid of your phone and go back to flip phone, or take the door off of your room. Like you're living with six dudes and you're all struggling with the same thing, maybe privacy is not your most important need. So, we move from the theological stuff to the practical stuff [emphasis added].

Interestingly, in Chris's account, the point of alleviating the shame in a man's life with the gospel was *so that* he can move toward the practical steps that will help the man quit porn. In Chris's experience, men who felt beaten down and defeated by pornography use would wallow in their sin and give up. But reminding them of God's love and acceptance could help them to get back in the fight. Thus, the practical goal motivated his theological emphasis.

Other pastors applied this logic as well, particularly when it came to shame—something that they believed perpetuates the pornography use. Blane, for example, explained: "What I counsel [is that] when you come to the fork in the road, one way will lead you further into shame, which will be a perpetual thing that'll lead you back into [porn]. The other road will be the road of the gospel, which will be the healing power to the shame, which then frees the individual to continue to fight." Like Chris, Blane's goal in preaching the gospel here is completely pragmatic: the gospel relieves the shame and enables these struggling men to keep taking steps to resist pornography.

But more often, beyond these initial explanations it was clear that pastors also emphasized behavioral change as a key factor, sometimes even *the* factor that would precede the heart transformation itself. Blane, for example, stressed the need to cut off access to pornography, using his own struggles with addiction as an example:

I think one of the important things is killing access to the pornography. Like, I had an addiction to tobacco, and it's not the same, but it is kinda the same in the sense of physiological desires. Porn has a connection with our physiological desires that God gave us. With tobacco, now, I have this physiological desire for it. As I was trying to fight it, one of the main things was access. If I could get access to it,

I would do it. There came a point where I had to get extreme. Like, even if I had the money—if I had the money, I was going to buy it. And so, with my wife [I] essentially [gave] her all the finances, and she knows where all of it is going, and if a charge comes up somewhere, she would know. And so I wouldn't have any access to money to buy it. And that helped tremendously. *At least it brought me to a place where I could sort of apply some of these other things (the gospel).* But if that wasn't the case, and I continued to have access, then it wasn't going to work. I was going to keep running back to it. *Once I killed that access, then that helped me deal with the deeper issues that were causing me to run toward it.* So I think that's really important initially [emphasis added].

Blane's last few sentences here are instructive. Even though he had communicated earlier that the key to long-term freedom from pornography is the redeeming, shame-killing truth of the gospel, he now indicates that what needed to happen *first* in his own struggle with nicotine addiction was for him to take a behavioral step—cutting off access. The behavioral change came first; the heart work followed. Indeed, the heart transformation depended on the behavioral change.

Similarly, Matthew indicated that before he digs into the theological realities of the gospel, he discusses behavioral modifications that might give these men some initial victory over pornography:

A question I've found helpful is, "Tell me about when you've had some victory." Cuz, usually that's the first step, the baby step for helping them get out of it. So, they'll say, "Well I was at camp, and man, there wasn't any TV and there was all these solid dudes." So I'll say right there are two easy things to implement. So I think that's number one: learning about the struggle, when it's happening. Sometimes it's just having other people around. Don't go home when there's no one there. [For] married guys, it's easier; don't go home [when] their wife isn't there. I didn't do this personally, but I've had guys put a password on their TV or put a password on their internet that their wives know. So any time they're online, their wives know—so, any time he's on the internet his wife knows.

As Matthew indicates, the "first step," or "baby step," or "number one" action for these men to experience some initial freedom from porn is to think about "easy things to implement."

Other pastors described an approach that appears to integrate a variety of theological terms with more therapeutic, psychological techniques similar to cognitive behavioral therapy. Contrary to the biblical counseling approach, which stresses identifying sin and quickly calling believers to repentance and faith, Beau, an evangelical Presbyterian pastor in South Carolina, explained that:

> I don't see pornography as something that's disconnected from either their stage of life or something unique going on in their life. Pornography is something that holds out some sort of promise to them, whether they've lost their job or they're lonely. All those things help me understand why this has a grip on them, and why they've become addicted to it. How's their marriage going? What are some earlier life factors? And once I have a better feel for those things, then I love to hear about how they're trying to battle it. What's the battle with it look like? Have they given up for a period? Are they trying to battle at all? Are they using different software? Are they sharing with others about it? Based on those factors, on a case-by-case basis, you're trying to discern how they could best fight this sin. So, while I think there are some obvious universal things, there are also a lot of nuanced things. Cuz, people are looking at pornography for different reasons; they're looking at different types of pornography. On and on we go.

Notably, with the exception of his reference to "sin," Beau does not mention spiritual concerns explicitly. Certainly, he acknowledges that there are "some obvious universal things" that he will use to advise the men he counsels, which likely means the theological truths just described. But he stresses that there will be tremendous nuance, since porn use could stem from a variety of psychological stressors and hangups, including issues with parents, job troubles, loneliness, control issues, and so on. Knowing these different contributing factors helps Beau develop a specialized, personal plan with these men.

Similarly, Matthew, even as he sought to stress that pornography use is a symptom of spiritual realities, often probed his parishioners with statements that focus on triggers and recognizing what sorts of situations could be changed practically speaking. He explained:

> Before I give any statements, I'll try to ask as many questions as possible. And I tend to not be very shy about the questions I ask. So, I'll even say, "I'll ask you some hard questions." I'll ask, How often? When is it? How are you accessing it? So, that's some practical, environmental things. But I'll also ask, What are you feeling the moment before you give in? I think that could potentially tell you about the deeper why. Because I think dudes who are Christians unless they are enslaved—I think there's a feeling like, "I probably shouldn't do this." So, what do you feel that pushes you toward the pornography in that moment? I don't ask about what kind, because I don't really want that information in my head and I don't need to know. But, How often? When? Is it after a stressful day, or in the shower? In those moments of crisis, I want to get into their head. So, [I'm] putting together their story a little bit.

Indeed, Matthew volunteers that this is actually how he begins his conversations with these men—not with theological statements, diagnostics, and Bible verses, but by assessing the particularities of their situations and whether there are special circumstances that might direct his counsel.

Others more explicitly adopted practical approaches. For instance, even as Chris stressed how he wanted to focus on theological truths, his practical counsel seemed to advocate a "tapering down" approach to defeating sexual sin, which was shaped by his pragmatic understanding of how his parishioners would inevitably and repeatedly fail. He explained:

> One thing that has been helpful has been [that] we think through chronologically, like a timeline. So, okay, you watch porn and

masturbated, and you feel terrible about it. And two weeks go by, and you don't read your Bible and you don't speak up in Bible study because you have this shame, and then finally you've had enough so you come and talk to me, your college pastor. So, if that's a two-week window, what if next time it was a one-week window, so there wasn't two weeks of shame—it was one week of shame? And what if the next time it was three days? And what if the next time it was one day? And what if you had that thought before you watched porn, "This is not a healthy deal"? So, if it took two weeks, then one week, then one day, and before you even sinned? So, [it's] almost with the assumption that they're going to mess up again. So, it's almost giving them permission to mess up, with this confidence to approach the throne. Hopefully that opens their eyes to this new reality of, "Okay, I don't want to go here anymore."

The ultimate goal is abstinence from pornography and masturbation. But Chris indicates that it is more effective to systematically reduce the time between failures (which he assumes they're going to have) than to demand that they quit cold turkey. Eventually, he believes, they will get out of the unhealthy shame cycle he describes.

My goal in letting these pastors speak for themselves is not necessarily to point out contradictions but, rather, to highlight how their counsel itself represents a tension between an adherence to certain theological commitments (reflecting pietistic idealism and biblicism) and pragmatic concerns. Contrary to thought leaders like Challies and Chester, these pastors don't assume that simply memorizing Bible verses or otherwise internally repenting of wrong beliefs and embracing the right beliefs will address the porn use of men in their churches. They don't even believe that doing those things is of primary importance, at least as the *initial step*. While they obviously affirm that those things are important, for these pastors in the trenches there is a clear emphasis on practical changes that need to take place in a person's life for the individual to overcome the pornography use. Sometimes, in fact, the pragmatic and the practical necessarily *precede* the heart transformation, rather than the other way around.

Moving further down the leadership hierarchy, we can ask, How do lay conservative Protestants describe their thought processes and practices when fighting porn in their own lives? What changes took place for them to gain "freedom"?

What Works in the Pews?

As mentioned, I left my interviews with lay conservative Protestants as open-ended as possible. After inquiring about how often men or women used pornography, I asked those who reported using pornography frequently in the past, but not anymore, to "tell me about how that happened." To be sure, not all of them required support from other Christians or a drastic change of any sort; some just stopped by sheer will. Mike, a Baptist college student whom we met in chapter 3 (he considers himself addicted to porn, though views it quite rarely), just decided to not look at porn anymore. When I asked him if he'd ever done anything specifically to stop, he explained:

> No [internet] blocks or anything like that. I've heard of, like, friends, like, giving someone their laptop, you know, just so they wouldn't [watch porn]. I didn't do that. I don't know that that's necessarily best for me. [Sam: Why not?] Cuz, I just made myself stop. And I definitely fell off at points, but I just think that I got more out of it and benefited from it more by keeping [the computer] around, by having that temptation around, and just saying, like, "I believe in myself more than I believe in this"—you know, if that makes sense. Like, I am strong enough.

On the flip side of this, as biblical counseling advocates would surely point out, half-heartedly taking practical steps to quit masturbating to pornography will do little good if someone does not *really* want to stop. Daniel, whom we met in the previous chapter, recounted:

> At different times in my life I've had accountability software. Both X3Watch and Covenant Eyes. But I got rid of those things quickly. I wasn't ready to get better, and I didn't like the thought of having to report to guys—mostly because I was still looking at porn. Like

I said, I've been, I guess, *am* pretty enslaved to it. Accountability groups have been somewhat helpful when I'm being honest, but the typical pattern is [that] it starts off strong and then I just start hiding again. It gets old being the guy who can't stop looking at porn and jerking off. And I haven't been willing to do the difficult thing and get rid of [the] internet, or get a flip phone, or put locks and accountability software on the computer.

But most conservative Protestant men I spoke with, at least the ones who had experienced some success in quitting porn, were not like Mike or Daniel. Most sincerely wanted to stop, and most sought help of some sort. While they certainly made reference to God's empowerment in their answers, none described a significant change in their beliefs and values at any point in time. Rather, virtually all seemed to recall a catalog of practical steps they took to either (1) eliminate access to the source of their struggle or (2) talk about their temptations with other Christians.

One Baptist male college student in Texas told me matter-of-factly: "I did lots of different things. Mostly behavior modification. Nothing major." When I asked him to elaborate, he explained: "I put Covenant Eyes on every device. The only unprotected device I have is my phone, and I report monthly to an accountability partner how I am doing in this area—like, if there are any compromises whatsoever. That pretty much eliminated any temptation I have." Another student said, "I called the phone company and asked them what it would cost monthly, the service, to turn off any access to the internet, to cellular data, so I couldn't have [internet] access after I got out of class in college, and then it would shut off at 9:00 p.m. at night. I was so gung-ho about it. I was, like, we're going to do this and it's going to work!"

A Baptist graduate student from Oklahoma recounted, "I took some practical steps like throwing away movies when I became disgusted at myself or felt guilty for viewing them again. And I got into accountability relationships with other Christian men, and that has worked to some degree. Those accountability relationships have helped me to make instances in which I have engaged in pornography less prolonged and much less interested in what could be considered 'different' sexual interests." I asked, "Like gay porn?" The student responded, "Yeah, mostly." While this last student may occasionally falter, having open relationships with other Christian men, he feels, has effectively curbed his binges and even dissuaded him from viewing porn that he would consider especially immoral.

Dean, a Presbyterian man in Georgia who struggled with porn a great deal when he was single, said he now only occasionally "relapses." Describing what changed for him, he recalled: "My apartment (before marriage) became a technological fortress against porn. Randomized passwords, hidden in a safe in a communal area, protected the router, which locked out any naughty websites. Unfortunately, I am a computer programmer. It is impossible to prevent me from doing anything on a computer." I asked, "So, what did you do then?" Dean explained, "I also used accountability groups and moved my computer to an open place that was not hidden or private." While these steps to eliminate access and lean on close relationships with other men greatly reduced Dean's pattern of porn use, he added, "[Those changes] helped a great deal, but of course, it's not 100% effective."

Each of these explanations are indicative of the broader trend that "success" in the fight against porn (either eliminating the temptation or greatly reducing the failures) usually followed talking openly with peers about it and eliminating opportunities to access it.

Sometimes, the actual means through which men and women stopped viewing porn had not been intended for that goal originally, but nonetheless they seemed to have had the same result. Devon, a 27-year-old single man in a nondenominational congregation in Chicago, said he quit pornography late in high school when he became a Christian. But he did not attribute his quitting porn to any belief change. Rather, upon thinking it over, he attributed it to the change in his social influences and the media consumption change he happened to make:

It was maybe junior, senior year of high school when I became a Christian. I started, like, a Bible study; I was doing several Bible studies and went to multiple church camps—that kind of thing— and just, like, kind of stopped [looking at porn]. I didn't watch any at all. [Sam: So, what do you think it was that made you stop?] We went to church and a lot of my friends were very religious, so it was just kind of, everyone I knew was just a group of religious people. So, that just kind of pushed me away from it. I also listened to more music, tried to get new video games, tried different things with the video games and stuff. And then I even stopped listening to, like, some of my favorite bands—you know, rappers, that sort—because they talked about sex, drugs, that kind of thing. So we just stopped watching, listening to all that kind of stuff, and, like, go to Mardel's and get all your new stuff [laughs].

Unlike the previous men who all consciously did things to break their porn habit, such as installing accountability software, pursuing connections with other groups of men, and taking drastic steps to eliminate access, Devon's story seems to suggest that the same things—social pressure and removing the source of temptation—were operative in his life as well, though they were not sought out intentionally.

To be sure, several men and women I interviewed emphasized spiritual changes that helped, but even these could be embedded in behavioral changes. For example, one college man explained, "I unfollowed scandalous [Twitter] accounts, and started following accounts with Bible verses or inspiring quotes or positive vibes. This was really helpful because the verses remind me who I am, and not seeing those images are really out of sight, out of mind." Not necessarily attributing his abstinence from porn to some sort of heart transformation, this man explained that simply getting rid of the "scandalous" material popping up on his Twitter feed and replacing it with Bible verses helped keep his mind from temptation. Other respondents sought to emphasize God's role in their recovery from porn use, even as they described how they restructured their lives to avoid temptation.

Megan, for example, is a 23-year-old recent college graduate who had regularly masturbated to porn for years during high school and into college. In her story, she outlined a variety of practical steps she took that were beneficial, but also emphasized conversations that she had with women about the gospel and sought to give credit to God for his transforming work:

I deleted Twitter forever off my phone, because it is too enabling. I went through phases where I deleted Instagram as well, and there are accounts or types of accounts that I block so they can't pop up, like, even if I were to search for them. I told other girls and [have] been able to process and walk through the issue together with them. I sought out accountability from older women and developed a system where I text them a specific emoji [laughs], like, praying hands, when I feel tempted to look at porn or masturbate, because attempting to overcome the temptation alone is so much harder than if someone else knows about it. Those text messages also were always followed by intentional conversations where we'd talk about what I was doing that led to the temptation, what I was believing, how or why I was seeking fulfillment or my hope or identity in something the world offers rather than in the Lord. Also, I have confessed all of it to the Lord. These strategies have definitely been effective. . . . [W]alking through this with the help and prayer and accountability of other women and girls was hugely helpful and empowering. I believe it's foolish to think that I could overcome pornography on my own. Healing and redemption only come through Jesus and the Holy Spirit, and so the best ways to move in that direction are to talk to him about it and to his people.

Megan described what many would characterize as an ideal relationship of accountability with the older women in her life—one that would be envied by others who struggle with pornography. Along with limiting access to tempting media, she texts her support team in moments of temptation and they respond with questions about the internal or practical sources of those struggles. Certainly, she cites her relationship with God as a source of strength, helping her to avoid temptation, but it seems that God works primarily through intentional, supportive relationships with fellow Christian women.

The trends illustrated in these statements are also supported by national data. Psychologist Kyler Rasmussen and sociologist Alex Bierman conducted a series of studies on what religious factors seem to reduce pornography use among young adults as they aged over time. They found that regular religious service attendance reduces the likelihood that men and women will increase in their porn viewing as they age. But is this due to something internal, like a belief or value, or something more social? The authors also found that more private, devotional religious behaviors like prayer and Bible reading also predict that young adults will view porn less often, *but only* if they are also attending church frequently. For those who were not closely connected to their church, porn use increased no matter how often they prayed and read their Bibles.[34] What does this mean? Just as the men and women here have expressed, along with eliminating access to the source of temptation, the *primary* weapon against porn is not necessarily private communion with God (though that is obviously a component for them) but, rather, close relationships with fellow believers. Indeed, it seems to be *through* those close personal relationships that one's communion with God can have an effect.

Conclusion

Pietistic idealism and biblicism, while they can be quite motivating, can also be ineffective. They force conservative Protestants to embrace certain approaches because they seem more oriented toward the heart or explicitly connected to a Bible verse, rather than because they work.[35] Porn-recovery manuals that embrace pietistic idealism and biblicism most strongly—the growing majority—certainly acknowledge that practical steps like accountability and eliminating access play a role in obtaining freedom from porn. But they are firmly committed to the belief that these methods cannot (indeed, *should* not) be the primary ones by which men and women achieve sexual purity. True growth, they stress, only comes through forsaking idols, believing the gospel, and valuing God more than porn. Biblical beliefs and values influence behaviors, not the other way around.

My interviews with pastors and lay conservative Protestants, however, suggest that quitting pornography—assuming people *want* to stop—may be far more about the willingness to take practical steps than any sort of change in beliefs or values. Indeed, men and women take practical steps to quit porn because they *already* believe watching porn to be wrong. Whether their motivations stem from "godly guilt," as one pastor put it, or one's spouse drawing a hard line in the sand on the porn issue, or the sort of unconscious social pressure that comes from surrounding oneself with other Christians who take sexual purity seriously, taking steps to eliminate access to porn and opening up to others about one's temptations seems to be the most effective techniques.

Conservative Protestants face a challenge. Biblical counseling likely offers a number of helpful spiritual and relational tools for Christian men and women to use in reorienting their lives around the gospel and in carefully diagnosing the spiritual roots of their moral failures. But within the biblical counseling community, there appears to be a growing unwillingness to acknowledge the wholeness of human beings, or that human beings are social creatures, and that quite often our physical bodies and social relationships influence the spiritual and moral realms, not the other way around.

In C. S. Lewis's *Screwtape Letters*, the senior devil (Screwtape) is advising his mentee (Wormwood) on how to tempt and destroy his assigned human. He remarks that, "at the very least, [your Christian] can be persuaded that the bodily position makes no difference to their prayers; for they forget, what you must always remember, that they are animals and that whatever their bodies do affects their souls."[36] Holding firmly to pietistic idealism and biblicism, writers like Challies, Chester, and others seem convinced that spiritual realities are primarily at play in why men and women continue to view pornography. To the extent that this position makes conservative Protestant thought leaders unwilling to acknowledge the reality, that intentional steps involving opportunity and social support seem to play a stronger role in helping people eliminate porn from their lives than any sort of belief/value change, their counsel will be less effective. And the fact that this group is gaining more influence within conservative Protestant circles means this ineffectiveness will become more widespread.

Conclusion

Between these two (Jekyll and Hyde), I now had to choose. . . . Strange as my circumstances were, the terms of this debate are as old and common-place as man; much of the same inducements and alarms cast the die for any trembling sinner; and it fell out with me, as it falls with so vast a majority of my fellows, that I chose the better part and was found wanting in the strength to keep to it.

—Robert Lewis Stevenson, *Dr. Jekyll and Mr. Hyde*, pp. 90–91

For I do not understand my own actions. For I do not do what I want, but I do the very thing I hate. . . . For I know that nothing good dwells in me, that is, in my flesh. For I have the desire to do what is right, but not the ability to carry it out. For I do not do the good I want, but the evil I do not want is what I keep on doing. Now if I do what I do not want, it is no longer I who do it, but sin that dwells within me. So I find it to be a law that when I want to do right, evil lies close at hand. . . . Wretched man that I am! Who will deliver me from this body of death?

—Apostle Paul, *Letter to the Romans* 7:15, 18–21, 24

COMMITTED CHRISTIANS ARE WELL acquainted with the sentiments the Apostle Paul describes in this epigraph—namely, the bewilderment, frustration, and discouragement that comes from knowing an activity is contrary to God's moral will, and yet repeatedly engaging in it anyway. Paul writes as if there were two persons battling away inside him, a spiritual Jekyll and Hyde: the godly one controlling his moral values and the sinful one controlling his body. The latter all too often overpowers the former.[1] Struggles with sexual lust have long caused committed Christians, and men in particular, to experience firsthand the spiritual distress Paul describes.

Importantly, this experience of moral incongruence—not only personally and spiritually but also socially and culturally—is rapidly growing worse for conservative Protestants. Their sexual ethic has remained the same, but the sexual temptation has evolved in every respect. The phenomenon of modern internet pornography, and the cultural context in which it now thrives, is different from anything committed Christians faced in centuries prior. Even as late as the mid-1990s, the perceived risks and costs involved in accessing pornographic material were great enough to preclude access for most faithful churchgoers. But those barriers are gone in a world where the most basic smartphone can show Christians (and their children) limitless, free, digital-quality adult content whenever they have a spare second alone—during a bathroom break, in their dorm room, when their spouse and kids are in bed, when their parents are at work. Paul's words in Romans 7:15–24 have likely never been so real for so many.

Revisiting the Focus and Argument

The paradox at the heart of this book—that conservative Protestants think pornography is immoral and yet succumb to its lure all the time—leads to effects that are (1) unique compared to other Americans (including other conservative religious groups); and (2) uniquely damaging to their mental health, spiritual lives, and interpersonal relationships. Whatever negative effects pornography may have on Americans' lives, they are decidedly worse for conservative Protestants. This is due to a combination of moral incongruence and other subcultural particularities that exacerbate the shame, isolation, and relational conflict conservative Protestants experience in porn use. Specifically, we have seen at least four ways in which conservative Protestants experience pornography use as uniquely caustic to their mental health and personal relationships.

First, unlike the growing numbers of American men and women who are unbound to a traditionalist Christian sexual ethic—and thus are less likely to equate their self-worth with their private sexual practices—conservative Protestants largely subscribe to sexual exceptionalism, counting sexual sin as the most corrupting and damnable of all sins. Consequently, pornography use—not anger, greed, selfishness, racism, pride, or envy—often becomes a proxy for measuring the quality of a believer's spiritual life. In other words, as one's battle with lust goes, so goes their relationship with God and their perceived worth as a Christian. A pattern of porn-fueled masturbation, even if somewhat infrequent, can provoke powerful feelings of shame, self-loathing, and isolation in conservative Protestant men and women. This experience of violating one's own moral values in pornography use—what I and others have called "moral incongruence"—is the key factor connecting pornography use with depression-related symptoms, and as Joshua Grubbs and colleagues have shown, provokes a variety of spiritual struggles as well. Indeed, the personal dissonance from these sorts of repeated failures can even lead conservative Protestant men and women to back away from their faith altogether in an attempt to resolve the inconsistency.

Second, as distressing as the moral incongruence may be for conservative Protestant men who view pornography, the complementarian sexual ideology pervading that subculture creates a situation in which women who view pornography experience arguably even worse shame and isolation than their male counterparts. While conservative Protestant men often find ample opportunities to discuss and process their struggles with pornography use, and may also counterintuitively have their God-given masculinity validated by the struggle (after all, God designed men especially to be visually stimulated and pursue sexual fulfillment), women who feel tempted to view pornography often wrestle in silence and private shame for violating not only God's sexual standard but also their own femininity. Indeed, much of their shame and isolation stems not from the porn use itself but from feeling abnormal, "like a freak," struggling with "a dude thing." That conservative Protestants continue to reinforce these patterns informally means that, unlike conservative Protestant men for whom most porn-recovery groups and materials are designed, the growing number of conservative Protestant women who view pornography will have few social or spiritual resources with which to process their struggles.

Third, conservative Protestant relationships seem particularly vulnerable to pornography's negative effects, for at least three interrelated reasons.

1. The combination of sexual exceptionalism and moral incongruence make conservative Protestant husbands feel particularly ashamed of their pornography use, likely decreasing their enjoyment of their relationship and certainly lowering their evaluation of themselves as husbands and fathers.

2. Compared to wives and partners who are not conservative Christians, conservative Protestant women virtually always interpret their husbands' pornography use as both a betrayal and adultery (sometimes not only metaphorically, but quite literally). Consequently, the repercussions of discovering one's spouse using pornography are more hurtful and damaging, on the whole, for conservative Protestant couples.

3. Conservative Protestant men, because of their own shame and fear of their spouse's response to their porn use, are unlikely to talk about porn with their spouse and would never expect to reach a compromise on the issue. While some men and women I interviewed who were not conservative Protestants were able to discuss the issue of pornography and negotiate its use, this is virtually impossible for conservative Protestants. Consequently, while some research suggests that couples who talk about pornography or even view erotic material together may actually experience some benefits, among conservative Protestants pornography is almost always consumed in isolation and in ways that are wholly negative for their intimate relationships.

Finally, because of the perceived threat of pornography to the spiritual life and relationships of people in the church, a cottage industry has emerged in the past few decades to help conservative Protestant men (less so women) stop viewing porn. But among a number of thought leaders in this field, and particularly those reflecting the growing influence of neo-Calvinism, commitments to pietistic idealism and biblicism essentially require them to emphasize certain "gospel-centered," "biblical" philosophies of change and recovery. These philosophies are not only inconsistent with how mainstream psychology advises people with these sorts of problem behaviors (by design, since secular psychology is viewed as unbiblical and wrongheaded) but also are not consistently applied by pastors and lay conservative Protestants. Indeed, while conservative Protestant pastors often espouse these philosophies formally, their practical counsel is often far more pragmatic and "ends driven," emphasizing actionable steps oftentimes *before* spiritual transformation. More than this, lay conservative Protestants seem to try anything at all that might help them fight off their temptation to view pornography, without much regard for whether they are believing the gospel or clinging to idols. The potential challenge here is that thought leaders' disregard (even disdain) for evidence-based, secular strategies for helping people overcome problem behaviors ultimately ensures that a muddied message will filter down into the pews, as struggling porn users deploy a "kitchen sink" of strategies to combat their porn habit. To the extent that conservative Protestants increase their adherence to the "biblical counseling" model to the neglect of more evidence-based therapies, their struggle with porn use will likely get worse.

Religion and the Experience of Moral Incongruence

How might the idea of moral incongruence help advance our understanding of religious experience? How could this concept be expanded to other groups, situations, and contexts?

In a much-cited essay, sociologist Mark Chaves rightly critiques religion scholars for frequently committing what he calls the "religious congruence fallacy." Researchers often assume there will be a close connection between actors' religious beliefs or values and their behaviors, which in reality is often untrue. Notably, however, the instances of religious *in*congruence Chaves cites as examples are unlikely to be the sorts of incongruences that would bother people tremendously. He gives an example of a divinity school student who is conflicted about going into the ministry because she no longer believes in God. But she is told by several denominational ministers that it's no big deal because lots of them don't believe in God, either. In this example, we see an apparent incongruence that turns out *not* to be incongruent socially.

He cites another story of a conservative rabbi in Israel who is chanting, and in the middle of his chant, he stops and says he doesn't believe any of what he's saying. But then the rabbi adds, "in Judaism, it doesn't matter what you believe. What's important is what you do."[2] Again, there is an apparent example of incongruence that turns out *not* to be incongruent socially.

Moral incongruence, as I've described it in this book, is more than just one more instance of religious incongruence in which the conflict between one's values and one's behavior doesn't really matter much socially or personally. This is because moral incongruence involves the violation of moral values that are deeply held and socially reinforced. These are values that a community (ourselves included) expects us to uphold and rebukes those who fail to uphold them. Conservative Protestants' pornography use shows how powerfully moral incongruence influences peoples' lives and social relationships. But there could be other examples beyond pornography use that should be explored. For theologically conservative Christians, because of pervasive sexual exceptionalism, committing numerous other sexual sins would also occasion the experience of moral incongruence. Indeed, findings from previous studies showing that premarital sex or cohabitation contributes to lower levels of religious participation over time suggests that these studies may have been describing the consequences of moral incongruence involving religious values and sexual behavior.[3]

I have argued that conservative Protestant women who willingly violate complementarian gender expectations through porn use feel even more acute moral incongruence. Similarly, men in these communities might experience the intrapersonal or social consequences for violating their gender expectations as well—say, for not leading their family spiritually, not providing financially, or otherwise not consistently performing what the culture categorizes as a characteristically masculine role. We might be able to observe these sorts of "role strain" experiences and their consequences for men and women within other traditionally patriarchal religions like Islam and conservative Judaism.

Related to this, while conservative Protestants have provided an ideal group to explore the social and personal consequences of moral incongruence because of their large numbers and extensive writings on issues of sexual purity, one of the next steps in this research will be to consider how moral incongruence works within non-Western contexts and non-Christian religions. What does it look like for Muslims, traditional

Catholics, or conservative Jews to willfully violate their sacred values or face a situation in which members of the group are regularly doing so? The experience will no doubt be different for other religions that may be more practice-oriented and/or less bound to a particular set of doctrines or creeds than is conservative Protestantism. For those in other traditions, incongruence may involve aspects of bodily practice or impurity that violate sacred values. Nevertheless, psychological and personal results may be the same.

Clinical psychologist David Paul Fernandez and his coauthors conducted a study of porn users in Malaysia. The authors found that porn users who disapproved of pornography use were more likely to report greater emotional distress when they failed to abstain, even though their actual use frequency did not register as compulsive.[4] Importantly, this sample was made up of people outside the Christian religion and outside the Western cultural context, suggesting that the consequences of moral incongruence are not unique to conservative Protestants or Americans.

Last, sociologists of religion should consider how the experience of moral incongruence may change over time owing to transformations in the cultural landscape. In the case of conservative Protestants, moral incongruence is likely only becoming worse as broader American society gradually, but undeniably, becomes less bound to a traditionalist sexual ethic. It is possible that religious Americans, or simply those with deeply held moral convictions that are becoming difficult to uphold in practice because of cultural marginalization, will experience increasingly acute moral incongruence in ways that provoke severe personal consequences, collective responses, or capitulation.

Where Moral Incongruence Fits into Research on Pornography's "Effects"

Focusing on conservative Protestants' interpretations of and experiences with pornography provides a unique opportunity for scholars of pornography use and sexual behavior more broadly to have a more nuanced discussion about pornography's effects. Much of pornography research tends to fall along one of two lines of inquiry. One line, the more empirical and quantitatively oriented of the two, tends to focus almost exclusively on the individual (or perhaps a couple), hoping to discern whether viewing erotic images does something to a person's brain or affects cognitive processes in ways that shape their attitudes or behaviors. The other line of research, more qualitatively oriented and steeped in critical theory, has focused on issues of cultural meaning and power, deconstructing "pornography" as a concept and often rejecting the idea that "pornography" has a concrete reality at all. Rather, "pornography" is whatever groups in power call sexual images and ideas they don't like.

In this book, I have sought to integrate both perspectives by arguing that "pornography" does indeed have concrete, negative effects on peoples' mental health and personal relationships, but much of that negative effect stems from the cultural meaning this activity has for a group in combination with the various cultural idiosyncrasies of that group that exacerbate its influence (e.g., sexual exceptionalism, complementarianism, pietistic idealism, biblicism). Both camps, in other words, are correct in some respects. But both are wrong to the extent that they fail to recognize how social meanings themselves, and our experiences of transgressing them, have very real consequences in peoples' lives. Whether "pornography" is "a thing" that has its own concrete reality beyond social definitions doesn't matter so much as whether a group of people (e.g., my faith community, my spouse, myself) agree that it is unequivocally immoral, and respond with real consequences when group members consume it.

Correspondingly, studies of pornography's "effects" on individuals' cognitive or relational outcomes may misidentify a key mechanism at work if so much of individuals' responses are powerfully moderated by their religious and moral context. Religious factors, in other words, cannot merely be thrown into regression models as something to control away. Nor can biased samples drawn from "Christian universities" be used to characterize how people in general respond to pornography use. Rather, religion, and the moral interpretations that it engenders with respect to sexual behavior, should be of paramount concern as a potential moderating variable in studies of pornography's "effects."

But here I need to qualify my argument, lest I be misunderstood as dismissing all research that seems to show frequent porn use as contributing to some undesirable outcomes. I certainly do not deny that pornography consumption, especially if it is habitual and compulsive, can have negative consequences in people's lives and relationships, *regardless of their religious or moral leanings.* For example, numerous studies, including some of my own, have found that more frequent pornography use can negatively influence Americans' romantic relationships, and sometimes these results do not seem to vary by whether or not viewers are conservative Protestants, frequent worship attendees, Bible believers, or think porn is morally wrong.[5] So, I certainly do not mean to say that the *only* people whom pornography negatively influences are religious hypocrites who just feel really guilty about watching porn. More accurately, rather, what a growing body of evidence suggests is that scholars cannot ignore the multifarious influence of culture, and particularly of religion and morality, in assessing the very real consequences of pornography use in peoples' lives.[6]

A Way Forward for Conservative Protestants?

Conservative Protestants are in a dilemma, and one that is likely to get more challenging for them. On the one hand, becoming more accommodating to the idea of pornography use is not an option. Sexual purity has remained at the core of Christian values and identity for centuries. There can be no truce with pornography.

Yet, despite conservative Protestants' past political efforts, the surrounding Western society is clearly growing more comfortable with pornography's growing ubiquity.[7] The recent spate of red-state legislatures issuing public resolutions that declare pornography a "public health crisis"[8] is, in the end, mostly political posturing with no legal teeth. Though anti-porn activist groups are excited about these resolutions as a way to decrease the demand for pornography, outlawing pornography (assuming it is the kind including only adults) or even strongly restricting its availability is unlikely to happen, especially given how each telecommunications advance has simultaneously melted away all the previous hindrances to access.[9] Conservative Protestants are as much aware of this as anyone. In the preface to Barna Group's *The Porn Phenomenon*, Josh McDowell laments where the advent of new technologies like virtual reality would take pornography:

Pornography is not new. However, the digital tools that deliver and propagate it today are new, and they have fundamentally changed the landscape. But not even the ubiquity and easy access of smartphone and tablet apps will be able to compete with the coming advancements in virtual reality (VR) technology. VR systems such as Oculus Rift, Samsung Gear VR, and HoloLens immerse the user visually and sonically in a virtual world. In the near future, all three systems will have add-on devices that bring other parts of the user's body into the virtual space—meaning a user won't just see and hear but also touch and feel virtual objects and people as if they were real. This technology has promising implications for manufacturing design, the medical field, and other sciences and the arts. But it is not difficult to imagine the devastating capacity of VR devices to lure an entire generation deeper into a virtual world of pornography, turning what is already a crisis into an epidemic of addiction.[10]

McDowell is likely not too far off in extrapolating the future uses of virtual reality devices for porn. Indeed, to the infamously irrefutable "Rule 34" (if you can imagine it, there's internet porn about it) we could add a "Rule 35": every advance in media technology will somehow be used for porn.[11] In fact, some have even argued that porn itself now *drives* tech advances, not the other way around.[12]

So, while conservative Protestants will continue to categorically condemn pornography, it's not going away. But then, conservative Protestants do not seem to be going anywhere, either—at least in terms of their participation in mainstream media and technology. One conservative Christian commentator, Rod Dreher, who argues with familiar language "the scourge of pornography is destroying the imagination of millions," and "pornography literally rewires the brain," has recommended what he calls "The Benedict Option" for dealing with this growing problem.[13] Along with fighting pornography tooth and nail at every opportunity, Dreher prescribes that conservative Christians should take voluntary fasts from the internet; take smartphones away from kids; keep things like social media out of worship; develop a more contemplative lifestyle that values simplicity and disengages from the frenzy of the modern internet age; and be among those who are generally skeptical about the unassailable goodness of "progress" for its own sake.[14]

Being myself skeptical of the social value of most things on the internet, part of me is inclined to agree with Dreher's prescription—and not just for conservative Protestants who hate pornography. A number of secular commentators have suggested that similar practices and orientations toward the internet and technology would be beneficial for all of us.[15] Yet most conservative Protestants are unlikely to embrace Dreher's plan. First, most conservative Protestants are closely tied to the world and the myriad resources and entertainment options it provides; comparatively few actually choose to consume whatever the evangelical subculture produces.[16] Conservative Protestants are different enough from the larger culture to be completely at odds with its dominant sexual ethic, but too identical in their addiction to modern technology and media to abandon the source of their ills. Second, many would reject Dreher's suggestions since retreat from secular society might preclude conservative Protestants' ability to impact their neighbors, coworkers, and broader culture with the gospel.

Given these realities, what can conservative Protestants do?

Reconsidering Sexual Exceptionalism

Pornography, and sexual temptation more broadly, is a problem that will never go away for conservative Protestants. But certain changes to conservative Protestant culture could help mitigate the effects of pornography.

Sexual exceptionalism—the extreme emphasis on sexual sin above all other sins—lies at the core of the torment experienced by men and women in this study; it likely plays a strong role in conservative Protestants' tendency to regard themselves as "addicts" despite their relatively infrequent porn use; and it inflames conflict and isolation among conservative Protestant couples where one partner is wrestling with pornographic temptation.

Conservative Protestants are not going to condone sexual practices they find unbiblical. But the emphasis they put on sexual purity above all other sins leads to greater harm among the faithful. Some conservative Protestant leaders have begun to seek change. They argue that sexual exceptionalism is not only unhelpful it is also not essentially Christian. As biblical counselor David Powlison has pointed out, sexual exceptionalism reflects a largely Western evaluation of moral priorities that appears to be missing among Christians in other non-Western contexts.[17] But even within Western expressions of conservative Christianity, there have been dissenting voices like C. S. Lewis, who have held that internal sins of pride and selfishness tell us more about a Christian's true spiritual state than his or her private sexual mistakes.[18]

None of this is to suggest that conservative Protestants should just accept that porn use will become more commonplace among a growing number of Christians. But it seems that the emphasis on sexual sin—to the extent that young Christian men and women commonly evaluate their own spiritual lives by whether they have viewed porn recently and show a pattern of either obsessing unhealthily over porn or backing away from their faith due to the personal dissonance this causes in their lives—is undeniably counterproductive to helping young Christians live out their faith as conservative Protestant communities would hope.

The Usefulness of Complementarian Assumptions

The largest and most influential camps of conservative Protestantism are formally committed to complementarianism, and they often re-affirm that commitment when given opportunity. This is unlikely to change anytime soon. The complementarian assumption that men *tend to* be more visually oriented than women, and therefore tend to view pornography more than women, may have long been true in a statistical sense, but this view is coming to reflect the present reality less and less. Visual pornography, the kind that primarily men were thought to be interested in because of how "God designed them" is now a problem for conservative Protestant women.

But beyond causing conservative Protestants to largely ignore the growing challenges and temptations confronting younger conservative Protestant women, maintaining these pervasive stereotypes about men's and women's sexual tendencies has been completely counterproductive in meeting the needs of this population. Starting from the assumption that "God designed" men to be visual and interested in physical inti-macy, and "designed" women to be interested in emotional connections and to be sexual responders for men has caused women who wrestle with visual, physical temptation to feel even more abnormal and, consequently, less willing or able to process that struggle with others in their faith community.

While complementarianism may be a core biblical belief for many conservative Protestants, in terms of dealing with pornography, the associated assumptions about men's and women's sexual tendencies have proven unhelpful. In contrast, we saw that pastors who were willing to openly discuss the issue of sexual temptation and pornography with women, assuming their temptations can be just as strong as those in men, were able to more effectively minister to those women. The more leaders in congregations can acknowledge that men and women are both sexual beings with a broad spectrum of sexual profiles and tastes, the easier it will be for women in those congregations to become more open about those temptations and get the resources they need to continue walking in faith.

Structuring Openness into Faith Communities

Among the greatest torments for conservative Protestants when it comes to pornography is the feeling of isolation—the resignation that they must wrestle with their temptation and failures alone. Readers will recall that a number of those I interviewed and presented in the book expressed fear that other church members would judge them for their porn struggles and, consequently, fellow parishioners would be the last people they would want to ask for accountability or counsel. Part of the problem is the sexual exceptionalism I already addressed: if sexual sin is the most shameful and stigmatizing of all sins, porn users will be less eager to acknowledge their struggles. But this problem is compounded by the *perception* that fellow Christians do not battle the same temptations, or do not struggle to the same extreme, and thus would either not understand or would view the confessor as lesser, spiritually and morally. This only increases their shame and isolation. Whether their perception is true or not, it is obviously counterproductive and contrary to what most conservative Protestant churches would like to be characterized by—namely, openness and restoration.

But I should clarify. For conservative Protestants, not all shame and bad feelings stemming from porn use are negative. Rather, as one pastor explained, there is "the shame and guilt that accompany those that are true Christians and especially Christians who think [porn is] wrong and know it's wrong." Within the conservative Protestant subculture, true believers *should* feel guilty about their porn use at some level. But to the extent that these negative feelings stem from a perception that fellow Christians either cannot or are unwilling to identify with the same struggle, it only hinders opportunities for openness and mutual support. Conversely, throughout my interviews, it seemed that the following practices are helpful:

• Talking through the temptation with others
• Thinking together about what emotions or past hurts might fuel acting out or shame
• Strategizing about concrete steps that can be taken to avoid temptation
• Openly confessing to one another when someone had a "bad weekend"
• Accepting one another as works-in-process

These practices, done regularly, not only diminish the unhealthy suffering but seem to foster more practical success in avoiding future failures with pornography.

Recognizing this, some churches have devised ways to structure openness into their congregations and small groups. One congregation, for example, implemented a regular gathering in which pastors and other leaders were invited to discuss their own present or past sexual struggles, and how they personally fight those battles. Those in attendance could ask advice or share about their own personal experiences in ways that could be helpful to others. These discussions were gender specific, and women's sexual temptation was addressed in some form as well.

Openness and interaction among members has also been accomplished through small groups. While the gradual shift in the American religious landscape toward megachurches can in some ways contribute to an individualist, isolated, antiseptic feeling among churchgoers, small groups may provide opportunities to develop deeper, interdependent, familiar relationships with fellow Christians. Because opportunities for confession and counsel in the area of pornography use may be limited if one happens to be in a group where few others are struggling with the same issue, recovery-focused ministries have been helpful. Parts of these ministries function as support groups for those with similar struggles, and participation is confidential. A commitment to offering these sorts of stable options to Christian men and women have proven to be more effective ways of structuring openness into faith communities, rather than assuming those things are happening organically.

Appendix A
Methods and Data

There is no *single* type of data that can answer all research questions with complete confidence. Some types of data can give us assurance that our findings are generalizable (high reliability), but it is possible they do not accurately measure what we think they are measuring (low validity). Other types of data allow us to confirm what we are measuring, and with great nuance (high validity), but may generate findings that are impossible to replicate or generalize to a broader population (low reliability). Because of this problem, social scientists like myself often use different types of data to provide insights that are as comprehensive and nuanced as possible. This study includes both quantitative and qualitative components, and each contributes something unique to understanding pornography's relationship to conservative Protestant men and women.

Quantitative Data

One common limitation of research on pornography and its effects is that the data are often based on small, nonrandom, convenience samples of individuals. These have historically been college students or, more recently, panels of individuals who get paid money to take surveys. The quantitative data in this book all come from large, probability samples of American adults, allowing me to generalize to the broader population. These quantitative data are listed in table A.1.

TABLE A.1 Quantitative Survey Datasets with Chapters Cited

Survey	Chapter Cited
1973–2016 General Social Surveys (GSS)	Intro., 1, 4, 5, Conc.
2000 Politics of Character Survey	2
2003, 2005, and 2007/2008 National Study of Youth and Religion (NSYR)	3
2006 and 2012 Portraits of American Life Study (PALS)	2, 3, 5
2012 New Family Structures Study (NFSS)	2, 3, 5
2014 Relationships in America (RIA) Survey	2, 3, 4, 5
2005, 2007, and 2017 Baylor Religion Survey	2, 5

With the exception of the 2014 Relationships in America Survey,[1] which I accessed directly from the survey's proprietor, each of the quantitative data sets I use are publicly available for download at the ARDA website (Association of Religion Data Archives): www.thearda.com. Under the leadership of Roger Finke, Christopher Bader, and Andrew Whitehead, The ARDA is an invaluable repository for religion data that can essentially be used like Google for searching out variables and datasets one might need. Because I use so many different datasets, and because they are all publicly available online, I will not take up more book space with an exhaustive list describing these data or the variables I use. Interested readers can easily find that information at the ARDA website along with the data for replicating whatever I have presented. Appendix B provides the tables behind a number of the figures presented throughout the book.

Qualitative Data

While quantitative data from large, representative surveys allowed me to establish that conservative Protestants often experience more severe consequences for their porn use compared to other Americans, the qualitative data were crucial for answering the question: Why? One of the challenging aspects of gathering good qualitative data is ensuring that what you are observing in the data is *reliable*—that is, the findings illustrate something true about more than just that one person or source. One does not have the same standards for being "representative" as one does with quantitative data. But qualitative data should not be wildly "unrepresentative," or based on a handful of abnormal or extreme cases. One way to confirm reliability with qualitative data is to triangulate with a variety of types. My qualitative data included semi-structured, in-person interviews with 132 men and women; qualitative content analyses of conservative Protestant monographs on sexuality and pornography; participant observation at conservative Protestant events where pornography was explicitly addressed; and focus groups with conservative Protestant men.

Interviews

RECRUITMENT

As I expressed in the book's preface, my interview sample was somewhat selective in that the vast majority lived in urban or suburban areas and were college educated (or at least pursuing a college degree), mostly because I tended to recruit participants through my own personal and professional networks. Consequently, lower-educated, working-class individuals from rural areas are not well represented in this study. While acknowledging that this limits the qualitative findings somewhat, research shows that the sorts of individuals I interviewed (educated, urban/suburban, possessing greater familiarity with technology) are the group most likely to consume pornography, and thus one could also argue that this would be the most appropriate group on which to focus. More limiting, I would argue, would be the potential lack of interviewees from Pentecostal or charismatic backgrounds who are more prevalent in rural, working-class areas of the country. While it is true that a larger majority of my conservative Protestant respondents came from Baptist, evangelical Presbyterian, or nondenominational evangelical traditions, my interviews with those from a Pentecostal background provided findings that were consistent with the others.

INTERVIEWING

Asking people to be candid about their pornography use (or even broaching the subject itself) can be touchy. Some earlier studies have that found that both young people and women tend to be reticent to discuss issues like porn use and masturbation.[2] My experiences with recruiting interview participants only matched those studies partly. For example, while I did not interview teens in high school, I found college students, and especially conservative Protestant men, to be quite willing to share details and feelings about their pornography use. I certainly had no shortage of young Christian men willing to speak with me about how porn had shaped their lives. I attribute this to their experiencing pornography use as something that deeply bothered them, and they felt that talking through those issues with a perceived "expert" would be helpful to their recovery. Indeed, several expressed that they found the interview experience cathartic and helped recruit their friends. This trend in my interviews actually confirmed findings from recent studies showing that religious Americans tend to be more open and less influenced by social desirability in reporting their porn use.[3] Relatively less religious men were also fairly open about their pornography use, but not as a means of "confession." More often, rather, they seemed more defensive, holding that their pornography use was harmless and no big deal.

I found just the opposite in my interviews with women. Irreligious or nominally religious women tended to be quite open about their pornography use, either talking about it matter-of-factly or in some cases almost boasting about it as if to affirm their sexual freedom. Conservative Protestant women, however, because of the reasons I discussed in chapter 4, were the most unwilling to share about their pornography use. I also experienced challenges recruiting conservative Protestant women to talk about their husband's pornography use, as that is also a sensitive and potentially shameful subject for those women.

In order to maximize the possibility of adult's being willing to participate in the interviews and, beyond that, being as honest as possible about their experiences with pornography, I leveraged several strategies. These strategies included alternatives for potential interviewees to decide which scenario would be more disarming for them. For example, when interviewing people locally in Oklahoma, I offered interviewees the choice of being interviewed by myself or by one of my two female research assistants. While most people were fine to be interviewed by me, a number of individuals chose to be interviewed by my assistants. I personally trained both those assistants and, upon reading the transcripts of their conversations, was able to confirm that the information they were getting was no different from that gained in my interviews.

When I conducted interviews with persons outside of Oklahoma, in Texas, Illinois, Georgia, South Carolina, or elsewhere, I offered participants the opportunity to participate in an interview with me personally (either over phone or video call) or they could complete an online questionnaire with the same open-ended questions I would ask in an interview (see appendix C). A relatively small percentage of interviewees took the online survey option (15%). All pastors out of state completed interviews with me over the phone, and also answered follow-up questions via email.

Table A.2 provides a breakdown of the interview sample by gender, religion, and whether they were pastors/ministers or laypersons. The vast majority of non-conservative Protestants were in the category of agnostic or atheist, followed by mainline Protestant or Catholic. Less than a handful of these participants were Muslim, Hindu, or Buddhist, none of whom regularly used pornography but each took a completely nonjudgmental approach to others watching it. While I occasionally had to make a judgment call as to whether I considered, say, a faithful Methodist a "conservative Protestant," the vast majority of designations were easily made.

TABLE A.2 Breakdown of Interview Sample

Description	Number of Participants
Conservative Protestant pastors/ministers	35
Men	(30)
Women	(5)
Lay conservative Protestants	45
Men	(36)
Women	(9)
Non-conservative Protestants*	52
Men	(27)
Women	(25)
Total	132 Participants

Note: *Non-conservative Protestants included self-described atheists, agnostics, Muslims, Buddhists, and Hindus, as well as nominal or liberal Catholics or Methodists.

Interviews that took place in person, over the phone, or via video call were digitally recorded and professionally transcribed by a transcription service that signed a confidentiality agreement. I read through the transcripts several times and oftentimes listened to the recording again to confirm where an interviewee was placing his or her emphasis. I coded the interviews along a number of salient themes that were emerging from the data.

Qualitative Content Analysis of Conservative Protestant Monographs

There is growing opinion among sociologists of culture that in-depth interviews, while an important data source, must be triangulated with other data sources where researchers can observe participants in a more naturalistic setting without overreliance on interviewees' self-explanations, which may be biased or invalid.[4] This is especially important for a study of conservative Protestants and pornography, where my interviewees' accounts of their "struggles" may be influenced by their own unique subcultural interpretations of sexuality.

For this reason, conservative Protestant monographs provide an extremely valuable source of data because they allowed me to view how conservative Protestants talk *to one another* about topics like masturbation and pornography use, and how these topics intersect with other important institutions like gender and marriage. Because there is no official database of such literature, and because quantifying the content was not my goal, I started accumulating titles from bibliographies provided by recent sociological studies of religion and sexuality, particularly those that focus on conservative Protestants.[5] I also followed the bibliographies of the monographs themselves in order to see whom the Christian authors were in dialogue with. I also followed the "also purchased" links on Amazon whenever buying these titles to ensure that I was not missing relevant and popular books. Lastly, I would often ask my interviewees if they had read particular books or other resources that shaped their thinking about issues of sexuality, pornography, and masturbation.

Table A.3 lists the fifty-five monographs arranged chronologically and topically, including titles that (1) focus exclusively on issues of

TABLE A.3 List of Conservative Protestant Monographs by Focus and Publication Date

About pornography and/or masturbation explicitly

1. David Powlison. 1999. *Pornography: Slaying the Dragon.*
2. Steve Gerali. 2003. *The Struggle.*
3. Craig Gross and Carter Krummrich. 2006. *The Dirty Little Secret: Uncovering the Truth Behind Porn.*
4. Michael Leahy. 2008. *Porn Nation: Conquering America's # 1 Addiction.*
5. Mark Driscoll. 2009. *Porn-Again Christian: A Frank Discussion on Pornography & Masturbation.*
6. William Struthers. 2009. *Wired for Intimacy: How Pornography Hijacks the Male Brain.*
7. Tim Challies. 2010. *Sexual Detox: A Guide for Guys Who Are Sick of Porn.*
8. Tim Chester. 2010. *Closing the Door: Steps to Living Porn Free.*
9. Craig Gross and Jason Harper. 2010. *Eyes of Integrity: The Porn Pandemic and How It Affects You.*
10. Craig Gross and Steven Luff. 2010. *Pure Eyes: A Man's Guide to Sexual Integrity.*
11. Michael John Cusick. 2012. *Surfing for God: Discovering the Divine Desire Beneath Sexual Struggle.*
12. Heath Lambert. 2013. *Final Free: Fighting for Purity with the Power of Grace.*
13. Jen and Craig Ferguson. 2014. *Pure Eyes, Clean Heart: A Couple's Journey to Freedom from Pornography.*
14. J. S. Park. 2015. *Cutting It Off: Breaking Porn Addiction and How to Quit for Good.*
15. Douglass Weiss. 2015. *Lust Free Living.*
16 Barna Group. 2016. *The Porn Phenomenon: The Impact of Pornography in the Digital Age.*
17. John Foubert. 2017. *How Pornography Harms: What Today's Teens, Young Adults, Parents, and Pastors Need to Know.*

About sexual purity broadly, including chapters on pornography and/or masturbation

18. Josh McDowell. 1987. *How to Teach Your Child to Say "No" to Sexual Pressure.*
19. Stephen Arterburn. 1992. *Addicted to Love: Recovering from Unhealthy Dependencies in Love, Romance, Relationships, and Sex.*

(continued)

TABLE A.3 **Continued**

20.	Lewis Smedes. 1994. *Sex for Christians: The Limits and Liberties of Sexual Living.*
21.	Harry Schaumburg. 1997. *False Intimacy: Understanding the Struggle of Sexual Addiction.*
22.	Russell Willingham. 1999. *Break Free: Understanding Sexual Addiction & the Healing Power of Jesus.*
23.	Stephen Arterburn, Fred Stoker, and Mike Yorkey. 2000. *Every Man's Battle: Winning the War on Sexual Temptation One Victory at a Time.*
24.	Bob Gresh. 2001. *Who Moved the Goal Post?*
25.	Douglass Weiss. 2002. *Sex, Men, and God.*
26.	Stephen Arterburn, Fred Stoeker, and Mike Yorkey. 2002. *Every Young Man's Battle: Strategies for Victory in the Real World of Sexual Temptation.*
27.	Shannon Ethridge. 2003. *Every Woman's Battle: Discovering God's Plan for Sexual and Emotional Fulfillment.*
28.	Joshua Harris. 2003. *Sex is Not the Problem (Lust Is): Sexual Purity in a Lust-Saturated World.*
29.	Clifford and Joyce Penner. 2003. *The Gift of Sex: A Guide to Sexual Fulfillment.*
30.	Shannon Ethridge and Stephen Arterburn. 2004. *Every Young Woman's Battle: Guarding Your Mind, Heart, and Body in a Sex-Saturated World.*
31.	Robert Daniels. 2005. *The War Within: Gaining Victory in the Battle for Sexual Purity.*
32.	John Piper and Justin Taylor (Eds.). 2005. *Sex and the Supremacy of Christ.*
33.	Lauren Winner. 2005. *Real Sex: The Naked Truth About Chastity.*
34.	James Jackson. 2006. *Revolutionary Purity* (True Love Waits).
35.	Fred Stoker and Mike Yorkey. 2006. *Tactics: Securing the Victory in Every Young Man's Battle.*
36.	Steve Gallagher. 2007. *At the Altar of Sexual Idolatry.*
37.	Stanton and Brenna Jones. 2007. *How & When to Tell Your Kids about Sex.*
38.	Stephen Arterburn, Fred Stoker, and Mike Yorkey. 2010. *Preparing Your Son for Every Man's Battle: Honest Conversations about Sexual Integrity.*
39.	Fred and Brenda Stoker, Stephen Arterburn, and Mike Yorkey. 2010. *Every Heart Restored: A Wife's Guide to Healing in the Wake of a Husband's Sexual Sin.*
40.	Douglas Weiss. 2013. *Clean: A Proven Plan for Men Committed to Sexual Integrity.*
41.	Stephen Arterburn and Jason Martinkus. 2014. *Worthy of Her Trust: What You Need to Rebuild Sexual Integrity and How to Win Her Back.*

TABLE A.3 Continued

About broader Christian issues, including chapters on sexual purity, pornography, and/or masturbation

42. Jerry Falwell. 1980. *Listen, America!*
43. David Jeremiah. 1982. *Before It's Too Late: Crises Facing America.*
44. Tim LaHaye, 1982. *The Battle for the Family.*
45. Tim LaHaye, 1985. *Sex Education is for the Family.*
46. Richard Foster. 1985. *The Challenge of the Disciplined Life: Christian Reflections on Money, Sex, and Power.*
47. James Dobson. 1997. *Solid Answers.*
48. Tim and Beverly LaHaye. 1998. *The Act of Marriage: The Beauty of Sexual Love.*
49. James Dobson. 2006. *Preparing for Adolescence. How to Survive the Coming Years of Change.*
50. Brenda Stoeker and Susan Allen. 2008. *The Healing Choice: How to Move Beyond Betrayal.*
51. Tim Chester. 2010. *You Can Change: God's Transforming Power for Our Sinful Behavior and Negative Emotions.*
52. Mike Wilkerson. 2011. *Redemption: Freed by Jesus from the Idols We Worship and the Wounds We Carry.*
53. Mark and Grace Driscoll. 2012. *Real Marriage: The Truth about Sex, Friendship & Life Together.*
54. David Platt. 2015. *Counter Culture: Following Christ in an Anti-Christian Age.*
55. Tony Reinke. 2017. *12 Ways Your Phone Is Changing You.*

pornography and masturbation; (2) focus on Christians and sexuality more broadly but include discussions of pornography and masturbation; and (3) focus on Christians and a variety of social issues, but also include discussions of sexuality, pornography, and/or masturbation. Some of these books I do not cite in the chapters and thus they are not included in the book's references.

I read through each of these books carefully and hand-coded their contents much like I had for the interview data. Important quotes and ideas were noted and catalogued in a database for use in the book. In addition to these monographs, I incorporated other complementary data sources, including all of the *Christianity Today* articles from 1956 to 2017 that discuss pornography (taken from Thomas 2013 and 2016, and my own compilation) and blog posts from various conservative Protestant groups writing about pornography, such as Covenant Eyes and Focus on the Family. While I do not cite these data sources extensively outside of chapters 1 and 5, they nonetheless provided a useful comparative reference for the monographs.

Participant Observation

Between 2015 and 2017, I conducted participant observation at three separate events in Oklahoma, South Carolina, and Texas, which were hosted by conservative Protestants. Each was intended to provide a venue for corporately discussing pornography. Two took place at churches; the other at a large conference. One of the church events was a men's retreat that also included discussions about other men's issues, like being a husband and father. These events included speakers on the topic of pornography in the lives of Christians, as well as Q&A sessions. The two church events also included panel discussions during which men from the church were asked to talk about their own experiences with pornography. One of the church events also had a separate women's time that I was not allowed to attend. However, I later asked questions about what was discussed from women who were willing to share information about that time. I also had dozens of informal conversations with men and women at each event. I took copious notes during and after these times in order to organize my thoughts and reconcile what I observed at the events with what was being discussed in my interviews and the monographs.

Focus Groups

Focus groups can provide an opportunity to observe not only how participants discuss topics in one-on-one settings with an interviewer but how they discuss those topics with one another.[6] I conducted three focus groups with sixteen men total. Two groups took place in Oklahoma (five men each) and one in Texas (six men). I was unable to recruit enough conservative Protestant women to conduct a focus group, and because of the extreme reluctance of conservative Protestant women to open up about their porn use with one another, and especially strange men, focus groups would likely not have been a good venue for gathering data from this population anyway. My list of focus group questions (see appendix C) was not as extensive as it was for one-on-one interviews because I could expect that men would share information in a more dialogical, back-and-forth manner. I treated these focus groups like participant observations, not digitally recording the events but taking extensive notes. And while this was not where the brunt of the qualitative data came from for this book, these data also, like those from my participant observation, allowed me to corroborate the discourses I had observed in the monographs and the concepts that had been discussed in the interviews.

Appendix B
Tables

TABLE B.1 Ordinary Least Squares Regression Coefficients Predicting Religious Measures by Pornography Use for Conservative Protestants

Predictors	Religious Doubts (W2)	Imp. of Religion (W2)	Church Attendance (W2)
Pornography Viewing (W1)	.118***	−.146***	−.303***
	(.026)	(.036)	(.057)
Religious Doubts (W1)	.307***		
	(.042)		
Importance of Religion (W1)		.553***	
		(.048)	
Church Attendance (W1)			.689***
			(.038)
Age	−.009***	.009*	.016**
	(.003)	(.004)	(.006)
Male	.004	.129	.294
	(.082)	(.115)	(.188)
Married	−.188*	.038	.121
	(.090)	(.760)	(.203)
Number of Children	−.019	.003	−.027
	(.021)	(.029)	(.568)
Bachelors or Higher	.152+	−.117	−.209
	(090)	(.124)	(.204)
Household Income	−.004	.016	.030
	(.010)	(.014)	(.023)
White	.252**	−.329**	−.390*
	(.082)	(.113)	(.188)
Southern Residence	.018	−.008	−.002
	(.073)	(.105)	(.167)
Intercept	1.344***	1.591***	.976*
	(.187)	(.288)	(.976)
Adjusted R^2	.296	.374	.552
N	370	387	386

Note: Corresponds with figure 3.2. Unstandardized regression coefficients with standard errors in parentheses. All predictor variables are from Wave 2 (2012) PALS unless otherwise indicated.

+ $p < .10$; * $p < .05$; ** $p < .01$; *** $p < .001$ (two-tailed test).

Source: Portraits of American Life Study, 2006 and 2012.

TABLE B.2 Fixed Effects Regression Estimates Predicting Religious Measures by Pornography Use for Conservative Protestants

Predictor	Church Attendance		Importance of God		Prayer Frequency		Closeness to God		Religious Doubts	
	Model 1	Model 2	Model 1	Model 2	Model 1	Model 2	Model 1	Model 2	Model 1	Model 2
Pornography Viewing	-0.133**	-.091	-.056*	-.046	-.153***	-.164***	-.048*	-.042	.088***	.077*
	(.048)	(.106)	(.024)	(.031)	(.037)	(.047)	(.021)	(.029)	(.024)	(.030)
Porn Viewing × female		-.104		-.027		.029		-.015		.026
		(.098)		(.048)		(.077)		(.043)		(.050)
18 or older	-.725***	-.726***	-.080	-.081+	-.147+	-.147	-.243***	-.243***	.003	.003
	(.105)	(.106)	(.049)	(.049)	(.089)	(.089)	(.061)	(.061)	(.062)	(.062)
Southern residence	.547+	.554+	-.013	-.011	.310	.308	-.051	-.050	.177	.175
	(.317)	(.314)	(.110)	(.110)	(.242)	(.243)	(.162)	(.162)	(.183)	(.184)
Parent in home	.440**	.436**	.022	.020	.082	.083	-.147+	-.147+	.005	.006
	(.147)	(.146)	(.068)	(.068)	(.117)	(.118)	(.081)	(.081)	(.008)	(.088)
Constant	3.887	3.879	3.163	3.161	4.150	4.152	3.732	3.731	.547	.549
Rho	.485	.484	.528	.528	.544	.543	.511	.511	.511	.511
R²	.629	.629	.644	.644	.665	.665	.622	.623	.612	.612
Adjusted R²	.412	.413	.437	.436	.469	.469	.401	.401	.386	.385
Within R²	.156	.158	.021	.021	.043	.043	.032	.032	.019	.019

Note: Corresponds with figure 3.3. Unstandardized regression coefficients with robust standard errors in parentheses. There is no main effect term for gender because it is time invariant. Thus, it is only interacted with porn viewing. + p < .10; * p < .05; ** p < .01; *** p < .001 (two-tailed test).
Source: National Study of Youth and Religion, 2003, 2005, 2007/2008; N = 442.

TABLE B.3 Binary Logistic Regression Coefficients Predicting Serving in Leadership Positions Between 2006 and 2012 by Pornography Use for Conservative Protestants

Predictor	Held Leadership Position (W2)	Served on Committee or Board (W2)
Held Leadership Position (W1)	2.332***	
	(.401)	
Served on Committee (W1)		1.897***
		(.400)
Pornography Viewing (W1)	−.448*	−.625*
	(.192)	(.263)
Age	.006	.032*
	(.013)	(.014)
Male	.728+	.907*
	(.425)	(.409)
Married	.533	−.133
	(.413)	(.433)
Children Living in Home	−.460	.007
	(.423)	(.426)
Bachelors Degree or Higher	.482	.462
	(.434)	(.447)
White	−.105	−.495
	(.789)	(.401)
Southern Residence	.190	.339
	(.360)	(.372)
Household Income	.006	.030
	(.033)	(.036)
Attendance Frequency	.564***	.606***
	(.127)	(.138)
Prayer Frequency	.051	.284*
	(.118)	(.139)
Scripture Fully Inspired	.301	−.400
	(.650)	(.705)
Constant	−5.558***	−7.896***
	(1.380)	(.1.651)
Nagelkerke Pseudo R^2	.548	.525

Note: Corresponds with figure 3.4. Unstandardized regression coefficients with standard errors in parentheses. All predictor variables are from 2006 to establish temporal precedence. + $p < .10$; *$p < .05$; ** $p < .01$; *** $p < .001$ (two-tailed test).
Source: Portraits of American Life Study, 2006 and 2012; $N = 287$.

TABLE B.4 Correlations Between Pornography Viewing Frequency and Marital Outcomes for 2006 PALS, 2012 NFSS, and 2014 RIA

2006 PALS	Full Sample	Men	Women
How often spouse expressed affection in past year	−.01	−.01	−.02
How often spouse compliments you for the work you do	−.03	−.08*	−.09*
How often spouse performs acts of kindness	.02	−.04	−.08*
How often insults or harshly criticizes	.08**	.03	.06
How often spouse hits or slaps	.06*	.04	.04
How happy with relationship	−.10***	−.17***	−.08*
How satisfied with affection received from spouse	−.13***	−.22***	−.06
How satisfied with sex life with spouse	−.12***	−.20***	.01
How satisfied with decision-making	−10***	−.15***	−.11**
Believes spouse has cheated	.13***	.25***	.06
Respondent cheated	.19***	.19***	.08
Experienced marital separation	.06*	.06	.12***

2012 NFSS	Full Sample	Men	Women
Ever thought about leaving your spouse?	−.01	−.05	−.08
Have you and your spouse talked about separating?	.08	.15	.11
How often have you thought your relationship is in trouble?	.15***	.21***	.16***
How often have you and your spouse discussed ending the relationship?	.15***	.17***	.20***
How often have you broken up and then got back together?	.15***	.09*	.30***
Agree/Disagree: we have a good relationship.	−.09**	−.08	−.15***
Agree/Disagree: our relationship is very healthy.	−.07*	−.10*	−.10*
Agree/Disagree: our relationship is strong.	−.06*	−.07	−.10*
Agree/Disagree: my relationship makes me happy.	−.09**	−.06	−.19***

(continued)

TABLE B.4 Continued

2012 NFSS	Full Sample	Men	Women
Agree/Disagree: I feel like part of a team with partner.	−.08**	−.06	−.17***
Agree/Disagree: our relationship is pretty much perfect.	−.14***	−.22***	−.13***
Marital Happiness Scale (1 = worst, 10 = best)	−.04	−.08	−.07

2014 RIA	Full Sample	Men	Women
Ever thought about leaving your spouse?	.09***	.18***	.12***
Have you and your spouse ever talked about separating?	.07***	.07***	.15***
Respondent cheated sexually?	.16***	.20***	.16***
Experienced physical violence in current marriage?	.11***	.12***	.08***
Marital Happiness Scale (1 = worst, 10 = best)	−.09***	−.15***	−.09***

Note: Corresponds with table 5.2. * $p < .05$; ** $p < .01$; *** $p < .001$ (two-tailed test). PALS = Portraits of American Life Study; NFSS = New Family Structures Study; RIA = Relationships in America Survey.

TABLE B.5 Binary Logistic Regression Predicting Marriage Being "Very Happy" in Relation to Pornography Use for Conservative Protestants

Predictors	Evangelical[b]		Protestant "Fundamentalist"	
	Model 1	Model 2	Model 2	Model 2
Porn Viewing	.826***	.868***	.826***	
	(.029)	(.043)	(.037)	
Evangelical	1.086*	1.127***		
	(.033)	(.037)		
Porn × Evangelical		.825*		
		(.080)		
Prot. Fundamentalist			1.060+	1.093*
			(.033)	(.036)
Porn × Fundamentalist				.845*
				(.079)
Worship Attendance	1.071***	1.071***	1.070***	1.070***
	(.006)	(.006)	(.006)	(.006)
Age	1.002+	1.002+	1.002*	1.002*
	(.001)	(.001)	(.001)	(.001)
Female	.777***	.777***	.780***	.781***
	(.029)	(.029)	(.029)	(.029)
Black[a]	.521***	.525***	.524***	.528***
	(.050)	(.050)	(.051)	(.051)
Other[a]	.771***	.771***	.768***	.768***
	(.065)	(.065)	(.065)	(.065)
Number of Children	.940***	.940***	.939***	.939***
	(.009)	(.009)	(.009)	(.009)
Years of Education	1.030***	1.030***	1.029***	1.030***
	(.005)	(.005)	(.005)	(.005)
Year of Survey	.993***	.993***	.992***	.992***
	(.001)	(.001)	(.001)	(.001)
Constant (coefficient)	15.216***	15.258***	15.579***	15.608***
	(2.333)	(2.333)	(2.342)	(2.342)
Nagelkerke Pseudo R^2	.036	.036	.035	.036
N	19,413	19,413	19,251	19,251

Note: Corresponds with figure 5.1. Odds ratios with standard errors in parentheses. [a] Reference category is White; [b] Steensland et al. 2000. + $p < .10$; * $p < .05$; ** $p < .01$; *** $p < .001$ (two-tailed test).
Source: General Social Surveys, 1973–2016.

TABLE B.6 Binary Logistic Regression Predicting
Women Wanting a Divorce Because of Their Spouse's
Pornography Use

Predictors	Wanted Divorce Because of Spouse's Porn Use
Evangelical Protestant	2.814**
	(.386)
Worship Attendance	1.006
	(.056)
Age	.931***
	(.014)
Any Children	1.256
	(.378)
White	1.169
	(.339)
High School[a]	11.052*
	(1.136)
Some College[a]	12.016*
	(1.137)
Bachelors or Higher[a]	9.524+
	(1.158)
Constant (coefficient)	−2.190+
	(1.246)
Nagelkerke Pseudo R^2	.113
N	988

Note: Corresponds with figure 5.2 Odds ratios with standard errors in parentheses. Sample only includes women who indicated they had been divorced at some point. Almost no men in the survey (and zero conservative Protestant men) indicated they had wanted a divorce because of their spouse's pornography use. [a] Reference category is Less Than High School. * $p < .05$; ** $p < .01$; *** $p < .001$ (two-tailed test).
Source: Relationships in America Survey, 2014.

Appendix C
Interview Guides

1. General Interview Guide

Demographics

- What is your age?
- What is your gender?
- What is your race/ethnicity?
- What is your current marital status?
- How would you identify yourself religiously?
- Is there a particular denomination or theological tradition you identify with?
- How important would you say your religion is to you?

Definitions and Views of Pornography

- How would you define the word "pornography?"
- What makes something pornographic by definition? (For example, how would you distinguish "art" from "porn"?)
- What do you think about porn morally?
- Where did that moral perspective come from? Parents? Some other source? Have you always felt that way or did that perspective develop over time?

Experiences with Pornography

- When was the first time you ever looked at pornography? Can you describe that experience?
- How frequently would you say you looked at pornography earlier on? Under what circumstances?
- Would you describe your porn use as habitual at any time? What does that mean to you?
- Would you ever use the word "addiction" to describe your porn use now or ever? What does that mean to you?
- Describe your frequency of porn use within the past year? Occasionally? Monthly? Weekly? Daily? Under what circumstances do you typically use it?
- Has your use of pornography over the years been consistent or inconsistent? If it's been inconsistent, what factors were associated with you either using or deciding not to use pornography?
- Was porn use always connected with sexual gratification, either masturbation or during sex with a partner? Did you ever just watch it to pass the time?
- What types of pornography do you find yourself watching? (You can be as specific as you feel comfortable being.) Softcore? Hardcore? Fetish? Have your tastes in porn changed over the years?
- Have you ever been caught using porn? Can you describe that situation and whether there was any fallout?

Personal Evaluations of Pornography Use

- Would you say that viewing pornography has ever benefited you in some way? If yes, how so?
- Has your use of pornography ever conflicted with your moral principles? If so, has that ever bothered you?
- Did you ever think you had a problem **not** using pornography, like you wanted to stop but couldn't?
- [If the respondent stopped using pornography] Tell me about how that happened?

Pornography and Personal Relationships

- How has your personal pornography use influenced your romantic relationships over the years?
- Have you ever voluntarily used pornography with a partner as a part of lovemaking? If yes, on whose initiation? More than once?
- [If the person is married] How has your pornography use influenced your marriage?
    o Do you hide it? Why? How does that affect the relationship?
    o Do you use it together? Why? How does that affect the relationship?
    o What would happen if your spouse caught you using it without them?
    o Do you see it as cheating? Would you see it as cheating if your spouse was using pornography without you?
- [If the person has children] How has your pornography use influenced your relationship with your children?
    o Do you hide it from your children?
    o Has it ever influenced the way you relate to your children? Lower frequency? Guilt or embarrassment?
    o Do you think you'll talk about it with your children? What would you say?
    o How would you feel if you came to find out your children frequently used pornography when they grew up because of your use?
- What role does pornography play in your relationships with close friends? Ever talk about it? Why or why not? If yes, under what circumstances?
- How has pornography use influenced your relationship with strangers or acquaintances? Does it affect the way you see people?

Pornography and Religious Faith

- Do you feel that your religious views have something to say about your pornography use? Like what? Or is pornography a non-issue for you religiously?

- Do you feel that regular pornography use could be compatible with being a faithful [your religious identity] for you? How so?
- [If they are Christians] Has your pornography use ever negatively affected your relationship with God or the practice of your faith? If yes, how so? Try to be specific.
- Have you ever turned down an opportunity to practice your faith because of your pornography use? If yes, please describe those situations.
- Has viewing pornography ever benefited your religious faith in some way? If yes, how so?

2. Interview Guide for Wives/Partners of Pornography Users

Demographic Questions are the same as for General Interview Guide.

Definitions and Views of Pornography

- How would you define the word "pornography?"
- What do you think about porn morally?

Personal Experiences with Pornography

- Have you ever intentionally sought out pornography? Please describe that experience.
- Is watching pornography something that you still do? If yes, how frequently? Under what circumstances.

Pornography and Personal Relationships

- Have you ever voluntarily used pornography with a partner as a part of lovemaking? If yes, on whose initiation? More than once?
- Have you ever had a romantic partner whom you knew used pornography alone? If yes, how did you find out about it? Did that activity (or your knowledge of that activity) affect your relationship in any ways?
- If you had a spouse or partner who used pornography alone, please explain how you responded when you first found out. What did you say? How did they respond?

- If you did not approve of your spouse or partner's porn use, what is it explicitly that you did not like about it? What bothers you exactly? You can give more than one reason.
- If your spouse/partner continues to use pornography despite your wishes, what do those conversations look like now?
- Have you ever issued an ultimatum?
- Have you ever tried to discover whether your spouse/partner is using pornography without asking him? If yes, how did you do so?
- Do you feel that your spouse's/partner's pornography use has had a lasting impact on your relationship today?

3. Interview Guide for Pastors/Ministers

Demographic/Professional Questions

- What is your age?
- Where do you serve as a pastor/minister?
- How long have you been serving there?

Pornography Use in Your Ministry

- Where would you rank pornography in terms of issues that you hear about people dealing with in your church/ministry?
- What are the circumstances under which you normally have people come to you? (Do they come voluntarily? Are they being forced to by parent or spouse?)
- When people come to you, do you ever have to convince them that what they're doing is wrong? Or do they usually know and are looking for help?
- So walk me through your counsel when men or women come to you? What do you tell them? What does the process look like? As many details as possible would be helpful.
- It's often pastors' experience that they talk more to men on this issue than women? Has that been your experience? Why do you think that is?
- How do your own personal experiences with pornography either in the past or currently factor into your counsel with these men

or women? Do you think those struggles make you more or less effective as a pastor?

- Usually when we talk about pornography, the idea of masturbation is sort of implied. But imagine the scenario where pornography is not in the picture. Perhaps a soldier is overseas and his wife gives him a picture of herself? Or the guy says he can masturbate without lusting or fantasies? Is masturbation wrong then? Why or why not?
- Do you think women experience any added barriers in their fight with pornography? If yes, like what?
- Do you think Christians and non-Christians may deal with pornography a little differently? How so?

4. Interview Guide for Focus Groups

Demographic Questions are the same as for General Interview Guide.

Pornography Questions

- Can you all share a little about your own histories with pornography over the years?
- [For married people who used porn apart from their spouse] Have you talked with your spouse about your struggles in this area?
  o How did s/he react?
  o What was the fallout there?
  o During times when you've watched pornography again, do you tell your spouse immediately? What do those conversations look like now?
- [If men/women disclosed they no longer used porn] What did the process of stopping porn use look like for you? What happened or changed? What did you do?
- What practical steps do you take to avoid porn now, if any?
- Do you think masturbation under certain circumstances could be okay? For example, if it was without porn?

NOTES

Preface

1. Defining "pornography" with specificity is notoriously difficult. When asked to define "hard-core pornography," Supreme Court Justice Potter Stewart famously wrote, "I shall not today attempt further to define the kinds of material I understand to be [hard-core pornography], and perhaps I could never succeed in intelligibly doing so. But I know it when I see it" (*Jacobellis v. Ohio*, 1964). The definition of pornography as "sexually explicit media intended for sexual arousal" is the basic definition employed by the majority of researchers on the topic and is found in most dictionary entries for the word itself. By defining pornography or "porn" in this way, I wish to distinguish it from more mainstream sexual media that are found on television. Conservative Protestants may not be a fan of the sexual images on television, but most recognize a difference between what is seen on Netflix and what is seen when they type "porn" into Google. Because the term "pornography" is freighted with moral connotations, some sexuality scholars choose to use more descriptive words like "sexually explicit media," or "sexually explicit Internet material," or "erotica." Because the surveys I use for this study employ the term "pornography" (as do the conservative Protestants I interviewed), I chose to use the term here.

2. Though related, "moral incongruence" should not be confused with "cognitive dissonance," the intrapsychic distress that stems from situations in which our behaviors do not match our beliefs (Festinger 1957). Properly understood, moral incongruence refers to the *situation* in which cognitive dissonance or mental stress is the resulting symptom. Also, unlike cognitive

219

dissonance theory, which largely terminates with the individual psyche, moral incongruence as a concept is intended to emphasize the socially embedded nature of our moral values, as well as the severe personal and social consequences that accompany our violations of those values.

3. The most vocal advocates for this view are radical feminists like Andrea Dworkin (1979) along with her frequent coauthor Catherine MacKinnon (1985); sociologist Gail Dines (1998, 2006, 2010); and journalism professor, Robert Jensen (2007). Sociologist of gender, Michael Kimmel (1990, 2008) could also be included in the camp of scholars who are highly critical of contemporary pornography and its influence on the culture.

4. This camp would include pro-sex feminist and critical sexuality scholars like Feona Attwood (2005, 2006, 2011), Mureille Miller-Young (2014, 2016), and most contributors and editors of the peer-reviewed journal *Porn Studies*.

5. Haidt (2012).

6. One need only follow the scientific and political controversies over the etiology and understanding of transgender issues to see how vitriolic (even malicious) debates in sexuality research can become (see Dreger 2015).

7. As confident as anti-porn advocates are about the ability of laws to curb the growing availability of pornography, I believe this is ultimately an unwinnable battle for them, since (1) the vast majority of American men (and I assume that includes policymakers) are now viewing pornography at least occasionally and likely have no desire to make it so that they could be arrested for doing so; and (2) people have long known that "pornography" in the sense of visual/literary material used for arousal can be made out of *anything* (the joke among teenage boys when I grew up was making use of the lingerie section of mom's JC Penney catalog), and thus, it's impossible to police fully. The philosopher, author, and cultural commentator Bertrand Russell (1929, 114–116) explained back in 1929:

> In spite of the law, nearly every fairly well-to-do man has in adolescence seen indecent photographs, and has been proud of obtaining possession of them because they were difficult to procure. . . . Undoubtedly [pornographic photos] stir a transient feeling of lust, but in any sexually vigorous male such feelings will be stirred in one way if not in another. . . . [T]he occasions which rouse such feelings in him depend upon the social conventions to which he is accustomed. To an early Victorian man a woman's ankles were sufficient stimulus, whereas a modern man remains unmoved by anything up to the thigh. . . . The more prudes restrict the permissible degree of sexual appeal, the less is required to make such an appeal effective. Nine-tenths of the appeal of pornography is due to the indecent feelings concerning sex which moralists inculcate in the young; the other tenth is physiological, and will occur in one way or another whatever the state of the law may be.

So, too, the English literary critic Walter Allen (1962, 144, 146) wrote:

> One knows very well that the mind intent on pornography
> will always find it, however innocent the material on which
> it is projected. . . . All we can say with any confidence is that
> [pornography] has always existed and always will, so long as men
> and women have sexual fantasies they cannot realise, for whatever
> reasons, in actual life. . . . And we ought by now to know enough
> about human behaviour not to be too impressed by the zeal of those
> who would vindictively suppress what they consider pornography.

8. Collins (2000), Dines (1998, 2006, 2010), Jensen (2007), Kimmel (2008), MacKinnon (1985).
9. Buzzell (2005a, 2005b), Doring (2009), Perry (2017a), Perry and Schleifer (2018a), Stack, Wasserman, and Kern (2004).
10. Using data from the 2010–2016 General Social Surveys, roughly 1% of American Protestants who affiliate with a "fundamentalist" denomination or who believe that the Bible must be interpreted literally, or who affiliate with an evangelical denomination (according to the Steensland et al. [2000] classification) also identify as "gay, lesbian, or homosexual."
11. Though I have heard this quote from Jim Elliot referenced numerous times, the only source I found citing it was Mitchell (1995).

Introduction

1. If those numbers seem implausibly large, they should. For over 6.3 trillion porn videos to have been watched in 2016 when McDowell said this, each of the 3.4 billion people on the planet with internet access would have to watch at least five pornographic videos every day. As we will see later, Christian anti-porn activists, and Josh McDowell most notoriously, have enlisted statistics in the fight against pornography, and are often more concerned with driving home the point of porn's pervasiveness than whether their statistics are accurate. Additionally, the idea that people are watching "videos" is a little misleading. Visitors to pornographic websites like *Pornhub* or *PornTube* rarely watch full videos, but often bounce around from clip to clip, taking in certain scenes. Thus, what amounts to a 15-minute session of porn viewing might involve 10 to 15 porn clips (Ogas and Gaddam 2011).
2. There were three non-evangelical speakers at the 2016 Set Free Summit. One was a Mormon neurosurgeon, Donald Hilton, who was invited for his expertise on how pornography affects the brain. He spoke on a panel with two evangelical experts on porn and addiction. While Hilton has written more religiously minded literature on pornography use, he did not speak on those things. Another non-evangelical speaker included another Mormon, Clay Olsen, founder of the activist organization Fight the New Drug, an ostensibly irreligious anti-porn advocacy group. The third

non-evangelical Protestant speaker was a Catholic priest, Sean Kilcawley. Though technically not an evangelical, his message emphasized theological teachings that would resonate with evangelicals, stressing the need to share the gospel with those enslaved by porn.

3. Thomas (2013 and 2016).
4. LaHaye (1982, 183).
5. Lykke and Cohen (2015), Price et al. (2016), Regnerus, Gordon, and Price (2016), Wright (2013), Wright, Bae, and Funk (2013).
6. Regnerus et al. (2016).
7. According to a report by Gallup released in the summer of 2018, the proportion of Americans who felt pornography is morally acceptable increased from 36% in 2017 to 43% in 2018. And over two-thirds (67%) of men under age 50 felt pornography was morally acceptable. See https://news.gallup.com/poll/235280/americans-say-pornography-morally-acceptable.aspx.
8. A meme has been bouncing around the internet since around 2005 that the average age of children's first exposure to pornography is 11. And some conservative Protestant commentators try to argue that the age could be more like 8 or 9 years old (Cutrer 2016). These claims have not been supported by any reliable, data-driven studies, however. In fact, they are likely to have originated from a religious group intending to scare parents about the threat of pornography (Lubov 2005). The earliest reliable studies on this topic suggested that boys are more likely to be exposed to pornography in their early to mid-teens, with girls being exposed a little later (Mitchell, Wolak, and Finkelhor 2007; Sabina, Wolak, and Finkelhor 2008; Wolak, Mitchell, and Finkelhor 2007; Ybarra and Mitchell 2005). While the age has likely been lowered by internet and smartphone use, no independent studies that I am aware of have found average exposure for young people in the pre-teen years.
9. Price et al. (2016) show that American men below age 27 who report viewing porn increased by roughly 16% from the mid-1970s to the mid-2000s, compared to only 6% for men ages 45–53 during that same time period. So, too, women below age 27 who view porn increased by 8% during that time period, while this percentage actually declined slightly for women 45–53 years old.
10. Price et al. (2016).
11. Barna Group's term "Practicing Christian" is most often (though not always) reserved for self-identified Christians (including Protestants and Catholics) who agree that their faith is "very important" to them and who attend church at least once a month (see Barna Group 2016, 46).
12. These figures can be found in Barna Group (2016, 81, 100–101, 150–152). By listing Barna's statistical claims, I do not mean to suggest that they are entirely reliable. I am merely pointing out that the evangelical polling firm

is reporting these statistics and the findings are being disseminated and read among conservative Protestants, shaping their view of pornography's pervasiveness.

13. For example, see Trevin Wax's post about pastors on social media for The Gospel Coalition (Wax 2014; see also Reinke 2017). Wax argues that evangelical pastors should be on social media because it allows pastors to speak the language of their culture, just as a missionary would seek to do. He also argued that the pastor's social media presence might become the "front door" of the church, the way newcomers find out about the church and then check out the website.

14. See the Christian Broadcasting Network interview with Josh McDowell, at http://www1.cbn.com/cbnnews/health/2016/april/alarming-epidemic-porn-the-greatest-threat-to-the-cause-of-christ.

15. For examples in which *all* these arguments are deployed against pornography, see Foubert (2016) or Wilson (2014). See also websites like www.yourbrainonporn.com.

16. For examples of these arguments, see Ley (2012), Prause and Pfaus (2015), and Staley and Prause (2013).

17. A long history of studies shows that certain types of pornography use and aggression are positively correlated with one another (see meta-analytic studies provided by Allen, D'Alessio, and Emmers-Sommer 1999; Seto and Lalumiere 2010). But does one really *cause* the other? This is where it is most appropriate to address the issue of *self-selection* in research on pornography use. When studies find, for example, that persons who use pornography are more likely to hold misogynistic attitudes or to have been convicted of sexual violence, it could just as well be that misogynistic, violence-prone persons seek out pornography in the first place, rather than pornography use being the thing that *caused* certain attitudes or behaviors. In fact, there is a whole line of research arguing that pornography does not lead to sexual violence, but in fact provides a sort of "mastubatory catharsis," in which persons who might have been tempted to act out certain violent sexual desires with actual human beings can "safely" find release through pornography (Wright, Tokunaga, and Kraus 2016). Pornography, then, would not be a catalyst for sexual violence; it is a safety valve. In support of this idea, some research finds that as pornography becomes more available in societies, sex crimes have either declined or remained the same (Diamond 2009; see also Diamond, Jozofkova, and Weiss 2011; and Kingston and Malamuth 2011). In this case, it could be the issue is not *too much* violent pornography contributing to sexual violence but, rather, that society is not providing *enough* access to mitigate outward expressions. This is a self-selection issue, and it is an enormously important problem for studies of pornography use to overcome. The best way for researchers to do this is with randomized experiments. Individuals should be randomly assigned to receive a "treatment" (exposure to sexually explicit

media) that a randomized control group does not receive, and then observe the outcomes.

18. For some early analyses, see Allen, D'Alessio, and Brezgel (1995); and Allen et al. (1995). For a more recent and exhaustive list of such studies, see Hald, Malamuth, and Yuen (2010) and Wright et al. (2016).

19. See the meta-analyses of Hald et al. (2010) and Wright et al. (2016).

20. Hald and Malamuth (2015); Malamuth, Hald, and Koss (2012); Wright et al. (2016). Media scholar Paul Wright (2011) has elaborated on the scripting framework by proposing what he calls the $_3$AM model of sexual script acquisition, activation, and application. One major takeaway of Wright's work is that viewers are more likely to acquire, activate, and apply pornography's sexual scripts when those scripts resonate with the values and beliefs that viewers have already internalized. In other words, pornographic media amplifies or slightly modifies sexual scripts far more often than it completely changes them. This helps us understand why pornography use might have a greater influence on violence for someone who is already predisposed toward such behavior.

21. Sociologists occasionally wade into researching *attitudes* toward pornography (e.g., Lykke and Cohen 2015; Sherkat and Ellison 1997; Wood and Hughes 1984), but few focus on actual pornography viewing. Although Gail Dines is a sociologist by training and position, her contribution to the discussion on pornography is primarily one of an anti-porn activist rather than a social scientist. And even as sociologist Mark Regnerus has written somewhat on pornography use (Price et al. 2016; Regnerus et al. 2016), it is noteworthy that his coauthors on those subjects are economists and Regnerus employs the market-based theories of an economist to explain porn use and relationships (see Regnerus 2017, chap. 4). Other important exceptions to sociology's relative silence on pornography include the work of Jeremy Thomas (2013, 2016; see also Thomas, Alper, and Gleason 2016); Burke (2016); Alex Bierman, in Rasmussen and Bierman (2016, 2017); and Sumerau and Cragun (2015a, 2015b).

22. Why have sociologists, of all scholars, been so remiss in studying a social phenomenon that is so manifestly present in the lives of American men and women? There are a few reasons for this, but the one I find most likely (and unfortunate) is that pornography puts most sociologists in a thorny *political* situation—one in which they are uncomfortable issuing public statements about porn's influence, either positive or negative. On the one hand, sociologists overwhelmingly align with feminist and anti-racist principles and goals, and the content of much pornography is notoriously misogynistic and racist. Consequently, sociologists do not wish to appear as though they wholeheartedly endorse an industry that profits from the onscreen degradation of women and the perpetuation of offensive ethnic stereotypes. But on the other hand, sociologists in general have long been committed to "sex positivity" (the idea

that sexuality should have few if any limits beyond being safe and consensual). As a result, sociologists are reluctant to argue that one's private sexual practices might somehow be dysfunctional for individuals or society. Related to this, sociologists are also reluctant to criticize porn, with the belief that the women working in this industry are being empowered to work on their own terms and express themselves sexually, and thus they should not be shamed or discouraged. These two general commitments put sociologists on the horns of a dilemma regarding pornography, and most have opted for another solution—write about something else.

23. I debated using the term "evangelical" here, as I have in a previous book (Perry 2017b). I opted not to for several reasons. First, while evangelicals are certainly conservative Protestants, the term "evangelical" emphasizes the witnessing, world-impacting aspect of Christian identity (Bebbington 1989; Lindsay 2007; Perry 2017b; Smith 1998). I prefer, rather, to emphasize the theological conservatism of these Protestants over their priority of evangelization. Second, several typologies that define evangelicals by certain denominational affiliations do not include all the conservative Protestants I describe in the book. The broader term "conservative Protestant" is thus more descriptively accurate. Lastly, leading up to and following the election of Donald Trump to become the 45th president of the United States, the term "evangelical" has increasingly become one consciously rejected by conservative Protestants themselves. A number of men and women I interviewed, in fact, while they would understand what I mean by the term, indicated they would rather not be referred to as "evangelical," owing to its pejorative connotations. Just as very few conservative Protestants in 2018 go around calling themselves "fundamentalists" anymore, likely because the term is widely associated with being culturally backward and probably bigoted, the term "evangelical" is taking on that sort of stigma as well. Using "conservative Protestants" helps avoid some of that negativity, I hope.

24. Sociologist and leading expert on American evangelicalism Christian Smith (2017, 55) argues that conservative Protestants are among the least "practice-oriented" religions, preferring instead to place emphasis on "certain correct beliefs, words, and spiritual attitudes, and on having the right, informal, not culturally prescribed, relationship with God."

Chapter 1

1. Wilson and Abelson (1973).
2. McKenna (2017).
3. See Strub's (2011) excellent analysis of pornography and the rise of the Religious Right. See also Regnerus and Smith (1998), Woodberry and Smith (1998).

4. Falwell (1980, 200).
5. LaHaye (1985, 119).
6. LaHaye (1982, 178).
7. LaHaye (1982, 178).
8. LaHaye (1982, 179).
9. LaHaye (1982, 181).
10. LaHaye (1985, 34).
11. LaHaye (1985, 117).
12. LaHaye (1985, 196).
13. LaHaye (1985, 118–119).
14. Jeremiah (1982, 63).
15. LaHaye (1982, 181) relayed a similar story in a section entitled "It Can Happen to You!" One Christian couples' sweet teenaged daughter got caught up in the wrong crowd at church. A boyfriend in that group invited all of them over to his house, and they began looking through his father's *Playboy* magazines. LaHaye explains: "they all began reading them until they got so worked up that they stripped off their clothes and performed sexual acts in front of each other. This was followed by sex orgies, until the daughter had run the gamut of sexual experience by seventeen." By 19, that girl left home to become a prostitute. LaHaye concludes: "Depravity never happens suddenly. It is a progressive process, but nothing speeds a normal person's decency into the maelstrom of indecency faster than pornography."
16. Jeremiah (1982, 71).
17. Falwell (1980, 198, 200).
18. By historical accounts, the trend of Nazis making pornography and alcohol available to the Poles was indeed a part of their plan to dominate them thoroughly. But porn and alcohol were part of a larger project that included prohibiting other forms of entertainment or access to museums or education, as a way to strip the Poles of any connection to their native culture (see Connelly 2012; Rylko-Bauer 2014, 60).
19. For thoughts from conservative Protestant commentators on censorship and pornography during the 1950s, see Cannon and Everette (1958) and Dawson (1959).
20. Falwell (1980, 203).
21. Falwell (1980, 198, 200).
22. LaHaye (1982, 178)
23. LaHaye (1982, 181–182).
24. LaHaye (1982, 183).
25. Cleath (1975, 21).
26. McKenna (2017).
27. This is not my preferred way of measuring "conservative Protestant," since it tells us little about their beliefs or level of commitment, but in this case

the results are virtually identical if I measure "conservative Protestant" by whether they affiliate with a traditionally "evangelical" denomination (following the Steensland et al. 2000 classification scheme) or believing in biblical literalism, with the latter question only being asked since 1984. In other words, regardless of how you measure "conservative Protestant," the group is not becoming more accepting of pornography, even as other Americans are.

28. The most famous articulation of this argument is found in the work of feminist author Andrea Dworkin (1979). This has been followed in recent years by anti-porn feminist authors Gail Dines (2010), Robert Jenson (2007), and Michael Kimmel (2008). Though anything but feminists themselves, traces of this narrative can also be found among fundamentalist writers. LaHaye (1982, 183; 1985, 196) and Jeremiah (1982, 67) repeatedly attributed rape, incest, and child molestation to pornography's corrupting influence. And Falwell (1980, 199–200), ironically, more explicitly denounced pornography's portrayal of women: "Pornography displays a distorted view of women. Women are shown as masculine wish fulfillment, or many times women are depicted as being so lust driven that they will stop at nothing to satisfy themselves."

29. Thomas (2016).

30. The questions about being "born again" or convincing someone to accept Jesus have not been asked in the General Social Surveys (GSS) very consistently, unfortunately. However, the trends for each shows that, on average, roughly 42% of Protestant men who have tried to convert someone to Christianity view porn in a given year, and this has not changed since 1988. And among "born-again" Protestant men, the trend in porn use has increased only slightly between 1988 and 2016, from 39% to 42%, on average. For a more thorough analysis of these trends, see Perry and Schleifer (2018b).

31. Other than the fact that the *frequency* of viewership is not asked, another important limitation of the GSS measure is obviously the dated language about watching an "X-rated movie." While I would argue that most American adults still know what "X-rated" means, they tend not to refer to pornography as "X-rated" anymore in casual conversation. Another limitation is that the question does not ask anything about the *context* of viewership or whether or not the viewing was even intentional. While the assumption is often that someone was intentionally watching porn alone for sexual arousal, it could be that the viewer was watching porn with a romantic partner, or saw it accidentally on Twitter. Despite these limitations, the GSS is the only data source that we can use to track the use of pornography over time.

32. Barna Group (2016, 100).

33. Published on the blog *Expastors.com* in 2014. See http://www.expastors.com/how-many-pastors-are-addicted-to-porn-the-stats-are-surprising/.

34. McDowell (2015). The claim that "47 percent of Christian homes now have a major problem with pornography" comes from a 2003 survey administered by the "Internet Filter Review," an organization that obviously has a vested interest in making sure Christians know about the threat of pornography.

35. McDowell (2015). McDowell likely pulled this last statistic from the Covenant Eyes 2015 report on "Pornography Statistics," available for free on the *Covenanteyes* website. Among the statistics on Christians, they state, "those self-identified as 'fundamentalists' are 91% *more* likely to look at porn" (emphasis theirs). The claim is based on a study of internet pornography use with data from the 2000 GSS (see Stack, Wasserman, and Kern 2004), where the authors found that after controlling for sociodemographic factors, those who identified themselves as "fundamentalist" had an odds ratio of 1.91 (odds ratios over 1 indicate that someone has higher odds of doing the thing in question—in this case, visiting a pornographic website). Importantly, however, this finding was *statistically nonsignificant*. In other words, it is a non-finding statistically.

36. Published on the *Huffington Post* in 2014. See https://www.huffingtonpost.com/elwood-d-watson/pornography-addiction-amo_b_5963460.html.

37. Morgan (2008); See also similar numbers cited in Chester (2010a).

38. Scott (2016).

39. Paul (2005, 20).

40. These statistics were published in a promotional flyer put out by Mark Driscoll. See http://parablesblog.blogspot.com/2017/10/pornography.html.

41. Published on the blog *Expastors.com* in 2016. See http://www.expastors.com/key-findings-in-landmark-pornography-study/.

42. McDowell (2015).

43. Gross (2010, 30).

44. Barna Group (2016, 32).

45. Rasmussen et al. (2018).

46. McKenna (2017).

47. McDowell (2015). Full transcript available at https://www.youtube.com/watch?v=oOSbUjmupWE.

48. Chester (2010a, 9). The statistic Chester cites is based on an unscientific poll conducted by *ChristiaNet.com* in 2006. The site asked visitors to complete a survey. It is sited in several articles written by conservative Protestants (https://www.huffingtonpost.com/elwood-d-watson/pornography-addiction-amo_b_5963460.html) and other porn recovery books (e.g., Ferguson and Ferguson 2014, 10).

49. See just about every book by Stephen Arterburn and Fred Stoeker in the "Every Man Series" series, most famously: *Every Man's Battle: Winning the War on Sexual Temptation One Victory at a Time* (2000). See also Barna Group (2016), Chester (2010a, 2010b), Driscoll (2009), Driscoll and Driscoll (2012), Ferguson and Ferguson (2014), Gallagher (2007), Gerali

(2003), Gross (2006, 2010), Gross and Luff (2010), Harris (2003), Lambert (2013), Park (2015), Wilkerson (2011), Willingham (1999).

50. Abell, Steenbergh, and Boivin (2006); Bradley et al. (2016); Burke (2016, 41); Grubbs, Exline, et al. (2015); Kwee, Dominguez, and Ferrell (2007); Levert (2007).

51. Covenant Eyes (2015).

52. Barna Group (2016, 81).

53. Grubbs, Exline, et al. (2015), Grubbs and Perry (2018).

54. Nelson, Padilla-Walker, and Carroll (2010); White and Kimball (2009).

55. Related to this idea, a number of clinical psychologists have considered whether a maladaptive coping strategy called "experiential avoidance" may be to blame for the shame–relapse cycle that conservative Protestants seem caught up in (Levin, Lillis, and Hayes 2012; Wetterneck et al. 2012). Experiential avoidance involves avoiding or escaping situations where one experiences uncomfortable emotions like the shame and condemnation. One possible example of this could be conservative Protestant men who seem to structure their lives around avoiding situations where they might be tempted to view pornography. In the extreme, psychologists argue, the experiential avoidance strategy ultimately ends up being maladaptive because it precludes individuals from processing their negative emotions and going to the root of their feelings, while also inclining individuals to fixate on the very activity they wish to avoid. In this case, regular relapses with pornography are simultaneously the source of conservative Protestants' deep shame and become their source of self-medication.

56. See MacInnis and Hodson (2015) and Whitehead and Perry (2018), both of whom use Google Trends data to show that states with higher numbers of religious conservatives also show higher numbers of searches for pornographic content on Google.

57. Remarking on the shift from viewing porn use as *sin* to viewing it as an *addiction*, Thomas (2016, 191) reasons: "The timing of this shift is significant because it suggests that the idea of sin was increasingly being perceived as an inadequate explanation for why so many evangelicals were using pornography. In other words, the notion that evangelicals might simply choose to collectively increase their engagement in sexual sin was largely incomprehensible. Rather, something else had to be at work, and the idea of pornography addiction offered just such an explanation."

58. Barna Group (2016, 100).

59. Josh McDowell has frequently quoted Chuck Swindoll as calling porn "the greatest cancer in the church today." See Falwell (1980, 200), Foubert (2016, 198), Gross (2006, 118). See also Mark Hitchcock, as quoted in Foubert (2016, ix).

60. Promotional blurb for Challies (2010).

61. Thomas (2016, 189–190).

Chapter 2

1. There is the possible exception of Lewis Smedes. In his popular book, *Sex for Christians*, the evangelical ethicist Smedes (1994) argued that pornography was "harmful" (p. 35) and "dangerous" (p. 190), but he also challenged the view that looking at a *Playboy* necessarily constituted "lusting" in the biblical sense. While racy pictures no doubt get viewers excited, Smedes felt the bigger harms of pornography were that it provided an incentive to escape from real relationships and it made sex mundane and uninteresting (see pp. 35–36, 189–190). Most conservative Protestant authors would feel he minimized the importance of sexual purity of mind.

2. In the 2006 Portraits of American Life Study and the 2005 Baylor Religion Survey, roughly three fourths of Americans in conservative Protestant denominations believed viewing porn to be *always* immoral, and that percentage increases to between 80 and 90 percent among those who believe the Bible is fully inspired, inerrant, or to be taken literally. Looking at more recent data, the 2012 New Family Structures Study and 2014 Relationships in America survey both showed only about 10 percent of Protestants who identify as "evangelical" or "fundamentalist" agreed that viewing porn is morally okay.

3. Other sociologists have observed this trend as well. In his study of religion and adolescent sexuality, Mark Regnerus (2007, 115) says that some conservative Protestant leaders teach that tolerating masturbation is preferable to making adolescents feel condemned and may actually provide a relatively harmless, solitary outlet for sexual energy that would otherwise be directed toward more risky (paired) forms of sexuality. Similarly, Sarah Diefendorf's (2015, 655–656) ethnographic account of evangelical men's accountability groups revealed that participants held conflicting opinions on masturbation. One man in Diefendorf's group expressed: "Simply pleasuring yourself without porn is fine, as long as you're not always relying on it or scheduling time around it." Others in her group, however, disagreed with this view and felt that masturbation in any form was bad. And last, in her book on evangelicals who frequent "Christian sexuality websites" (which are staunchly anti-porn), Kelsy Burke (2016, 46–47, 122–129) describes a good deal of ambivalence surrounding the subject of self-pleasure, with most affirming it was "wrong only sometimes." Some discouraged it, while others felt it was a gray issue, and still others expressed that it could afford a needed release for Christian singles, provided they are not objectifying others as is the case with porn or fantasy.

4. The New Family Structures Study (NFSS) and Relationships in America (RIA) survey both ask two questions about masturbation. First, they ask if someone has ever masturbated. Those who affirmed that they had ever masturbated were then asked about the last time they masturbated. In calculating the percentages for table 2.1, I included those who said they had "never" masturbated with the respondents who indicated their

frequency of masturbation, and thus, the percentages presented represent monthly masturbation in the total sample, not just for those who admit to masturbating ever.

5. Sewell (1992); see also Perry (2017b).

6. For reviews and seminal descriptions of the framing perspective, see Benford (1997), Benford and Snow (2000), Snow and Benford (1988), Snow et al. (1986, 2014).

7. An illustration of this principle, in his comparative study of conservative Protestant and Sunni Muslim schools, sociologist Jeff Guhin (2016) observed that even though both groups tend to be "creationists" theologically, only conservative Protestants tend to view evolutionary theory as a moral threat worth opposing, because it more explicitly violates something so uniquely central to their identity and daily practice (i.e., interpreting the Scriptures literally). By contrast, Sunni Muslims were less threatened by evolution, since they were more likely to value other boundaries like gender performance or practices likely prayer.

8. See, for example, Arterburn, Stoeker, and Yorkey (2002, 195–113); Challies (2010, 31–44); Daniels (2005, 185–192); Driscoll (2009, 27–30); Driscoll and Driscoll (2012, 181–185); Ethridge (2003, 39–43); Ethridge and Arterburn (2004, 43–50); Gallagher (2007, 37–48); Gresh (2001, 208–211); Harris (2003, 97–112); Jones and Jones (2007, 187–204); LaHaye and LaHaye (1998, 364–369); Penner and Penner (2003, 216–220); Smedes (1994, 137–142); Struthers (2009, 169–176); Weiss (2002, 75–92); Willingham (1999, 57–58); Winner (2005, 113–117).

9. LaHaye (1985, 188–189).

10. Bebbington (1989), Lindsay (2007), Malley (2004), Perry (2017b), Smith (2011), Sherkat and Ellison (1997).

11. Smith (2011, 4–5).

12. Driscoll (2009, 20). See also Driscoll and Driscoll (2012, 182), Gerali (2003, 89), Jones and Jones (2007, 200), Penner and Penner (2003, 219–220), Willingham (1999, 57), Winner (2005, 114–115).

13. Willingham (1999, 57).

14. Dobson (2006, 68).

15. Arterburn et al. (2002, 207).

16. Stafford, quoted in Winner (2005, 115).

17. Challies (2010, 37, 40).

18. LaHaye (1985, 81), emphasis added.

19. Driscoll (2009, 20), emphasis added.

20. Chester (2010a, 91), emphasis added.

21. Jones and Jones (2007, 200).

22. Harris (2003, 98), emphasis added.

23. Arterburn et al. (2002, 109), emphasis added.

24. One poignant example of this is found in Steve Gerali's *The Struggle* (2003), which argues that masturbation is a completely amoral practice

for Christians: "While Scripture speaks to almost every other sexual issue, it's silent on masturbation. So what do we do now? We make it a matter of wise choice" (26). Yet while Gerali argues throughout that masturbation is a morally neutral issue for Christians, viewing pornography (while masturbating), he argues, is completely out of bounds: "Looking at pornographic materials, having cyber-sex on the Internet, dialing up phone-sex numbers, and entertaining inappropriate sexual thoughts . . . cross the line" (114). But why? Because the Bible provides clearer instruction about the immorality of illicit sexual desire or "lust." Oftentimes, in conservative Protestant books on sexuality, particularly those specifically about pornography use, the connection between pornography and immorality is so taken for granted that authors may not mention it explicitly. Others, however, are quite explicit.

25. Driscoll and Driscoll (2012, 144).

26. Perry (2017b); see also Hunter (2010).

27. Gallagher (2007, 38).

28. As Mark and Grace Driscoll (2012, 144–145) explain, "The act of desiring the unclothed body of a person is not a sin. The issue is which person's body you are lusting after. If it is your spouse's, then you are simply making the Song of Songs sing again to God's glory and your mutual joy. If it is not your spouse's, then you are committing the sin of coveting. The Ten Commandments are clear that we should not commit adultery, including the lustful mental adultery of coveting our neighbor's spouse. Likewise, Jesus taught that sexual sins are committed not only in acts we commit, but also in our lustful thoughts."

29. Driscoll and Driscoll (2012, 184) follow a similar logic when outlining the possible circumstances in which masturbation would be permissible for married individuals: "At times when a couple cannot be together because of such things as distance, sickness, injury, or the six or seven weeks of abstention a woman's body requires after the birth of a child, masturbation can be an acceptable and helpful form of relief until normal sexual relations can be resumed. One question asked by the soldiers in our church is whether or not each spouse can masturbate while they are apart using images of their spouses in their mind, in a photo, or even through seeing each other live through the Internet. The answer is yes, providing, no one else is involved in any way, including viewing." Here again, the action of stimulating one's own genitals to the point of orgasm outside of the presence of one's spouse is not the primary issue, but whether one's desires are for someone else not including their spouse.

30. Challies (2010, 27).

31. Harris (2003, 99, 101).

32. Chester (2010a, 92).

33. For example, see Rossman (2009).

34. Thomas (2013).

35. See, for example, Barna Group (2016, 94–95), Chester (2010a, 26–28), Driscoll and Driscoll (2012, 139–142), Ferguson and Ferguson (2014, 38–40), Foubert (2016, 30–43), Gross and Luff (2010, 72–92), Park (2015, 19–24), Struthers (2009, 83–114).

36. Struthers (2009, 37). For works citing Struthers's work, see Driscoll and Driscoll (2012), Foubert (2017), Park (2015).

37. Struthers (2009, 106).

38. LaHaye and LaHaye (1998, 238).

39. Gallagher (2007, 44–45).

40. Dobson (2006, 69); also quoted in Challies (2010, 33), LaHaye (1985, 83).

41. For example, the authors in *Every Young Man's Battle* (Arterburn et al. 2002, 110–111) explained, "While Steve [Arterburn] believes masturbation nearly always involves sin, because of the shame associated with it, he prefers not to focus on the word sin, but on the heart. He has seen young men react negatively to harsh preaching about sexual sin, whereas a hopeful message about change and freedom, and honoring God and women, can result in positive change. The shaming approach only makes matters worse." See also Smedes (1994, 140–141), Struthers (2009, 174).

42. Peter Berger (1967, 121–124) famously identifies the Protestant Reformation (and the Renaissance) as the beginning of the secularization of the Western world. Unlike Catholics who were more likely to stress the physicality of faith and the "enchantment" of all life, Protestants were more likely to view God and spiritual things as "otherworldly."

43. See Winchester (2008, 2016).

44. As reformed Baptist pastor and author John Piper (2002, 33–34) explained to other pastors, "Why Christians do what they do is just as important as what they do. Bad motives ruin good acts. . . . Therefore, we (pastors) must not be content that our people are doing good things. We must labor to see that they do good things from God-exalting motives."

Chapter 3

1. See, for example, Chester (2010b, 53–54) and Driscoll (2009, 8).

2. Erickson (2013), Grudem (1994), Ryrie (1999).

3. Grudem (1994, 506).

4. Kilpatrick (2006, 122).

5. Powlison (2005, 84).

6. Powlison (2005, 84n6).

7. Yancey (2003, 81).

8. Barna Group (2016, 122).

9. The fall of celebrity Christian pastor Mark Driscoll, culminating in 2014, would be an exception to this trend, since he was asked to resign from his various leadership roles primarily for being prideful and overbearing. But his ministry also makes my point, since one could also argue that his rise to fame was due in large part to his no-nonsense, tell-it-like-it-is,

hyper-masculine attitude toward preaching and ministry. Had his ministry been characterized by sexual indiscretions, it would have ended much sooner.

10. One famous recent example was in 2014, when the registry of Ashley Madison, an online dating service that supposedly arranges extramarital affairs, was leaked and found to include around 400 Christian pastors. Southern Baptist research strategist Ed Stetzer went on record, stating that he thought the 400 pastors would soon resign in disgrace. While we have no way of knowing whether the pastors resigned, the assumption of Stetzer and others that those who were found out would (or should) resign is telling.

11. Driscoll and Driscoll (2012, 123–138).

12. Rossman (2009).

13. See Diefendorf's (2015) fascinating ethnography of evangelical men's accountability groups.

14. Powlison (2005, 97).

15. Piper (1995, 331).

16. Driscoll (2009, 8–9).

17. See Grubbs and Perry (2018) for a systematic review of this literature. See also individual studies: Diefendorf (2015); Edger (2009); Grubbs, Exline, et al. (2015); Grubbs, Stauner, et al. (2015); Grubbs, Volk, et al. (2015); Grubbs et al. (2017); Kwee, Dominguez, and Ferrell (2007); Nelson, Padilla-Walker, and Carroll (2010); and Short, Kasper, and Wetternick (2015).

18. Patterson and Price (2012).

19. Published in 2013, the *Diagnostic and Statistical Manual of Mental Disorders* (*DSM-5*) serves as a universal authority for psychiatric diagnosis. Sex addiction was actually included in the *DSM-III* in 1987, and was removed from the *DSM-IV* in 1994. See Regnerus (2017).

20. Hardy et al. (2013); Perry (2016); Perry and Schleifer (2018a, 2018b); Wright (2013); Wright, Bae, and Funk (2013).

21. See Abell, Steenbergh, and Boivin (2006); Bradley et al. (2016); Grubbs, Exline, et al. (2015); Kwee et al. (2007); and Levert (2007). And while not the focus of her study, Kelsy Burke (2016) also makes this observation about evangelical Christians' equating habitual porn use with "addiction." Another study (Hecker et al. 1995) showed that Christian therapists are also more likely to diagnose their patients with sex addiction.

22. Baltazar et al. (2010).

23. Short et al. (2015). For a discussion of "scrupulosity disorder," see Miller and Hedges (2008).

24. Grubbs et al. (2017).

25. Grubbs, Stauner, et al. (2015); Grubbs, Volk, et al. (2015).

26. See Perry (2017c).

27. See Perry (2018a).

28. Baier and Wright (2001), Johnson et al. (2000).

29. For example, in several longitudinal studies, sociologist Arland Thornton and his colleagues (Thornton, Axinn, and Hill 1992; Thornton and Camburn 1989) found that young persons who engage in nonmarital sex and cohabitation showed lower levels of religious participation over time. And in studies using panel data from the National Longitudinal Study of Adolescent Health, sociologists Mark Regnerus, Jeremy Uecker, and others (Regnerus and Smith 2005; Regnerus and Uecker 2006; Uecker, Regnerus, and Vaaler 2007) have shown that adolescents who participate in premarital sex show declines in religious service attendance and importance of religious faith later on.

30. For example, see Regnerus (2007, 53–54), Regnerus and Uecker (2011, 232), Smith and Denton (2005, 236–237), Smith and Snell (2009, 84), Uecker et al. (2007, 1684).

31. In this analysis I include those who were listed as evangelical or Black Protestant in the 2006 PALS. Including mainline Protestants in the models yielded substantively similar findings, possibly because mainline Protestants also tend to be opposed to porn use in national surveys (see Patterson and Price 2012). Including Catholics in the models largely washed out the effects most likely because there is a great deal of variance among Catholics in terms of traditional versus more progressive views of sexuality. The fact that the effects are highly statistically significant (all at 0.001 or higher) when *only* conservative Protestants are included in models is evidence for the robustness of the effect of porn use on religiosity for this group.

32. These analyses and findings are similar to those used by myself and George M. Hayward in a related study (Perry and Hayward 2017).

33. Kelsy Burke (2016, 97–98) describes similar accounts of Christians in online forums recounting how God delivered them from pornography addiction and now they walk more faithfully.

Chapter 4

1. See the meta-analytic reviews of research on gender differences in sexuality conducted by Petersen and Hyde (2010, 2011), as well as Chivers et al. (2004, 2010).

2. For example, Article IV of the 2017 Nashville Statement states, "We affirm that divinely ordained differences between male and female reflect God's original creation design and are meant for human good and human flourishing. We deny that such differences are a result of the Fall or are a tragedy to be overcome." See https://cbmw.org/nashville-statement/.

3. For example, Article VII of the 2017 Nashville Statement states, "We affirm that self-conception as male or female should be defined by God's holy purposes in creation and redemption as revealed in Scripture." Note that God's holy purposes in creating two genders are shown in "creation"

(Genesis 2:18) and "redemption" (Ephesians 5:22–33). See https://cbmw.org/nashville-statement/.

4. Though conservative Protestants' understanding and theology of transgender issues is still developing, conservative Protestant leaders have issued statements recently affirming that God intended for there to be two genders corresponding to male and female reproductive structures. For example, Article V of the 2017 Nashville Statement reads, "We affirm that the differences between male and female reproductive structures are integral to God's design for self-conception as male or female. We deny that physical anomalies or psychological conditions nullify the God-appointed link between biological sex and self-conception as male or female." See https://cbmw.org/nashville-statement/.

5. The Nashville Statement was written and published in the fall of 2017 as a declaration among conservative Protestants regarding their biblical perspective on gender, sexual orientation, and transgender men and women. It was affirmed by conservative Protestant pastors and leaders across a broad theological spectrum. Original signatories included several former presidents of the Southern Baptist Convention, James Dobson, and John Piper; presidents from a broad swath of Bible colleges and seminaries (including Dallas Theological Seminary, Moody Bible Institute, Southern Baptist Theological Seminary, Southern Evangelical Seminary, Union University, Southwestern Baptist Theological Seminary, Gateway Seminary, Southeastern Baptist Theological Seminary, New Orleans Baptist Theological Seminary, Phoenix Seminary, Union School of Theology); the president of the Gospel Coalition; and others. And according to the website, over 20,000 others had signed the Nashville Statement as of December 2017. Before the Nashville Statement, a previous document called the Danvers Statement (1987) had been affirmed as the primary statement of complementarian belief. Similar to the Nashville Statement, the Danvers Statement's Affirmation 1 declares, "Adam and Eve were created in God's image, equal before God as persons and distinct in their manhood and womanhood." See https://cbmw.org/about/danvers-statement/.

6. Gallagher and Smith (1999); see also Bartkowski's (2001) and Gallagher's (2003) more extensive study of evangelical identity and gendered family life, as well as W. Bradford Wilcox's (2004) study of conservative Protestant men.

7. See, for example, Grudem (2012).

8. See Bielo (2014) for an argument about Driscoll representing more mainstream conservative Protestant masculinity. See Johnson (2015, 2018) for an analysis suggesting Driscoll represents a particular extreme within conservative Protestantism. For evangelical articles condemning Driscoll's brand of complementarianism, see https://www.christianitytoday.com/news/2014/august/

mark-driscoll-crude-comments-william-wallace-mars-hill.html and https://
www.christianitytoday.com/news/2015/june/distraction-down-under-
hillsong-mark-driscoll-conference.html.

9. Getting married in order to avoid struggling with lust is a common reason
given for young Christian men's pursuing marriage at an early age. See
popular blogger Douglas Wilson's "7 Reasons Young Men Should Marry
Before Their 23rd Birthday," https://dougwils.com/s7-engaging-the-culture/
7-reasons-young-men-marry-23rd-birthday.html. Elsewhere, Christian
sociologist Mark Regnerus in 2009 wrote a cover story for the evangelical
flagship *Christianity Today* in which he advocates for early marriage, in
part so as to help young Christians stay sexually chaste; see http://www.
christianitytoday.com/ct/2009/august/16.22.html. His argument was
responded to and supported by several conservative Protestant leaders,
including Al Mohler (https://albertmohler.com/2009/08/03/the-case-for-
early-marriage/) and David Gushee (http://www.christianitytoday.com/ct/
2009/august/18.29.html).

10. Challies (2010, 51).

11. Arterburn, Stoeker, and Yorkey (2002, 95).

12. Stephen Arterburn cites these numbers in the foreword to *Every Woman's
Battle* (Ethridge 2003, xi).

13. Ethridge (2003, 1).

14. Ethridge (2008, 2014).

15. Ethridge (2003, 13), emphasis added.

16. Ethridge and Arterburn (2004, 36), emphasis added.

17. Ethridge (2003, 14).

18. Ethridge (2003, 26).

19. LaHaye (1982, 180), for example, acknowledged, "Pornography of course
is not limited to boys. It also corrupts the morals of girls and sears their
sensibilities. But due to a psychological difference between men and
women, it is more harmful to boys than girls." See also Harris (2003,
81) and Chester (2010a, 11).

20. These percentages are nearly identical when I look at respondents who
affiliate with "Evangelical" denominations according to the "RELTRAD"
classification scheme proposed by Steensland et al. (2000).

21. We can also see this reasoning repeated in conservative Protestant books
on pornography use. William Struthers (2009, 11), in *Wired for Intimacy*,
explains why his book is targeted toward men, even as he recognizes more
women are consuming porn: "While pornography ravages and destroys the
lives of both men and women, this book and the research within focuses
almost exclusively on pornography's impact on men. It is true that women
are increasingly becoming consumers of pornography, but there is little
doubt that it is primarily men who are hooked on it. And the reasons that
women view pornography are very different than the reasons men do.
Men seem to be wired in such a way that pornography hijacks the proper

functioning of their brains and has a long-lasting effect on their thoughts and lives." Struthers's use of the passive voice suggests that he thinks that God has uniquely designed ("wired") men to be simply more susceptible to porn's addictive and destructive effects than are women. Consequently, even if women are increasing their porn consumption, which Struthers acknowledges, men's porn viewing deserves greater attention.

22. Petersen and Hyde (2010, 2011).

23. Ogas and Gaddam (2011).

24. Several pornography-recovery manuals affirm these thoughts among women. While Joshua Harris (2003, 81), in his book *Sex Is Not the Problem (Lust Is)*, focuses almost exclusively on men's visual temptations, he acknowledges, "[M]any women struggle with lust in what you might call traditionally male ways—the temptation to view pornography, to masturbate, to focus on the intense physical desire for sex. These women are often hindered in their fight against lust because they're consumed with shame over the particular ways they struggle." Harris goes on to share some quotes from women he had spoken with in his church: " 'It feels like a guy thing to be battling,' one girl said. . . . Another woman named Kathryn said lust seemed like a taboo subject among her Christian girlfriends. 'Sometimes I get the distinct impression that I'm the only Christian female with this problem,' she explained." Similarly, in *Closing the Window*, Tim Chester (2010a, 12) provides a few brief quotes illustrating how "It can be especially hard for women to talk about an issue that is often seen as a 'male weakness.' " He quotes one woman who explains, "I would really like it to be acknowledged that [porn] can be a problem for women as well as men. . . . These issues are always assumed to be gender specific and, as such, it makes it even harder for women to admit when they're struggling in these areas." And elsewhere, quoting another, "I've never told another Christian. I think we're told so often that this isn't a problem for women and it makes it even harder to admit that actually it is a problem for me." In all these accounts, it is not only the sin of pornography use that haunts these women but also the violating of the normative expectations for what "normal" women *should* be struggling with.

25. See Assad's talk at http://qideas.org/videos/the-porn-epidemic/?inf_contact_key=ea3oef19bofdocd58e2ocebb812a16d67574f71875bbe4e1e384064bocc7b861.

26. Barna Group (2016, 58).

27. See note 25 for source of Assad's talk.

28. Barna Group (2016, 59).

29. Burke (2016, 57).

30. Arterburn et al. (2002, 109).

31. Ethridge (2003, 43).

32. Ogas and Gaddam (2011, 68–70).

33. Chivers et al. (2010).

34. See Arterburn et al. (2002, 110–111), Dobson (2006, 69), Smedes (1994, 140–141), Struthers (2009, 174).
35. Ethridge (2003, 41).
36. While this pastor articulated this philosophy in his own words, he later attributed this story to Lauren Winner's book *Real Sex*. I tracked down the story where she explains:

> One pastor I know told me he doesn't have a blanket rule on masturbation. "Unmarried men," he said, "are either going to masturbate or have wet dreams, because sperm has to get out somehow. So occasional—not habitual, but occasional— masturbation is probably OK. But I would urge a married man not to masturbate—for to do so would really be an act of infidelity to his wife." For women, this pastor reverses things. "Many married women," he says, "especially but not exclusively newly married women, may need to spend some time figuring their own bodies out," if only so that they can figure out what they like and how they like it—and teach their husbands how to make them feel good. (Winner 2005, 115–116)

37. This is such an obvious point that it seems unnecessary to document it, but readers can see the heterosexual standard laid out explicitly within the complementarian framework provided by the Nashville Statement (2017) cited in note 5 above.
38. LaHaye (1985, 196).
39. LaHaye (1985, 89–90).
40. For example, in *Porn-Again Christian*, Mark Driscoll (2009, 16) writes, "Lusting eyes may begin with a magazine, web site, or video and continue to view more magazines, web sites, or videos until they become bored and then descend into strip clubs, prostitutes, and/ or easy women, which will eventually become boring and lead to orgies . . . pedophilia, and wherever else a crooked heart can venture." References to "orgies" and "pedophilia" here likely hint at Driscoll's expectation that porn-addicted Christian men will be tempted to cross heterosexual boundaries.
41. Driscoll (2009, 31).
42. Barna Group (2016, 59).

Chapter 5
1. In order to preserve anonymity, not only are the names pseudonyms but also the stories are taken from different focus groups and several important details have been changed.
2. For systematic reviews and meta-analyses of this literature, see Campbell and Kohut (2017), Manning (2006), Newstrom and Harris (2016), Rasmussen (2016), Wright et al. (2017). For specific studies about

pornography's relationship to relationship stability, see: Perry (2018c), Perry and Davis (2017), and Perry and Schleifer (2018c).

3. For a thorough analysis of these trends in the GSS, see Doran and Price (2014).

4. In 1994, the GSS also asked respondents whether they had viewed pornography in a theater or on a VCR in the previous year. Married men who affirmed they had done this were roughly 20% less likely than abstainers to report being "very happy" in their marriage (47% compared to 66%, respectively). Married women were not significantly different in their marital happiness for this measure.

5. In their meta-analysis of cross-sectional, longitudinal, and experimental studies of porn use and relationship satisfaction, Wright et al. (2017, 336) conclude: "While there may be a reciprocal element to these dynamics (i.e., lower sexual and relational satisfaction leading to pornography consumption), the convergence of results across cross-sectional survey, longitudinal survey, and experimental results points to an overall negative effect of pornography on men's sexual and relational satisfaction." Several longitudinal studies were cited in the previous note. For experimental studies linking porn use with lower relationship satisfaction or satisfaction with one's partner, see Kenrick, Gutierres, and Goldberg (1989); Lambert et al. (2012); Weaver, Masland, and Zillmann (1984); Zillmann and Bryant (1988a, 1988b).

6. See Doran and Price (2014), Perry (2017d), Wright et al. (2017), Yucel and Gassanov (2010).

7. Wright (2011). See also Sun et al. (2016).

8. Maddox, Rhodes, and Markman (2011); Willoughby et al. (2016).

9. Bergner and Bridges (2002); Bridges, Bergner, and Hesson-McInnis (2003); Stewart and Szymanksi (2012); Zitzman and Butler (2009).

10. See the interviews in Paul (2005, 138–171).

11. Muusses, Kerkhof, and Finkenauer (2015) were the first I read to articulate this insight. See also findings from Peter and Valkenburg (2009).

12. Doran and Price (2014).

13. Perry and Whitehead (2018); Wright et al. (2017); Yucel and Gassanov (2010).

14. Perry and Whitehead (2018).

15. Perry (2018b).

16. Perry (2016).

17. The number of "fundamentalist" respondents to this question was too small to be helpful here, thus I only looked at those who indicated they were "evangelical" Protestants.

18. See http://www.covenanteyes.com/2015/01/19/using-porn-is-cheating/.

19. See http://www.covenanteyes.com/2013/09/03/shattered-a-letter-to-wives-after-the-betrayal-of-pornography/.

20. See http://www.covenanteyes.com/2016/05/10/betrayal-trauma-the-side-of-pornography-use-no-one-is-talking-about/.
21. See http://www.covenanteyes.com/2014/08/11/micahs-post/.
22. Arterburn and Martinkus (2014); Stoeker and Allen (2008); Stoeker, Stoeker, and Yorkey (2010).
23. See, for example, the discussions on Focus on the Family at https://www.focusonthefamily.com/family-q-and-a/relationships-and-marriage/pornography-as-grounds-for-divorce; Covenant Eyes at http://www.covenanteyes.com/2015/10/08/porn-use-as-grounds-for-divorce-how-my-opinion-changed/; and Pure Life Ministries at http://www.purelifeministries.org/blog/is-his-pornography-use-grounds-for-divorce.
24. See https://www.focusonthefamily.com/family-q-and-a/relationships-and-marriage/pornography-as-grounds-for-divorce.
25. See also http://www.purelifeministries.org/blog/is-his-pornography-use-grounds-for-divorce.
26. See http://www.covenanteyes.com/2015/10/08/porn-use-as-grounds-for-divorce-how-my-opinion-changed/.
27. Bridges and Morokoff (2011); Campbell and Kohut (2017); Newstrom and Harris (2016); Poulsen, Busby, and Galovan (2013).

Chapter 6

1. Gardner (2011) touches on some of this in her analysis of evangelical abstinence campaigns.
2. The most influential of these emerging institutions has likely been the software company Covenant Eyes. Founded by a successful businessman and Christian, Ron DeHaas, who is the president and CEO. According to DeHaas, Covenant Eyes was worth over 12 million dollars in 2011; see https://tedmiller3.com/about/. Covenant Eyes owns a patent on monitoring non-http protocols, and it was the first company to market products using machine-learning artificial intelligence to filter pornography. See https://www.corpmagazine.com/celebrating-growth-in-michigan-continues-with-this-years-economic-bright-spots/.
3. Lindsay (2007) identifies conservative Protestants preference for pragmatism particularly when it involves opportunities for political power. For discussions of conservative Protestants' commitment to pietistic idealism and biblicism, see Hunter (2010), Perry (2017b), Smith (1998).
4. For example, see Williams and Blackburn (1996).
5. My descriptions of each approach to Christian counseling are taken from Greggo and Sisemore (2012), Johnson (2010), and an article written by Tim Keller in 2004 found at http://www.nlcwh.org/files/counseling_toolbox/definition/4_models_of_counseling_in_pastoral_ministry_tim_keller_2.pdf.
6. The word "sufficient" serves as a code of sorts for those in the Christian counseling community. To those interested in pursuing a counseling

degree at a particular seminary, a description of the Bible as "sufficient" for counseling serves as a signal that the particular program does not advocate an integrationist approach.

7. For instance, as I was writing this chapter in September 2017, The Southern Baptist Theological Seminary (TSBTS), the flagship seminary for the Southern Baptist Convention, fired longtime professor Eric Johnson, the seminary's lone remaining proponent for the "Christian psychology" approach. By most accounts, the firing was a response to growing pressure from Heath Lambert, an unyielding advocate for the biblical counseling approach, which now completely dominates the faculty at TSBTS and most other seminaries affiliated with the Southern Baptist Convention.

8. Gresh (2001, 15).

9. Gresh (2001, 67).

10. Gresh (2001, 118–119).

11. Arterburn, Stoeker, and Yorkey (2002, 140–141).

12. Arterburn et al. (2002, 141–142). See pp. 145–146 for their discussion of "bouncing the eyes."

13. Weiss (2002, 9–10), emphasis added.

14. Tim Challies (2010, 70), for example, concludes his book, "[A]re you ready for the Great Concluding Insight? You need to stop looking at pornography. And you need to stop masturbating. Right now. As in, this instant. Not tomorrow. Today."

15. Arterburn et al. (2002, 143).

16. Arterburn et al. (2002, 175–176).

17. A strong proponent of the reformed, "biblical counseling" model, Heath Lambert (2013, 16) admits that in some extreme cases, men need to take steps to stop viewing pornography *before* they can be transformed spiritually. He writes, "Some of you will be so submerged in a pornographic lifestyle that the gospel teaching at the beginning (of the book) will best take root after you have taken some steps to remove porn from your life." But lest someone misunderstand that he thinks actions themselves can transform someone's sinful heart, Lambert quickly notes that these steps will not be a durable solution for their pornography habit, which only comes from believing the gospel. "Taking steps like the ones suggested [later in the book] will never be the long-term fix for your struggle, but doing so can create some space for you to be able to consider the gospel."

18. Challies (2010, 46).

19. Lambert (2013, 13).

20. Challies (2010, 19)

21. Piper (1995, 338).

22. Chester (2010b, 28).

23. Chester (2010b, 65–66).

24. For example, when explaining why Christians struggle to see genuine transformation in their lives, Chester (2010b, 41, 43) describes how he tried to change by expressing his commitment to sexual purity with a vow. "[W]e often try to change in the wrong way. Frustrated by my lust, I wrote out a vow. This was it. Never again. I noted the date and imagined looking back in months to come with satisfaction that my struggle was history. But it didn't last long. It didn't work. It couldn't work. . . . External activities can't change us, Jesus says, because sin comes from within, from our hearts. Our rituals might change our behavior for a while, but they can't change our hearts. And so they can't bring true and lasting holiness. We need heart change."

25. Chester (2010b, 46–47).

26. Chester (2010b, 140).

27. Chester (2010b, 69–70).

28. Also advocating this view, a group of pastors (in Introduction to Challies 2010, 8) declare confidently in *Sexual Detox* that reordering our beliefs and values not only makes victory over porn possible but also *inevitable*: "The bottom line is that when we believe in our hearts that the biblical view of sexuality is better than our sinful view of sex, we won't cease to be tempted, but we will stop indulging in sin. When we believe that the joy of obedience and the rewards of purity are greater, the draw of sexual sin will be lesser. When we believe all that God has planned for us and our sexuality we will, in Christ, become conquerors over temptation."

29. Chester (2010b, 134).

30. Lambert (2013, 16)

31. Challies (2010, 70).

32. Challies (2010, 71–72, 76).

33. Challies (2010, 81).

34. Rasmussen and Bierman (2016, 2017).

35. Perry (2017a).

36. Lewis (1942, ch. 4).

Conclusion

1. Some commentators argue that the Apostle Paul is describing a sort of spiritual battle that takes place in unbelievers' lives before they have the Holy Spirit. But this is unlikely, since (1) the Apostle Paul has already indicated in Romans 3:10–12 that unbelievers do not want to obey God, and thus, there would be no reason for them to be internally conflicted; and (2) Paul intentionally and abruptly changes tenses in Romans 7 from past tense (vv. 4–13) to the present tense (vv. 14–24) and thus it is more likely that he is describing his present struggle as a Christian.

2. Chaves (2010, 1).

3. Regnerus and Smith (2005); Regnerus and Uecker (2006); Thornton and Camburn (1989); Thornton, Axinn, and Hill (1992); Uecker, Regnerus, and Vaaler (2007).

4. Fernandez, Tee, and Fernandez (2017).

5. For example, see Perry (2017d, 2018b, 2018c) and Perry and Davis (2017).

6. This is a separate issue that I have not waded into in this book, but in thinking of the potentially negative personal and societal consequences of pornography, there is obviously the ethical dilemma of mainstream pornography's undeniably male-centered, misogynistic, and racist content (Collins 2000, 135–143; Jensen 2007; Kimmel 2008). Most of us would find it morally problematic for major studios like HBO, Showtime, or Netflix to make and broadcast shows that eroticize the exploitation and abuse of women, or fetishize minorities according to popular stereotypes (e.g., the hyper-sexed black Jezebel or the submissive Asian woman). Does our moral evaluation of those things suddenly become more positive when people are masturbating to it as internet pornography? I do not write this to suggest banning such pornography, as I've stated previously, but neither should we ignore the inconsistency in what we do and don't tolerate as a society.

7. Analyzing attitudes toward pornography's availability since the 1970s. Lykke and Cohen (2015) show that tolerance toward pornography has steadily increased over the past four decades, especially for men.

8. As of December 2017, Arkansas, Oklahoma, Utah, Virginia, South Dakota, and Tennessee had all passed resolutions declaring pornography a public health crisis, and resolutions have been considered in a number of others, including Pennsylvania, Missouri, Georgia, South Carolina, and elsewhere.

9. See the post on these state resolutions by NoFap at https://www.nofap.com/news/rnc-porn-platform/, and Fight the New Drug at https://fightthenewdrug.org/here-are-the-states-that-have-passed-resolutions/.

10. Barna Group (2016, 6).

11. Ogas and Gaddam (2011, 7–8).

12. In a 2010 piece for CNN, Gross argued that "On the internet, streaming video, credit-card verification sites, Web referral rings and video technology like Flash all can be traced back to innovations designed to share, and sell, adult content. See http://www.cnn.com/2010/TECH/04/23/porn.technology/index.html.

13. Dreher (2017, 195, 215).

14. Dreher (2017, 226–236).

15. See, for example, Carr (2010), Charlton (2014), and Newport (2016). For arguments from conservative Christians along these lines, see Foster (1981) and Reinke (2017).

16. Rossman (2009).

17. Powlison (2005, 84n 6).

18. Lewis (1943, 87, 102).

Appendix A

1. For a more exhaustive discussion of the Relationships in America (RIA) survey, see Litchi et al. (2014). The RIA survey was distributed to a national probability sample of 15,738 adults between the ages of 18 and 60 in January and February 2014. Data collection was sponsored by the Austin Institute for the Study of Family and Culture and conducted by the research firm GfK. GfK recruited the first online research panel that is representative of the U.S. population, called the KnowledgePanel. Members in the KnowledgePanel are randomly recruited by telephone and mail surveys. Those households are provided with access to the internet and computer hardware, if necessary. Unlike other internet research panels sampling only individuals with internet access who volunteer for research, this panel was based on a sampling frame that included both listed and unlisted numbers and those without a landline telephone; it was not limited to current internet users or computer owners, and it did not accept self-selected volunteers. The main survey completion rate for the RIA survey instrument was 62%. Cases in the RIA sample were assigned a weight based on the sampling design and their probability of being selected, ensuring a sample that was representative of American adults ages 18 to 60. These sample weights are used in all analyses with these data.

2. On young people being reluctant to discuss porn use, see Regnerus (2007) and Smith and Denton (2005). On women underreporting their porn use, see Ogas and Gaddam (2011).

3. Rasmussen et al. (2018).

4. Jerolmack and Khan (2014)

5. Burke (2016), DeRogatis (2015), Gardner (2011), Regnerus (2007), Thomas (2013, 2016).

6. See Sarah Diefendorf's rich data gained from sitting in on men's accountability groups (2015).

REFERENCES

Abell, Jesse, Timothy Steenbergh, and Michael Boivin. 2006. "Cyberporn Use in the Context of Religiosity." *Journal of Psychology and Theology* 34: 165–171.

Allen, Mike, David D'Alessio, and Keri Brezgel. 1995. "A Meta-Analysis Summarizing the Effects of Pornography II: Aggression after Exposure." *Human Communication Research* 22: 258–283.

Allen, Mike, David D'Alessio, and Tara M. Emmers-Sommer. 1999. "Reactions of Criminal Sexual Offenders to Pornography: A Meta-Analytic Summary." *Annals of the International Communication Association* 22(1): 139–169.

Allen, Mike, Tara M. Emmers, Lisa Gebhardt, and Mary A. Giery. 1995. "Exposure to Pornography and Rape Myth Acceptance." *Journal of Communication* 45(1): 5–26.

Allen, Walter. 1962. "The Writer and the Frontiers of Tolerance." In *"To Deprave and Corrupt . . . " Original Studies in the Nature and Definition of "Obscenity,"* edited by John Chandos, 139–152. New York: Association.

Arterburn, Stephen, and Jason B. Martinkus. 2014. *Worthy of Her Trust: What You Need to Do to Rebuild Sexual Integrity and Win Her Back.* Colorado Springs, CO: Water Brook.

Arterburn, Stephen, Fred Stoeker, and Mike Yorkey. 2000. *Every Man's Battle: Winning the War on Sexual Temptation One Victory at a Time.* Colorado Springs, CO: Water Brook.

Arterburn, Stephen, Fred Stoeker, and Mike Yorkey. 2002. *Every Young Man's Battle: Strategies for Victory in the Real World of Sexual Temptation.* Colorado Springs, CO: Water Brook.

Attwood, Feona. 2005. "What Do People Do with Porn? Qualitative Research into the Consumption, Use, and Experience of Pornography and Other Sexually Explicit Media." *Sexuality & Culture* 9(2): 65–86.

Attwood, Feona. 2006. "Sexed Up: Theorizing the Sexualization of Culture." *Sexualities* 9(1): 77–94.

Attwood, Feona. 2011. "The Paradigm Shift: Pornography Research, Sexualization and Extreme Images." *Sociology Compass* 5(1): 13–22.

Baier, Colin J., and Bradley R. E. Wright. 2001. "If You Love Me, Keep My Commandments: A Meta-Analysis of the Effect of Religion on Crime." *Journal of Research in Crime & Delinquency* 38(1): 3–21.

Baltazar, Alina, Herbert W. Helm Jr., Duane McBride, Gary Hopkins, and John V. Stevens Jr. 2010. "Internet Pornography Use in the Context of External and Internal Religiosity." *Journal of Psychology and Theology* 38: 32–40.

Barna Group. 2016. *The Porn Phenomenon: The Impact of Pornography In the Digital Age*. Ventura, CA: Barna Group.

Bartkowski, John P. 2001. *Remaking the Godly Marriage: Gender Negotiation in Evangelical Families*. New Brunswick, NJ: Rutgers University Press.

Bebbington, David W. 1989. *Evangelicalism in Modern Britain: A History from the 1730s to the 1980s*. New York: Routledge.

Benford, Robert D. 1997. "An Insider's Critique of the Social Movement Framing Perspective." *Sociological Inquiry* 67(4): 409–430.

Benford, Robert D., and David A. Snow. 2000. "Framing Processes and Social Movements: An Overview and Assessment." *Annual Review of Sociology* 26: 611–639.

Berger, Peter. 1967. *The Sacred Canopy: Elements of a Sociological Theory of Religion*. New York: Anchor.

Bergner, Raymond M., and Ana J. Bridges. 2002. "The Significance of Heavy Pornography Involvement for Romantic Partners: Research and Clinical Implications." *Journal of Sex & Marital Therapy* 28: 193–206.

Bielo, James S. 2014. "Act Like Men: Social Engagement and Evangelical Masculinity." *Journal of Contemporary Religion* 29(2): 233–248.

Bradley, David F., Joshua B. Grubbs, Alex Uzdavines, Julie J. Exline, and Kenneth I. Pargament. 2016. "Perceived Addiction to Internet Pornography among Religious Believers and Nonbelievers." Sexual Addiction & Compulsivity 23(2–3): 225–243.

Bridges, Ana J., Raymond M. Bergner, and Matthew Hesson-McInnis. 2003. "Romantic Partner's Use of Pornography: Its Significance for Women." *Journal of Sex & Marital Therapy* 29: 1–14.

Bridges, Ana J., and Patricia J. Morokoff. 2011. "Sexual Media Use and Relational Satisfaction in Heterosexual Couples." *Personal Relationships* 18: 562–585.

Burke, Kelsy. 2016. *Christians Under Covers: Evangelicals and Sexual Pleasure on the Internet*. Berkeley: University of California Press.

Buzzell, Timothy. 2005a. "The Effects of Sophistication, Access, and Monitoring on Use of Pornography in Three Technological Contexts." *Deviant Behavior* 26(2): 109–132.

Buzzell, Timothy. 2005b. "Demographic Characteristics of Persons Using Pornography in Three Technological Contexts." *Sexuality & Culture* 9(1): 28–48.

Campbell, Lorne, and Taylor Kohut. 2017. "The Use and Effects of Pornography in Romantic Relationships." *Current Opinion in Psychology* 13: 6–10.

Cannon, Ralph A., and Glenn D. Everett. 1958. "Sex and Smut on the Newstands." *Christianity Today*, February 17, pp. 5–8.

Carr, Nicholas. 2010. *The Shallows: What the Internet Is Doing to Our Brains.* New York: W. W. Norton.

Challies, Tim. 2010. *Sexual Detox: A Guide for Guys Who Are Sick of Porn.* Hudson, OH: Cruciform.

Chaves, Mark. 2010. "SSSR Presidential Address Rain Dances in the Dry Season: Overcoming the Religious Congruence Fallacy." *Journal for the Scientific Study of Religion* 49(1): 1–14.

Charlton, Bruce G. 2014. *Addicted to Distraction: Psychological Consequences of the Modern Mass Media.* Buckingham: University of Buckingham Press.

Chester, Tim. 2010a. *Closing the Window: Steps to Living Porn Free.* Downers Grove, IL: InterVarsity.

Chester, Tim. 2010b. *You Can Change: God's Transforming Power for Our Sinful Behavior and Negative Emotions.* Wheaton, IL: Crossway.

Chivers, Meredith L., Gerulf Rieger, Elizabeth Latty, and J. Michael Bailey. 2004. "A Sex Difference in the Specificity of Sexual Arousal." *Psychological Science* 15(11): 736–744.

Chivers, Meredith L., Michael C. Seto, Martin L. Lalumiere, Ellen Laan, and Teresa Grimbos. 2010. "Agreement of Self-Reported and Genital Measures of Sexual Arousal in Men and Women: A Meta-Analysis." *Archives of Sexual Behavior* 39(1): 5–56.

Cleath, Robert. L. 1975. "Pornography: Purulent Infection." *Christianity Today*, October 11, pp. 21–22.

Collins, Patricia Hill. 2000. *Black Feminist Thought: Knowledge, Consciousness, and the Politics of Empowerment.* 2nd. ed. New York: Routledge.

Connelly, John. 2012. "The Noble and the Base: Poland and the Holocaust." *The Nation*, November 14. https://www.thenation.com/article/noble-and-base-poland-and-holocaust/.

Covenant Eyes. 2015. "Pornography Statistics: 250+ Facts, Quotes, and Statistics about Pornography Use. 2015 Edition." http://www.covenanteyes.com/pornography-facts-and-statistics/.

Crouch, Andy. 2008. *Culture Making: Rediscovering our Creative Calling.* Downers Grove, IL: InterVarsity.

Cutrer, Corrie. 2016. "Parenting in a Porn-Saturated World." *Christianity Today*, June 30. https://www.christianitytoday.com/women/2016/june/parenting-in-porn-saturated-world-pornography-children-teen.html.

Daniels, Robert. 2005. *The War Within: Gaining Victory in the Battle for Sexual Purity.* Rev. ed. Wheaton, IL: Crossway.

Dawson, Joseph Martin. 1959. "The Problem of Censorship." *Christianity Today,* June 22, pp. 15–16.

DeRogatis, Amy. 2015. *Saving Faith: Sexuality and Salvation in American Evangelicalism.* New York: Oxford University Press.

Diamond, Milton. 2009. "Pornography, Public Acceptance and Sex Related Crime: A Review." *International Journal of Law and Psychiatry* 32(5): 304–314.

Diamond, Milton, Eva Jozifkova, and Petr Weiss. 2011. "Pornography and Sex Crimes in the Czech Republic." *Archives of Sexual Behavior* 40(5): 1037–1043.

Diefendorf, Sarah. 2015. "After the Wedding Night: Sexual Abstinence and Masculinities Over the Life Course." *Gender & Society* 29(5): 647–669.

Dines, Gail. 1998. "King Kong and the White Woman: Hustler Magazine and The Demonization of Black Masculinity." *Violence Against Women* 4(3): 291–307.

Dines, Gail. 2006. "The White Man's Burden: Gonzo Pornography and the Construction of Black Masculinity." *Yale Journal of Law & Feminism* 18: 283–298.

Dines, Gail. 2010. *Pornland: How Porn Has Hijacked Our Sexuality.* Boston: Beacon.

Dobson, James. 2006. *Preparing for Adolescence: How to Survive the Coming Years of Change.* Grand Rapids, MI: Revel.

Doran, Kirk, and Joseph Price. 2014. "Pornography and Marriage." *Journal of Family and Economic Issues* 35: 489–498.

Doring, Nicola M. 2009. "The Internet's Impact on Sexuality: A Critical Review of 15 Years of Research." *Computers in Human Behavior* 25: 1089–1101.

Dreger, Alice. 2015. *Galileo's Middle Finger: Heretics, Activists, and the Search for Justice in Science.* New York: Penguin.

Dreher, Rod. 2017. *The Benedict Option: A Strategy for Christians in a Post-Christian Nation.* New York: Sentinel.

Driscoll, Mark. 2009. *Porn-again Christian: A Frank Discussion on Pornography & Masturbation.* Seattle: Resurgent.

Driscoll, Mark, and Grace Driscoll. 2012. *Real Marriage: The Truth About Sex, Friendship & Life Together.* Nashville, TN: Thomas Nelson.

Dworkin, Andrea. 1979. *Pornography: Men Possessing Women.* New York: Penguin.

Edger, Kailla. 2009. "The Lived Experiences of Evangelical Christian Men Who Self-Identify as Sexual Addicts: An Existential-Phenomenological Study." *Sexual Addiction & Compulsivity* 4: 289–323.

Erickson, Millard J. 2013. *Christian Theology.* 3rd ed. Grand Rapids, MI: Baker.

Ethridge, Shannon. 2003. *Every Woman's Battle: Discovering God's Plan for Sexual and Emotional Fulfillment.* Colorado Springs, CO: Water Brook.

Ethridge, Shannon. 2008. *The Sexually Confident Wife: Connecting with Your Husband, Mind, Body, and Spirit.* New York: Broadway.

Ethridge, Shannon. 2014. *The Passion Principles: Celebrating Sexual Freedom in Marriage*. Nashville, TN: W Publishing Group.

Ethridge, Shannon, and Stephen Arterburn. 2004. *Every Young Woman's Battle: Guarding Your Mind, Heart, and Body in a Sex-Saturated World*. Colorado Springs, CO: Water Brook.

Falwell, Jerry. 1980. *Listen, America!* Garden City, NY: Doubleday.

Ferguson, Jen, and Craig Ferguson. 2014. *Pure Eyes, Clean Heart: A Couple's Journey to Freedom From Pornography*. Grand Rapids, MI: Discovery House.

Fernandez, David Paul, Eugene Y. J. Tee, and Elaine Frances Fernandez. 2017. "Do Cyber Pornography Use Inventory-9 Scores Reflect Actual Compulsivity in Internet Pornography Use? Exploring the Role of Abstinence Effort." *Sexual Addiction & Compulsivity* 24(3): 156–179.

Festinger, Leon. 1957. *A Theory of Cognitive Dissonance*. Stanford, CA: Stanford University Press.

Foster, Richard. 1981. *Freedom of Simplicity*. New York: HarperCollins.

Foster, Richard. 1985. *The Challenge of the Disciplined Life: Christian Reflections on Money, Sex, & Power*. New York: HarperCollins.

Foubert, John D. 2016. *How Pornography Harms: What Today's Teens, Young Adults, Parents, and Pastors Need to Know*. Bloomington, IN: LifeRich.

Gallagher, Sally K. 2003. *Evangelical Identity & Gendered Family Life*. New Brunswick, NJ: Rutgers University Press.

Gallagher, Sally K., and Christian Smith. 1999. "Symbolic Traditionalism and Pragmatic Egalitarianism: Contemporary Evangelicals, Families, and Gender." *Gender & Society* 13(2): 211–233.

Gallagher, Steve. 2007. *At the Altar of Sexual Idolatry*. Dry Ridge, KY: Pure Life Ministries.

Gardner, Christine J. 2011. *Making Chastity Sexy: The Rhetoric of Evangelical Abstinence Campaigns*. Berkeley: University of California Press.

Gerali, Steve. 2003. *The Struggle*. Colorado Springs, CO. NavPress.

Greggo, Stephen P., and Timothy A. Sizemore, eds. 2012. *Counseling and Christianity: Five Approaches*. Downers Grove, IL: InterVarsity.

Gresh, Bob. 2001. *Who Moved the Goal Post? 7 Strategies in the Sexual Integrity Game Plan*. Chicago: Moody.

Gross, Craig. 2006. *The Dirty Little Secret: Uncovering the Truth Behind Porn*. Grand Rapids, MI: Zondervan.

Gross, Craig. 2010. *Eyes of Integrity: The Porn Epidemic and How It Affects You*. Grand Rapids, MI: Baker.

Gross, Craig, and Steven Luff. *Pure Eyes: A Man's Guide to Sexual Integrity*. Grand Rapids, MI: Baker.

Grubbs, Joshua B., Julie J. Exline, Kenneth I. Pargament, Joshua N. Hook, and Robert D. Carlisle. 2015. "Transgression as Addiction: Religiosity and Moral Disapproval as Predictors of Perceived Addiction to Pornography." *Archives of Sexual Behavior* 44(1): 125–136.

Grubbs, Joshua B., Julie J. Exline, Kennth I. Pargament, Fred Volk, and Matthew J. Lindberg. 2017. "Internet Pornography Use, Perceived Addiction, and Religious/Spiritual Struggles." *Archives of Sexual Behavior* 46(6): 1733–1745.

Grubbs, Joshua B., and Samuel L. Perry. 2018. "Moral Incongruence and Pornography Use: A Critical Review and Integration." *Journal of Sex Research.* doi: 10.1080/00224499.2018.1427204

Grubbs, Joshua B., Nicholas Stauner, Julie J. Exline, Kenneth I. Pargament, and Matthew J. Lindberg. 2015. "Perceived Addiction to Internet Pornography and Psychological Distress: Examining Relationships Concurrently and Over Time." *Psychology of Addictive Behaviors* 29(4): 1056–1067.

Grubbs, Joshua B., Fred Volk, Julie J. Exline, and Kenneth I. Pargament. 2015. "Internet Pornography Use: Perceived Addiction, Psychological Distress, and the Validation of a Brief Measure." *Journal of Sex & Marital Therapy* 41: 83–106.

Grudem, Wayne. 1994. *Systematic Theology: An Introduction to Biblical Doctrine.* Grand Rapids, MI: Zondervan.

Grudem, Wayne. 2012. *Evangelical Feminism and Biblical Truth: An Analysis of More Than 100 Disputed Questions.* Wheaton, IL: Crossway.

Guhin, Jeffrey. 2016. "Why Worry about Evolution? Boundaries, Practices, and Moral Salience in Sunni and Evangelical High Schools." *Sociological Theory* 34(2): 151–174.

Haidt, Jonathan. 2012. *The Righteous Mind: Why Good People Are Divided by Politics and Religion.* New York: Pantheon.

Hald, Gert Martin, and Neil M. Malamuth. 2015. "Experimental Effects of Exposure to Pornography: The Moderating Effect of Personality and Mediating Effect of Sexual Arousal." *Archives of Sexual Behavior* 44: 99–109.

Hald, Gert Martin, Neil M. Malamuth, and Carlin Yuen. 2010. "Pornography and Attitudes Supporting Violence Against Women: Revisiting the Relationship in Nonexperimental Studies." *Aggressive Behavior* 36(1): 14–20.

Hardy, Sam A., Michael A. Steelman, Sarah M. Coyne, and Robert D. Ridge. 2013. "Adolescent Religious as a Protective Factor Against Pornography Use." *Journal of Applied Developmental Psychology* 34(3): 131–139.

Harris, Joshua. 2003. *Sex Is Not the Problem (Lust Is): Sexual Purity in a Lust-Saturated World.* Sisters, OR: Multnomah.

Hecker, Lorna L., Terry S. Trepper, Joseph L. Wetchler, and Karen L. Fontaine. 1995. "The Influence of Therapist Values, Religiosity and Gender in the Initial Assessment of Sexual Addiction by Family Therapists." *American Journal of Family Therapy* 23(3): 261–272.

Hunter, James D. 2010. *To Change the World: The Irony, Tragedy, and Possibility of Christianity in the Late Modern World.* New York: Oxford University Press.

Jacobellis v. Ohio. 1964. 378 U.S. 184, 84 S.CT. 1676, 12 L.Ed.2d. 793.

Jensen, Robert. 2007. *Getting Off: Pornography and the End of Masculinity.* Cambridge: South End Press.

Jeremiah, David. 1982. *Before It's Too Late: Crises Facing America.* Nashville, TN: Thomas Nelson.

Jerolmack, Colin, and Shamus Khan. 2014. "Talk Is Cheap: Ethnography and the Attitudinal Fallacy." *Sociological Methods & Research* 42(3): 178–209.

Johnson, Byron, Spencer De Li, David Larson, and Michael McCullough. 2000. "A Systematic Review of the Religiosity and Delinquency Literature: A Research Note." *Journal of Contemporary Criminal Justice* 16(1): 32–52.

Johnson, Eric L., ed. 2010. *Psychology & Christianity: Five Views.* 2nd ed. Downers Grove, IL: InterVarsity.

Johnson, Jessica A. 2015. "Porn Again Christian? Mark Driscoll, Mars Hill Church, and the Pornification of the Pulpit." In *New Views on Pornography: Sexuality, Politics, and the Law,* edited by Lynn Comella and Shira Tarrant, 125–146. Santa Barbara, CA: ABC-CLIO.

Johnson, Jessica A. 2018. *Biblical Porn: Affect, Labor, and Pastor Mark Driscoll's Evangelical Empire.* Durham, NC: Duke University Press.

Jones, Stanton, and Brenna B. Jones. 2007. *How & When to Tell Your Kids about Sex: A Lifelong Approach to Shaping Your Child's Sexual Character.* Colorado Springs, CO: NavPress.

Kenrick, Douglas. T., Sara E. Gutierres, and Laurie L. Goldberg. 1989. "Influence of Popular Erotica on Judgments of Strangers and Mates." *Journal of Experimental Social Psychology* 25: 159–167.

Kilpatrick, Joel. 2006. *A Field Guide to Evangelicals and Their Habitat.* San Francisco: HarperSanFrancisco.

Kimmel, Michael, ed. 1990. *Men Confront Pornography.* New York: Crown.

Kimmel, Michael. 2008. *Guyland: There Perilous World Where Boys Become Men.* New York: HarperCollins.

Kingston, Drew A., and Neil M. Malamuth. 2011. "Problems with Aggregate Data and the Importance of Individual Differences in the Study of Pornography and Sexual Aggression: Comment on Diamond, Jozifkova, and Weiss (2010)." *Archives of Sexual Behavior* 40: 1045–1048.

Kwee, Alex W., Amy W. Dominguez, and Donald Ferrell. 2007. "Sexual Addiction and Christian College Men: Conceptual, Assessment, and Treatment Challenges." *Journal of Psychology and Christianity* 26(1): 3–13.

LaHaye, Tim. 1982. *The Battle for the Family.* Old Tappan, NJ: Fleming H. Revell.

LaHaye, Tim. 1985. *Sex Education Is for the Family.* Grand Rapids, MI: Pyranee.

LaHaye, Tim, and Beverly LaHaye. 1998. *The Act of Marriage: The Beauty of Sexual Love.* Rev. ed. Grand Rapids, MI: Zondervan.

Lambert, Heath. 2013. *Finally Free: Fighting for Purity with the Power of Grace.* Grand Rapids, MI: Zondervan.

Lambert, Nathanial M., Sesen Negash, Tyler F. Stillman, Spencer B. Olmstead, and Frank D. Fincham. 2012. "A Love That Doesn't Last: Pornography Consumption and Weakened Commitment to One's Romantic Partner." *Journal of Social and Clinical Psychology* 31: 410–438.

Levert, Natasha Petty. 2007. "A Comparison of Christian and Non-Christian Males, Authoritarianism, and Their Relationship to Internet Pornography Addiction/Compulsion." *Sexual Addiction & Compulsivity* 14: 145–166.

Levin, Michael E., Jason Lillis, and Steven C. Hayes. 2012. "When Is Online Pornography Viewing Problematic Among College Males? Examining the Moderating Role of Experiential Avoidance." *Sexual Addiction & Compulsivity* 19(3): 168–180.

Lewis, C. S. 1942. *The Screwtape Letters.* New York: HarperOne.

Lewis, C. S. 1943. *Mere Christianity.* Westwood, NJ: Barbour.

Ley, David J. 2012. *The Myth of Sex Addiction.* Lanham, MD: Roman & Littlefield.

Lindsay, D. Michael. 2007. *Faith in the Halls of Power: How Evangelicals Joined the American Elite.* New York: Oxford University Press.

Litchi, Andrew, David Gordon, Austin Porter, Mark Regnerus, Jane Ryngaert, and Larissa Sarangaya. 2014. "Relationships in American Survey." Austin Institute for the Study of Family and Culture. http://relationshipsinamerica.com/.

Lubov, Seth. 2005. "Sex, Lies, and Statistics." *Forbes.* https://www.forbes.com/2005/11/22/internet-pornography-children-cz_sl_1123internet.html#4511244f51ba.

Lykke, Lucia C., and Philip N. Cohen. 2015. "The Widening Gender Gap in Opposition to Pornography, 1975–2012." *Social Currents* 2: 307–323.

MacInnis, Cara C., and Gordon Hodson. 2015. "Do American States with More Religious or Conservative Populations Search More for Sexual Content on Google?" *Archives of Sexual Behavior* 44: 137–147.

MacKinnon, Catherine. 1985. "Pornography, Civil Rights, and Speech." *Harvard Civil Rights/Civil Liberties Law Review* 20(1): 10–68.

Maddox, Amanda M., Galena K. Rhoades, and Howard J. Markman. 2011. "Viewing Sexually-Explicit Materials Alone or Together: Associations with Relationship Quality." *Archives of Sexual Behavior* 40: 441–448.

Malamuth, Neil M., Gert Martin Hald, and Mary Koss. 2012. "Pornography, Individual Differences in Risk and Men's Acceptance of Violence Against Women in a Representative Sample." *Sex Roles* 66(7–8): 427–439.

Malley, Brian. 2004. *How the Bible Works: An Anthropological Study of Evangelical Biblicism.* Walnut Creek, CA: AltaMira.

Manning, Jill C. 2006. "The Impact of Internet Pornography on Marriage and the Family: A Review of the Research." *Sexual Addiction & Compulsivity* 13(2–3): 131–165.

McDowell, Josh. 2015. Moody Bible Institute Chapel Address, February 4: https://s3.amazonaws.com/jmm.us.setfree/Josh+McDowell+-+Moody+Founders+Week+02.04.15.pdf.

McKenna, Chris. 2017. "Your Church Is Looking at Porn." *Covenanteyes* blog: http://www.covenanteyes.com/2017/05/18/your-church-is-looking-at-porn/.

Miller, Chris H., and Dawson W. Hedges. 2008. "Scrupulosity Disorder: An Overview and Introductory Analysis." *Journal of Anxiety Disorders* 22(6): 1042–1058.

Miller-Young, Mureille. 2014. *A Taste for Brown Sugar: Black Women in Pornography.* Durham, NC: Duke University Press.

Miller-Young, Mureille. 2016. "Porn Isn't a Public Health Hazard. It's a Scapegoat." *Washington Post*, May 23. : https://www.washingtonpost.com/news/in-theory/wp/2016/05/23/porn-isnt-a-public-health-hazard-its-a-scapegoat/?tid=a_inl.

Mitchell, Kimberly J., Janis Wolak, and David Finkelhor. 2007. "Trends in Youth Reports of Sexual Solicitations, Harassment and Unwanted Exposure to Pornography on the Internet." *Journal of Adolescent Health* 40(2): 116–126.

Mitchell, Mark. 1995. "Handling Life's Transitions." Peninsula Bible Church Cupertino. Catalog No. 1018. pbcc.org/learning/sermons/?download&file_name=1018.pdf. Morgan, Timothy C. 2008. "Porn's Stranglehold." *Christianity Today*, March 20. http://www.christianitytoday.com/ct/2008/march/20.7.html.

Muusses, Linda D., Peter Kerkhof, and Catrin Finkenauer. 2015. "Internet Pornography and Relationship Quality: A Longitudinal Study of Within and Between Partner Effects of Adjustment, Sexual Satisfaction and Sexually Explicit Internet Material Among Newly-weds." *Computers in Human Behavior* 45: 77–84.

Nelson, Larry J., Laura M. Padilla-Walker, and Jason S. Carroll. 2010. "I Believe It Is Wrong But I Still Do It": A Comparison of Religious Young Men Who Do Versus Do Not Use Pornography." *Psychology of Religion and Spirituality* 2: 136–147.

Newport. Cal. 2016. *Deep Work: Rules for Focused Success in a Distracted World.* New York: Grand Central.

Newstrom, Nicholas P., and Steven M. Harris. 2016. "Pornography and Couples: What Does the Research Tell Us?" *Contemporary Family Therapy* 38(4): 412–423.

Ogas, Ogi, and Sai Gaddam. 2011. *A Billion Wicked Thoughts: What the Internet Tells Us About Sexual Relationships.* New York: Plume.

Park, J. S. 2015. *Cutting It Off: Breaking Porn Addiction and How to Quit for Good.* Orlando, FL: The Way Everlasting Ministry.

Patterson, Richard, and Joseph Price. 2012. "Pornography, Religion, and the Happiness Gap: Does Pornography Impact the Actively Religious Differently?" *Journal for the Scientific Study of Religion* 51(1): 79–89.

Paul, Pamela. 2005. *Pornified: How Pornography is Transforming Our Lives, Our Relationships, and Our Families.* New York: Times.

Penner, Clifford, and Joyce J. Penner. 2003. *The Gift of Sex: A Guide to Sexual Fulfillment.* Nashville, TN: Thomas Nelson.

Perry, Samuel L. 2016. "From Bad to Worse? Pornography Consumption, Spousal Religiosity, Gender, and Marital Quality." *Sociological Forum* 31(2): 441–464.

Perry, Samuel L. 2017a. "Spousal Religiosity, Religious Bonding, and Pornography Consumption." *Archives of Sexual Behavior* 46(2): 561–574.

Perry, Samuel L. 2017b. *Growing God's Family: The Global Orphan Care Movement and the Limits of Evangelical Activism.* New York: New York University Press.

Perry, Samuel L. 2017c. "Pornography Use and Depressive Symptoms: Examining the Role of Moral Incongruence." *Society and Mental Health.* doi: 10.1177/2156869317728373

Perry, Samuel L. 2017d. "Does Viewing Pornography Reduce Marital Quality Over Time? Evidence from Longitudinal Data." *Archives of Sexual Behavior* 46(2): 549–559.

Perry, Samuel L. 2018a. "Not Practicing What You Preach: Religion and Incongruence between Pornography Beliefs and Usage." *Journal of Sex Research* 55(3): 369–380.

Perry, Samuel L. 2018b. "Pornography Use and Marital Quality: Testing the Moral Incongruence Hypothesis." *Personal Relationships* 25(2): 233–248.

Perry, Samuel L. 2018c. "Pornography Use and Marital Separation: Evidence form Two-Wave Panel Data." *Archives of Sexual Behavior* 47(6): 1869–1880.

Perry, Samuel L., and Joshua T. Davis. 2017. "Are Pornography Users More Likely to Experience a Romantic Breakup? Evidence from Longitudinal Data." *Sexuality & Culture* 21(4): 1157–1176.

Perry, Samuel L., and George M. Hayward. 2017. "Seeing Is (Not) Believing: How Viewing Pornography Shapes the Religious Lives of Young Americans." *Social Forces* 95(4): 1757–1788.

Perry, Samuel L., and Cyrus Schleifer. 2018a. "Race and Trends in Pornography Viewership, 1973–2016: Examining the Moderating Roles of Gender and Religion." *Journal of Sex Research.* doi: 10.1080/00224499.2017.1404959

Perry, Sameul L., and Cyrus Schleifer. 2018b. "Are the Sanctified Becoming the Pornified? Religious Conservatism, Commitment, and Pornography Use, 1984–2016." *Social Science Quarterly.*

Perry, Samuel L., and Cyrus Schleifer. 2018c. "Till Porn Do Us Part? A Longitudinal Examination of Pornography Use and Divorce." *Journal of Sex Research* 55(3): 284–296.

Perry, Samuel L., and Andrew L. Whitehead. 2018. "Only Bad for Believers? Religion, Pornography Use, and Sexual Satisfaction Among American Men." *Journal of Sex Research.* doi: 10.1080/00224499.2017.1423017

Peter, Jochen, and Patti M. Valkenburg. 2009. "Adolescents' Exposure to Sexually Explicit Internet Material and Sexual Satisfaction: A Longitudinal Study." *Human Communication Research* 35: 171–194.

Peterson, Jennifer L., and Janet S. Hyde. 2010. "A Meta-Analytic Review of Research on Gender Differences in Sexuality, 1993–2007." *Psychological Bulletin* 136(1): 21–38.

Peterson, Jennifer L., and Janet S. Hyde. 2011. "Gender Differences in Sexual Attitudes and Behaviors: A Review of Meta-Analytic Results and Large Datasets." *Journal of Sex Research* 48(2–3): 149–165.

Piper, John. 1995. *Future Grace*. Sisters, OR: Multnomah.

Piper, John. 2002. *Brothers, We Are Not Professionals*. Nashville, TN: Broadman & Holman.

Poulsen, Franklin O., Dean M. Busby, and Adam M. Galovan. 2013. "Pornography Use: Who Uses It and How It Is Associated With Couple Outcomes." *Journal of Sex Research* 50(1): 72–83.

Powlison, David. 2005. "Making All Things New: Restoring Pure Joy to the Sexually Broken." In *Sex and the Supremacy of Christ*, edited by John Piper and Justin Taylor, 65–106. Wheaton, IL: Crossway.

Prause, Nicole., and James Pfaus. 2015. "Viewing Sexual Stimuli Associated with Greater Sexual Responsiveness, Not Erectile Dysfunction." *Sexual Medicine* 3(2): 90–98.

Price, Joseph, Rich Patterson, Mark Regnerus, and Jacob Walley. 2016. "How Much More XXX Is Generation X Consuming? Evidence of Changing Attitudes and Behaviors Related to Pornography Since 1973." *Journal of Sex Research* 53(1): 12–20.

Rasmussen, Kyler. 2016. "A Historical and Empirical Review of Pornography and Romantic Relationships: Implications for Family Researchers." *Journal of Family Theory & Review* 8(2): 173–191.

Rasmussen, Kyler, and Alex Bierman. 2016. "How Does Religious Attendance Shape Trajectories of Pornography Use Across Adolescence?" *Journal of Adolescence* 49: 191–203.

Rasmussen, Kyler, and Alex Bierman. 2017. "Religious and Community Hurdles to Pornography Consumption: A National Study of Emerging Adults." *Emerging Adulthood* 5(6): 431–442.

Rasmussen, Kyler, Joshua B. Grubbs, Kenneth I. Pargament, and Julie J. Exline. 2018. "Social Desirability Bias in Pornography-Related Self-Reports: The Role of Religion." *Journal of Sex Research* 55(3): 381–394.

Regnerus, Mark D. 2007. *Forbidden Fruit: Sex & Religion in the Lives of American Teenagers*. New York: Oxford University Press.

Regnerus, Mark D. 2017. *Cheap Sex: The Transformation of Men, Marriage, and Monogamy*. New York: Oxford University Press.

Regnerus, Mark D., David Gordon, and Joseph Price. 2016. "Documenting Pornography Use in America: A Comparative Analysis of Methodological Approaches". *Journal of Sex Research* 53: 873–881.

Regnerus, Mark D., and Christian Smith. 1998. "Selective Deprivation Among American Religious Traditions: The Reversal of the Great Reversal." *Social Forces* 76(4): 1347–1372.

Regnerus, Mark D., and Christian Smith. 2005. "Selection Effects and Social Desirability Bias in Studies of Religious Influences." *Review of Religious Research* 47(1): 23–50.

Regnerus, Mark D., and Jeremy Uecker. 2006. "Finding Faith, Losing Faith: The Prevalence and Context of Religious Transformations during Adolescence." *Review of Religious Research* 47(3): 217–237.

Regnerus, Mark D., and Jeremy Uecker. 2011. *Premarital Sex in America: How Young Americans Meet, Mate, and Think about Marrying.* New York: Oxford University Press.

Reinke, Tony. 2017. *12 Ways Your Phone Is Changing You.* Wheaton, IL: Crossway.

Rossman, Gabriel. 2009. "Hollywood and Jerusalem: Christian Conservatives and the Media." In *Evangelicals and Democracy in America, Vol. 1: Religion and Society*, edited by S. Brint and J. R. Schroedel, 304–328. Thousand Oaks, CA: Russell Sage.

Russell, Bertrand. 1929. *Marriage and Morals.* New York: Liveright.

Rylko-Bauer, Barbara. 2014. *A Polish Doctor in the Nazi Camps: My Mother's Memories of Imprisonment, Immigration, and a Life Remade.* Norman: University of Oklahoma Press.

Ryrie, Charles C. 1999. *Basic Theology: A Popular Systematic Guide to Understanding Biblical Truth.* Chicago: Moody.

Sabina, Chiara, Janis Wolak, and David Finkelhor. 2008. "The Nature and Dynamics of Internet Pornography Exposure for Youth." *CyberPsychology & Behavior* 11(6): 691–693.

Scott, Halee Gray. 2016. "The Porn Paradox." *Christianity Today*, June 23. http://www.christianitytoday.com/ct/2016/julaug/porn-is-simultaneously-more-criticized-and-more-popular-tha.html.

Seto, Michael C., and Martin L. Lalumiere. 2010. "What Is So Special about Male Adolescent Sexual Offending? A Review and Test of Explanations Through Meta-Analysis." *Psychological Bulletin* 136(4): 526–575.

Sewell, William H. Jr. 1992. "Historical Events as Transformations of Structures: Inventing Revolution at the Bastille." *Theory and Society* 25: 841–881.

Sherkat, Darren, and Christopher G. Ellison. 1997. "The Cognitive Structure of a Moral Crusade: Conservative Protestantism and Opposition to Pornography." *Social Forces* 75: 957–980.

Short, Mary B., Thomas E. Kasper, and Chad T. Wetterneck. 2015. "The Relationship Between Religiosity and Internet Pornography Use." *Journal of Religion and Health* 54: 571–583.

Smedes, Lewis B. 1994. *Sex for Christians: The Limits and Liberties of Sexual Living.* Revised Edition. Grand Rapids, MI: Eerdmans.

Smith, Christian. 1998. *American Evangelicalism: Embattled and Thriving.* Chicago: University of Chicago Press.

Smith, Christian. 2011. *The Bible Made Impossible: Why Biblicism Is Not a Truly Evangelical Reading of Scripture.* Grand Rapids, MI: Brazos.

Smith, Christian. 2017. *Religion: What It Is, How It Works, and Why It Matters.* Princeton, NJ: Princeton University Press.

Smith, Christian, and Melinda Lundquist Denton. 2005. *Soul Searching: The Religious and Spiritual Lives of American Teenagers*. New York: Oxford University Press.

Smith, Christian, and Patricia Snell. 2009. *Souls in Transition: The Religious and Spiritual Lives of Emerging Adults*. New York: Oxford University Press.

Snow, David A., and Robert D. Benford. 1988. "Ideology, Frame Resonance and Participant Mobilization." *International Social Movement Research* 1: 197–217.

Snow, David A., Robert D. Benford, Holly McCammon, Lyndi Hewitt, and Scott Fitzgerald. 2014. "The Emergence, Development, and Future of the Framing Perspective: 25+ Years Since 'Frame Alignment'." *Mobilization* 19(1): 23–46.

Snow, David A., E. Burke Rochford Jr., Steven K. Worden, and Robert D. Benford. 1986. "Frame Alignment Process, Micromobilization and Movement Participation." *American Sociological Review* 51: 464–481.

Stack, Steven, Ira Wasserman, and Roger Kern. 2004. "Adult Social Bonds and Use of Internet Pornography." *Social Science Quarterly* 85: 75–88.

Staley, Cameron, and Nicole Prause. 2013. "Erotica Viewing Effects on Intimate Relationshipand Self/Partner Evaluations." *Archives of Sexual Behavior* 42(4): 615–624.

Steensland, Brian, Jerry Z. Park, Mark Regnerus, Lynn Robinson, W. Bradford Wilcox, and Robert Woodberry. 2000. "The Measure of American Religion: Toward Improving the State of the Art." *Social Forces* 79: 291–318.

Stewart, Destin N., and Dawn M. Szymanski. 2012. "Young Adult Women's Reports of Their Male Romantic Partner's Pornography Use as a Correlate of Their Self-Esteem, Relationship Quality, and Sexual Satisfaction." *Sex Roles* 67(5–6): 257–271.

Stoeker, Brenda, and Susan Allen. 2008. *The Healing Choice: How to Move Beyond Betrayal*. Colorado Springs, CO: Water Brook.

Stoeker, Fred, Brenda Stoeker, and Mike Yorkey. 2010. *Every Heart Restored: A Wife's Guide to Healing in the Wake of a Husband's Sexual Sin*. Colorado Springs, CO: Water Brook.

Strub, Whitney. 2011. *Perversion for Profit: The Politics of Pornography and the Rise of the New Right*. New York: Columbia University Press.

Struthers, William M. 2009. *Wired for Intimacy: How Pornography Hijacks the Male Brain* Downers Grove, IL: InterVarsity.

Sumerau, J. Edward, and Ryan T. Cragun. 2015a. "Avoid that Pornographic Playground' Teaching Pornographic Abstinence in The Church of Jesus Christ of Latter-day Saints." *Critical Research on Religion* 3(2): 168–188.

Sumerau, J. Edward, and Ryan T. Cragun. 2015b. "Don't Push Your Immorals on Me': Encouraging Anti-Porn Advocacy in The Church of Jesus Christ of Latter-Day Saints." *Sexualities* 18(1–2): 57–79.

Sun, Chyng, Ana Bridges, Jennifer Johnason, and Matt Ezzell. 2016. "Pornography and the Male Sexual Script: An Analysis of Consumption and Sexual Relations." *Archives of Sexual Behavior* 45(4): 983–994.

Thomas, Jeremy N. 2013. "Outsourcing Moral Authority: The Internal
    Secularization of Evangelicals' Anti-Pornography Narratives." *Journal for the
    Scientific Study of Religion* 52: 457–475.
Thomas, Jeremy N. 2016. "The Development and Deployment of the Idea of
    Pornography Addiction within American Evangelicalism." *Sexual Addiction &
    Compulsivity* 23(2–3): 182–195.
Thomas, Jeremy N., Becka A. Alpert, and Shane A. Gleason. 2017. "Anti-
    Pornography Narratives as Self-Fulfilling Prophesies: Religious Variation
    in the Effect that Pornography Viewing Has on the Marital Happiness of
    Husbands." *Review of Religious Research* 59(4): 471–497.
Thornton, Arland, and Donald Camburn. 1989. "Religious Participation and
    Adolescent Sexual Behavior and Attitudes." *Journal of Marriage and Family*
    51(3): 641–653.
Thornton, Arland, William G. Axinn, and Daniel H. Hill. 1992. "Reciprocal
    Effects of Religiosity, Cohabitation, and Marriage." *American Journal of
    Sociology* 98(3): 628–651.
Uecker, Jeremy E., Mark D. Regnerus, and Margaret L. Vaaler. 2007. "Losing
    My Religion: The Social Sources of Religious Decline in Early Adulthood."
    Social Forces 85(4): 1667–1692.
Wax, Trevin. 2014. "4 Things a Pastor Should Consider Before Engaging Social
    Media." The Gospel Coalition. https://www.thegospelcoalition.org/blogs/
    trevin-wax/4-things-a-pastor-should-consider-before-engaging-social-media/.
Weaver, James B., Jonathan L. Masland, and Dolf Zillmann. 1984. "Effect
    of Erotica on Young Men's Aesthetic Perception of Their Female Sexual
    Partners." *Perceptual and Motor Skills* 58(3): 929–930.
Weiss, Douglas. 2002. *Sex, Men, and God.* Lake Mary, FL: Siloam.
Weiss, Douglas. 2013. *Clean: A Proven Plan for Men Committed to Sexual
    Integrity.* Colorado Springs, CO: Thomas Nelson.
Wetterneck, Chad, Angela J. Burgess, Mary B. Short, Angela H. Smith, and
    Maritza E. Cervantes. 2012. "The Role of Sexual Compulsivity, Impulsivity,
    and Experiential Avoidance in Internet Pornography Use." *Psychological
    Record* 62: 3–18.
White, Mark A., and Thomas G. Kimball. 2009. "Attributes of Christian
    Couples with a Sexual Addiction to Internet Pornography." *Journal of
    Psychology and Christianity* 28: 350–359.
Whitehead, Andrew L., and Samuel L. Perry. 2018. "Unbuckling the Bible
    Belt: A State-Level Analysis of Religious Factors and Google Searchers for
    Porn." *Journal of Sex Research* 55(3): 273–283.
Wilcox, W. Bradford. 2004. *Soft Patriarchs, New Men: How Christianity Shapes
    Fathers and Husbands.* Chicago: University of Chicago Press.
Wilkerson, Mike. 2011. *Redemption: Freed by Jesus from the Idols We Worship and
    the Wounds We Carry.* Wheaton, IL: Crossway.
Williams, Rhys H., and Jeffrey Blackburn. 1996. "Many Are Called but Few
    Obey: Ideological Commitment and Activism in Operation Rescue." In

Disruptive Religion: The Force of Faith in Social Movement Activism, edited by C. Smith, 167–188. New York: Routledge.

Willingham, Russell. 1999. *Breaking Free: Understanding Sexual Addiction & the Healing Power of Jesus*. Downers Grove, IL: InterVarsity.

Willoughby, Brian J., Jason S. Carroll, Dean M. Busby, and Cameron C. Brown. 2016. "Differences in Pornography Use among Couples: Associations with Satisfaction, Stability, and Relationship Processes." *Archives of Sexual Behavior* 45(1): 145–158.

Wilson, Gary. 2014. *Your Brain on Porn: Internet Pornography and the Emerging Science of Addiction*. Kent: Commonwealth.

Wilson, W. Cody, and Herbert I. Abelson. 1973. "Experience with and Attitudes toward Explicit Sexual Materials." *Journal of Social Issues* 29(3): 19–39.

Winchester, Daniel. 2008. "Embodying the Faith: Religious Practice and the Making of a Muslim Moral Habitus." *Social Forces* 86(4): 1753–1780.

Winchester, Daniel. 2016. "A Hunger for God: Embodied Metaphor as Cultural Cognition in Action." *Social Forces* 95(2): 585–606.

Winner, Lauren F. 2005. *Real Sex: The Naked Truth about Chastity*. Grand Rapids, MI: Brazos.

Wolak, Janis, Kimberly Mitchell, and David Finkelhor. 2007. "Unwanted and Wanted Exposure to Online Pornography in a National Sample of Youth Internet Users." *Pediatrics* 119: 247–257.

Wood, Michael, and Michael Hughes. 1984. "The Moral Basis of Moral Reform: Status Discontent vs. Culture and Socialization as Explanations of Anti-Pornography Social Movement Adherence." *American Sociological Review* 49(1): 86–99.

Woodberry, Robert D., and Christian Smith. 1998. "Fundamentalism et al: Conservative Protestants in America." *Annual Review of Sociology* 24: 25–56.

Wright, Paul J. 2011. "Mass Media Effects on Youth Sexual Behavior: Assessing the Claim for Causality." *Communication Yearbook* 35: 343–386.

Wright, Paul J. 2013. "U.S. Males and Pornography, 1973–2010: Consumption, Predictors, and Correlates." *Journal of Sex Research* 50: 60–71.

Wright, Paul J., Soyoung Bae, and Michelle Funk. 2013. "United States Women and Pornography Through Four Decades: Exposure, Attitudes, Behaviors, and Individual Differences." *Archives of Sexual Behavior* 42: 1131–1144.

Wright, Paul J., Robert S. Tokunaga, and Ashley Kraus. 2016. "A Meta-Analysis of Pornography Consumption and Actual Acts of Sexual Aggression in General Population Studies." *Journal of Communication* 66(1): 183–205.

Wright, Paul J., Robert S. Tokunaga, Ashley Kraus, and Elyssa Klann. 2017. "Pornography Consumption and Satisfaction: A Meta-analysis." *Human Communication Research* 43(3): 315–343.

Yancey, Philip. 2003. *Rumors of Another World*. Grand Rapids, MI: Zondervan.

Ybarra, Michelle L., and Kimberly J. Mitchell. 2005. "Exposure to Internet Pornography among Children and Adolescents: A National Survey." *Cyberpsychology & Behavior* 8: 473–486.

Yucel, Deniz, and Margaret A. Gassanov. 2010. "Exploring Actor and Partner Correlates of Sexual Satisfaction Among Married Couples." *Social Science Research* 39(5): 725–738.

Zillmann, Dolf, and Jennings Bryant. 1988a. "Pornography's Impact on Sexual Satisfaction." *Journal of Applied Social Psychology* 18(5): 438–453.

Zillmann, Dolf, and Jennings Bryant. 1988b. "Effects of Prolonged Consumption of Pornography on Family Values." *Journal of Family Issues* 9(4): 518–544.

Zitzman, Spencer T., and Mark H. Butler. 2009. "Wives' Experience of Husbands' Pornography Use and Concomitant Deception as an Attachment Threat in the Adult Pair-Bond Relationship." *Sexual Addiction & Compulsivity* 16: 210–240.

INDEX

⟨⟩